Cowboys, Ranchers and the Cattle Business

Cross-Border Perspectives on Ranching History

Editors

SIMON EVANS • SARAH CARTER • BILL YEO

Cowboys, Ranchers and the Cattle Business

Cross-Border Perspectives on Ranching History

Simon M. Evans
Sarah Carter
and Bill Yeo
(editors)

University of Calgary Press
University Press of Colorado

University of Calgary Press
2500 University Drive N. W.,
Calgary, Alberta, Canada T2N 1N4

University Press of Colorado
5589 Arapahoe Avenue, Suite 206C
Boulder, Colorado 80303

Cataloguing in Publication Data

Main entry under title:
Cowboys, ranchers and the cattle business

Papers from a conference held at the Glenbow Museum in Sept. 1997.
Includes bibliographical references and index.
ISBN 1-55238-019-X (University of Calgary Press)
ISBN 0-87081-594-6 (University Press of Colorado)

1. Ranch life—Canada, Western—History—Congresses. 2. Cowboys—Canada, Western—History—Congresses. 3. Cattle industry—Canada, Western—History—Congresses. 4. Ranch life—West (U.S.)—History—Congresses. I. Evans, Simon M. II. Carter, Sarah, 1954. III. Yeo, W. B. (William Bradbury), 1942. IV. Glenbow Museum.
FC3209.R3C68 1999 636.2'01'09712 C99-911221-X
F1060.C68 1999

Canada We acknowledge the financial support of the Government of Canada through the Book Publishing Industry Development Program (BPDP) for our publishing activities.

This project has been supported in part by the Alberta Historical Resources Foudation.

Printed and bound in Canada by Hignell Book Printing.
(∞) This book is printed on acid-free paper.

Cover design by Robyn Herrington and Cliff Kadatz.
Typesetting and page design by Cliff Kadatz.

Contents

Introduction
Simon M. Evans vii

Does the Border Matter?
Cattle Ranching and the 49th Parallel
Terry G. Jordan-Bychkov 1

Charles M. Russell, Cowboy Culture,
and the Canadian Connection
Brian W. Dippie 11

Not an Old Cowhand – Fred Stimson and the Bar U Ranch
Alan B. McCullough 29

George Lane: From Cowboy to Cattle King
Joy Oetelaar 43

Tenderfoot to Rider: Learning 'Cowboying' on the
Canadian Ranching Frontier during the 1800s
Simon M. Evans 61

The Untamed Canadian Ranching Frontier, 1874–1914
Warren M. Elofson 81

A Century of Ranching at the Rocking P and Bar S
Henry C. Klassen 101

The Impact of the Depression on Grazing Lease Policy
in Alberta
Max Foran 123

Wild West Shows and the Canadian West
Lorain Lounsberry 139

The Canadian Cowboy Exhibition
Richard W. Slatta 153

Postscript: 'He Country in Pants' No Longer — Diversifying Ranching History
Sarah Carter 155

Postscript: Ranching History: Have We Covered the Ground Yet?
Bill Yeo 167

Notes on Contributors 169

Selected Bibliography 171

Notes 181

Index 221

This book is dedicated to

Lewis Gwynne Thomas,

born and brought up at
Cottonwoods Ranch on Sheep Creek, Alberta.
His early work on ranching history
sparked interest in the topic, which he nurtured
during some three decades as Professor of History
at the University of Alberta.

Acknowledgements

The editors wish to recognize the role played by Donna Livingstone, formerly of the Glenbow Museum, whose idea it was to organize a conference on ranching history as a complement to the Museum's 1997 exhibit on The Canadian Cowboy. Doug Cass and Lindsay Moir, also at Glenbow, played an invaluable role in bringing the idea to fruition. This conference, a sequel to the 'Ranching in the Americas' program at the 1994 annual meeting of the Canadian Historical Association, was sponsored by Glenbow, the University of Calgary and Parks Canada. To these institutions we express our thanks, and also to the conference organizing committee and the many volunteers who assisted in running the program.

This book is the direct result of the success of the Canadian Cowboy Conference and the support of the contributing authors. In addition to their scholarly work we would like to acknowledge their co-operation and patience while the publication took shape. To Walter Hildebrandt and the University of Calgary Press, thanks for adopting the project at a crucial time.

Introduction

Simon Evans
Memorial University

The Glenbow Museum mounted an exhibition on The Canadian Cowboy as one of their major initiatives for 1997.[1] This many faceted and extremely popular celebration of the cowboy provided an excellent opportunity for a review of some contemporary research being conducted on ranching history. A partnership was established between the Glenbow, the University of Calgary and Parks Canada to mount a conference under the general umbrella of the exhibition. This was duly held at the end of September 1997. The 17 papers presented were splendidly eclectic and contributed to our understanding of the working cowboy, the performing cowboy and the cowboy of the imagination. Several of the papers, like George Lyon's singing and poetry reading, Peter Wesley's personal recollections of Stoney cowboys, and Sherm Ewing's evocation of the rancher as an endangered species, were 'performances'—you had to be there! Some of the other papers have been published elsewhere. However, the nine articles presented in this collection provide a balanced, if not complete, record of the proceedings.

The aim of the Cowboy Conference, and of this book which grew out of it, was to present some new perspectives on Canadian ranching history. It was to reflect contemporary research interests and for this reason was not organized round a single thesis. This emphasis on a variety of themes, places, and time periods, seems—perhaps fortuitously—congruent with the progress of the historiography of ranching in the 1990s.

More than a quarter of a century has passed since David H. Breen proposed his thesis that the ranching frontier evolved in very different ways to the north and south of the international border.[2] Building on the work of L. G. Thomas, Breen demonstrated that, far from being a simple case of the diffusion of a land use type from the northern great plains, ranching in Canada developed within a political and legislative framework which had no parallel in the United States.[3] He also evaluated the social milieu which sprang up in the Alberta foothills during the 1880s, and concluded that it differed fundamentally from ranching communities south of the 49th parallel. In general, the decade of the 1980s was characterized by a period

of consolidation rather than innovation as ideas were reiterated and illustrated using new data.[4] What had been a rather radical revisionist approach had become the accepted paradigm. When he returned to Alberta to lecture on ranching in 1993, after an intensive period of research into the history of the oil industry, Breen expressed surprise, perhaps tinged with disappointment, that his ideas had not been challenged or substantially extended.[5]

In his opening address to the conference, Terry Jordan-Bychkov asked the question, "Does the border matter?" He reviewed the real differences in national origins north and south of the 49th parallel, but he went on to point out that any classification of major agricultural types revealed distributions unaffected by the border. He reached the conclusion that none of the three systems of cattle ranching which he had identified "seemed much affected by the international boundary; the border played no consequential role." He was speaking at a high level of generalization and challenged our more regional or nationalistic perspectives. As the conference unfolded, Professor Jordan-Bychkov must have been amused by the number of Canadian researchers who disputed his conclusion either implicitly or explicitly. As a geographer, he would probably have explained these contrasting viewpoints as a 'scale problem,' for while he was dealing with broad continental patterns, several of us were wrestling with the characteristics of a particular ranch or group of individuals. If the conference failed to reach a neat evaluation of the degree to which the international border has influenced ranching, we are in good company. Victor Konrad concludes his introduction to *Borderlands: Essays in Canadian–American Relations* with the observation that, "the borderlands between Canada and the United States largely remain open to interpretation, and subject to debate."[6] Jordan-Bychkov's overview, positing a more or less homogeneous ranching frontier across the border, contradicted Breen's thesis. Nevertheless both scholars adopted an 'Olympian' viewpoint to provide them with a stimulating means of organizing their ideas.

The western grasslands of North America consist of a complex mosaic of varied physical environments (a fact brought home to me recently when I drove down the spine of the ranching country from the foothills of Alberta, through Montana, Idaho, Utah and Arizona to New Mexico). Imposed upon this ecological heterogeneity is an equally diverse web of administrative structures bolstered by more than a hundred years of regional lore and tradition. There is not one 'west' but many. There are not two 'ranching frontiers' divided by a national boundary, but rather a number of regional variations. This number can be increased almost indefinitely as the scale of the inquiry is increased. For example, the Canadian range area is small when compared with that of the United States, but there are easily recognizable and important differences between the ranching systems of the interior valleys of British Columbia; the foothills of

Alberta; and the short-grass prairies of south-eastern Alberta and south-western Saskatchewan.[7] This diversity and complexity is increasingly reflected in the historiography of the range. Terry Jordan's *North American Cattle Ranching Frontiers* stresses the variety of origins and regional adaptions of ranching. Richard Slatta's *Cowboys of the Americas* compares and contrasts the cowboy experience throughout the hemisphere. Perhaps Paul F. Starrs' recent book *Let the Cowboy Ride* is the most directly pertinent, for the core of the book is a set of case studies of five very different ranching systems from Texas and New Mexico to Wyoming, Nebraska and Nevada.[8]

I would argue that it is now time to set aside sweeping comparisons between ranching in Canada and the United States. The model has proved useful, but now we need to look for new ones, and to frame questions in a different context. Above all, we need to get to know our own range story better, and we need both precise 'head knowledge' and 'heart knowledge' which knows the country "bones and soul" as Dan Flores puts it.[9] How did and how do ranchers hold their land? What administrative arrangements were established to regulate the use of the commons? What organizations did cattlemen develop to protect their interests? Who were the men and women who established ranches? What were their goals and strategies? And what traditions and attitudes did they bring with them? The papers collected here provide some of the answers to questions like these, and their value is in the detailed picture they provide of significant figures, particular ranches, and issues of importance. A clear and detailed picture of the Canadian range is a necessary prerequisite for careful comparisons of the variety of ways ranching is carried out in North America.

But what is ranching? It is a word which evokes a variety of powerful images in the minds of those who use it. The term is heavily larded with mystique and obscured with cultural overtones. Nevertheless, we need to be clear about what we are discussing. Ranching involves the rearing of livestock for commercial purposes. It implies the sale of animal products: at first these were hides, horns and tallow; later meat became the principal output and gradually improved in quality. For all their vaunted independence, ranchers are securely tied to their markets and are prey to fickle changes in public taste and the seemingly inevitable progression of business cycles.

Ranching is particularly associated with grassland biomes, but not exclusively so, for it is found both on the desert margins and in high valleys and montane forests. These semi-arid regions of broken topography provide refugia for a land use type which, for a brief historical period, dominated the great plains and prairies.

The land base used for ranching can also be defined in economic terms, for range is found in those hinterland areas far removed from markets where other more intensive forms of commercial agriculture are unable to

compete.[10] Historically, this zone has been constantly redefined as transport networks have matured and population has spread. Ernest Staples Osgood described the cattlemen as, "merely the advanced screen ahead of the real conquerors of the land, the pioneer farmers."[11] Since he wrote in 1929, it has become clear that the boundary between unimproved pasture land and arable farm land has moved back and forth in response to ecological vagaries and technological advances. The consolidation and reseeding of community pastures in southwestern Saskatchewan after the dirty thirties would be an example of expanding range acreage.[12] One might also expect a retreat from some irrigated areas as water costs soar.

Ranching is an extensive rather than an intensive form of land use. An animal may require anywhere from 20 to 100 acres of range to support it. For this reason land holdings tend to be large, and the better measure of ranch size is the number of cattle in the herd rather than the acreage controlled.[13] This does not mean that there are no small ranches, but rather that even a small herd of 50 head will require access to a substantial area of range.[14] A typical ranch would have a core area of deeded land surrounding the 'home place,' and have access to public lands through leases or permits. Ranching differs from mixed farming and from stock farms because it involves cattle grazing 'unimproved' grass for a considerable period of the year.[15] It is essential to remove the bulk of the herd from bottomland pastures to allow them to be cropped for hay and fodder crops.

This need for access to huge areas of range has meant that ranchers have always been dependent on public lands. In Canada, a lease system established in 1881 proved a powerful incentive for eastern entrepreneurs to invest risk capital in what was then the North-West Territories.[16] Almost as soon as this lure had proved successful, the regulations were modified in favor of farm settlement. Ranchers have been fighting with federal and provincial governments for secure tenure of their range ever since.[17] In the United States, no provision was made for cattlemen to acquire the large acreages of marginal land necessary for them to pursue their avocation. This led to all manner of 'creative manipulations' of the land laws so that large units of rangeland could be pieced together. Today, fully a third of the land in the United States is publicly owned. The balance of this huge acreage is in the western states and is used for grazing.[18] It is administered by a bevy of agencies, particularly the Bureau of Land Management and the United States Forest Service. Private use, by ranchers, of public lands has become a bitterly contested issue south of the border and it seems likely that the same arguments and issues will be debated with increasing acrimony in Canada during the next few years.[19]

To summarize, ranching is a commercial activity which involves the raising of a preferred species for sale; it is extensive in nature; and is located in areas which are too dry or too hilly to be suitable for more intensive land uses; these are hinterland areas far from markets. Ranchers make use of

lands which have remained in the public domain and the terms of their tenure have been the subject of ongoing debate.

And now it is my privilege to introduce the papers presented here. Mention has already been made of Terry Jordan-Bychkov's keynote address which reactivated methodological debate, Richard Slatta also helped to shape and direct our thinking. In a light hearted but penetrating lunch-time presentation, he reviewed with us some of the pitfalls and pleasures of carrying out research on cowboys.[20] He pointed out that the highly mobile cowboy tended to live in isolated rural environments, and often escaped the attempts of governments to record their comings and goings. He illustrated the ways in which photographs, art, and the study of material culture can sometimes make up for deficiencies in the written record. Serious historical study, he concluded, can be illuminated by examining the intersection between cowboy social history, popular culture, and mythology, but our task is always to distinguish between myth and history. "In recapturing the real cowboy past we enhance our understanding of and appreciation for today's vibrant cowboy culture throughout the Americas."[21] (Figure 1)

Figure 1. Important guests at the first Calgary Stampede, 1912, included several of the protagonists discussed in these papers. (Left to right:) White-Headed Chief; Unknown; Mr. Galbraithe, friend of George Lane; Inspector James Spalding, NWMP; George Lane; Unknown; Mrs. Nancy Russell; Mr. Blackstock, Medicine Hat; Hon. Archie McLean; Alex Newton; Pat Burns; Charlie Russell; Unknown; A. E. Cross; Unknown; Edward Borein. (Glenbow Archives, Calgary, Canada NA-2376-1)

Both Jordan-Bychkov and Slatta make full use of the study of material culture as they explicate the origins and diffusions of ranching frontiers. Brian Dippie's encyclopedic knowledge of Charlie Russell's life and work enables him to use 'Kid Russell' as a contemporary trained observer of ranching culture. Russell was, he points out, obsessed with accuracy and authenticity, he even did a series of studies of the regional variations in cowboy dress and 'rig.' Dippie concludes: "For Russell, the cowboy on either side of the forty-ninth parallel was interchangeable. Canadian or American, he looked alike and went about his business the same way."[22] However, it is perhaps significant that Russell's most frequent excursions onto Canadian range came during the first decade of the 20th century, and occurred in the Milk River country along the Montana border north of his ranch in the Sweetgrass Hills. Like Wallace Stegner on the Whitemud River further east, Russell was observing the wholesale movement of ranchers from the United States onto under-used Canadian grass which was specific in place and time.[23] However, in another context, the artist, by his choice of subject, brought out the contrasts on either side of the line. Russell's studies of the North-West Mounted Police in action against whiskey traders and horse thieves may well reflect his canny understanding of what would sell in the Dominion! But it also suggests that he, like other contemporary observers, perceived the 'Medicine Line' as a real border between two very differently administered states.

In their papers, Alan McCullough and Joy Oetelaar flesh out the characters and contributions of two figures who have been significant 'names' rather than 'real people' for far too long. Fred Stimson epitomized the role played by eastern capital in the development of ranching in western Canada during the 1880s, and he managed the most successful of the 'Big Four' ranches for twenty years. He deserves the careful attention he is accorded by McCullough. It would be difficult to overestimate the importance of George Lane to ranching, and indeed to the development of Alberta, during the years leading up to the First World War. Oetelaar is the first contemporary historian to 'take on' this giant figure.[24] She balances an overview of his early years with an exploration of his contributions as rancher, horse breeder, spokesperson for the ranchers' interests, farmer, businessman, politician, and friend of princes.

Simon Evans focuses his attention on the working lives of immigrant cowboys and examines how they learned their new trade. In so doing he attempts to convey a more balanced view of their experiences, moving away from the focus on their social lives, which characterizes earlier accounts. He points out that many of the men who passed on their skills to the newcomers had been making a living on the plains for a decade or more before the 'beef bonanza.' Continuity and adaption were powerful forces shaping men's lives on the frontier. On the other hand, Evans concludes that many of the big corporate ranches employed American cowboys to manage their herds. Most of

Figure 2. A group of cowboys from the Bar U Ranch relax after a day on the roundup, c. 1902. They represent the ethnic mix of the Canadian range, having been born in Canada, Great Britain, Mexico and the United States. (Left to right:) Unknown, Unknown, Fred Robertson (in tent doorway), Kid Smith (standing), Eddie Moreno (sitting in front), a transient Englishman gathering information, Miles Clink, and A. Melross. (Glenbow Archives, Calgary, Canada, NA-285.4)

these men were from the northern ranges and exemplified what Jordan-Bychkov called 'the Midwestern tradition' of cattle rearing. (Figure 2)

Warren Elofson takes on another myth, the contention that the Canadian west was orderly, law-abiding and peaceful. He suggests that the North-West Mounted Police were spread too thinly, and were too poorly equipped to fulfil the role which had been thrust upon them. Guns were omnipresent in range country and prompted dangerous 'high-jinks' and occasional blood-letting, while all strata of western society, including the police, connived to insure the illegal import of 'booze' was not interrupted. This is not the genteel image of emerging Alberta that has sometimes been projected.

Henry Klassen's study of the Rocking P and the Bar S Ranches breaks new ground in two directions. First, it is a study of medium-sized family ranches, when so much of our attention has been focused on a few big operations. By the turn of the century the growing numbers of smaller ranches collectively ran more cattle than did the few remaining huge

operations. Moreover, we have tacitly assumed that continuity of settlement is the norm in the foothills and that each generation passes on their land to the next. Here we have a detailed study of how the process works, and of how an extended family coped with boom and bust. Secondly, as Klassen follows the fortunes of his chosen ranches into the modern era, he stresses continuity, evolution and adaption.

Max Foran builds on this trend, for he describes the ways cattlemen tried to protect their interests through negotiations with governments during the 1920s and 1930s. In particular, he elucidates three themes: the struggle to achieve some measure of security of tenure for their leases in the face of expanding crop farming; the growing concern among ranchers with regard to land taxes and rents; and the gradual emergence of new and more sophisticated ideas about how the productivity of the range could be measured and enhanced. Foran charts the changing strategies of the Western Stock Growers Association as the physical, economic and social impacts of the Great Depression made themselves felt.

Lorain Lounsberry's research into wild west shows in Canada appears to be the first scholarly investigation of this interesting phenomenon.[25] Like ranching, it was rooted and grounded in the United States, but Lounsberry shows that a distinctive variation of the Real Wild West did develop in Canada. These cross-border relationships are illustrated by the careers of Jim and Stastia Carry from Kew, Alberta.

As we reflect on the Cowboy Conference, it is clear that our illumination of some 'dark corners' merely draws attention to what remains to be done.[26] Nothing could be more stultifying than the perception that 'it has all been done before.' New descriptive models need to be calibrated using more well-researched case studies. We need to extend our time line to trace the fortunes of cattlemen into the modern era. Moreover, we must broaden our spatial perspective to move out of the foothills, onto the plains to the east and westward to the intermontane valleys, where ranching in western Canada began.[27] It is clear that there is considerable popular interest in grassland environments and their management.[28] This presents historians with both an opportunity and a responsibility. For example, we need to build partnerships with the scientists who are refining our understanding of the ecology of Palliser's Triangle.[29] They need to know who arrived: when? in what numbers? and armed with what ideas and technology? We need to know more about native and exotic grasses, rainfall cycles and variability, and mean and absolute variations in temperature.[30] Finally, if we seek to be more far ranging with respect to space and time, we should also be aware of the valuable perspectives to be gained by including issues of gender, race and class.[31]

Does the Border Matter? Cattle Ranching and the 49th Parallel

Terry G. Jordan-Bychkov
Walter Prescott Webb Professor
University of Texas at Austin

International boundaries often influence spatial patterns of land use, society, culture, politics, and humanized landscapes. Geographers have long assumed that such borders can exert a shaping influence on human occupance. As early as 1935, Derwent Whittlesey penned an article entitled 'The Impress of Central Authority upon the Landscape,' a sentiment more recently echoed by geographer David B. Knight, who wrote of 'The Impress of Authority and Ideology on Landscape.'[1] Canadian geographer Deryck W. Holdsworth found 'Architectural Expressions of the Canadian National State.'[2]

Yes, borders do matter to the cultural geography and history of any region they bisect. But does the particular border under consideration here—the Canadian–United States boundary west of the Lake of the Woods—matter, and did it matter over a century ago when cattle ranchers established their enterprises on both sides of the line? After all, this particular boundary is so artificial in its perfect straightness and disregard for the lie of the land as to raise questions concerning its relevance to the cultural geography of North America. A thoughtful observer might even conclude that the Canadian and American Wests have more in common with each other than either does with its respective East. The presence of English-speaking peoples, on both sides of the line, who have always been at peace with each other, maintaining a demilitarized boundary, further undermines the notion that the 49th parallel possesses much significance.

And yet this border does, demonstrably, make a difference. Canadians are not like Americans in a variety of ways, perhaps most obviously in terms of the Old World national origins of the population (Table 1). In particular, the proportions of French, German, Irish, African, and Hispanic ancestry differ markedly between the two countries. In the United States, persons of German and Irish origin account for fully 41 percent of the population, while in Canada these two groups comprise less than 9 percent of the total. Truly, we are not the same people.

Table 1
Ten Largest Groups of Origin

Canada – 1991		United States – 1990	
French	33.8%	German	23.3%
English	26.3%	English	18.4%
German	5.0%	Irish	17.8%
Oriental	4.8%	African	11.7%
Scottish	4.8%	Hispanic	9.0%
Italian	3.9%	Italian	5.9%
Irish	3.9%	French	5.3%
Ukrainian	2.3%	Scottish	4.4%
Native American	2.1%	Polish	3.8%
Jewish	1.4%	Oriental	2.9%

Source: Terry G. Jordan-Bychkov, Mona Domosh, and Lester Rowntree, *The Human Mosaic*, 7th ed., New York: Longman, 1999, p. 348. The criteria are not identical in the respective national censuses, but the message is basically accurate.

View this contrast as a geographer does, by mapping it, and the 49th parallel springs to life (Figure 1, A). Along most of its course west of the Lake of the Woods, the border presents a fault line of national origin, mainly separating a huge zone of German dominance in the northern United States from English majorities in Canada.[3] Nor should we ignore the substantial Ukrainian presence on the Canadian side of the line. Along the entire length of the 49th parallel, national origins match up in only three narrow corridors: a tiny German area in the Red River Valley, a miniscule Norwegian corridor connecting parts of North Dakota and Saskatchewan, and a narrow Pacific Coastal English belt. Elsewhere the boundary divides Germans from English, perhaps helping explain the American propensity for marching mindlessly off to war led by generals and admirals bearing surnames such as Schwarzkopf, Eisenhower, Pershing, Nimitz, and Custer. If any cultural continuity exists between the Old World and the New, then yes, the border should matter.

The 49th parallel even seems to possess a behavioral aspect. Geographer John Hudson recently pointed out that the American side of the border seemed to attract assorted nut-case loners and anarchist groups.[4] Consider the activities of the Aryan Nation Nazis at Sand Point, Idaho; the dustup at Ruby Ridge in the same state; Ted Kazinski busily building bombs in his isolated cabin; the Montana militia holed up in their ranch forts, and assorted survivalists playing at the 'rape of the Sabine women.' No comparable aberrant behavior seems to occur on the Canadian side of the line, as Hudson observed.

A. National Origin Groups

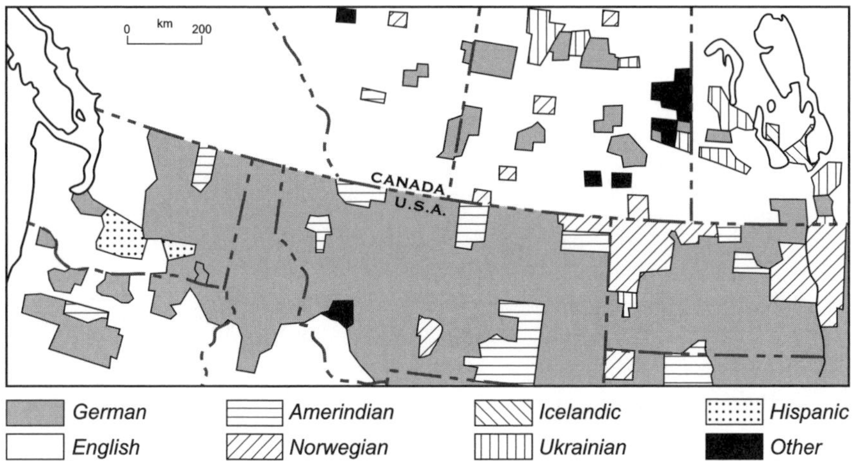

B. Selected Terrain Features and River Systems

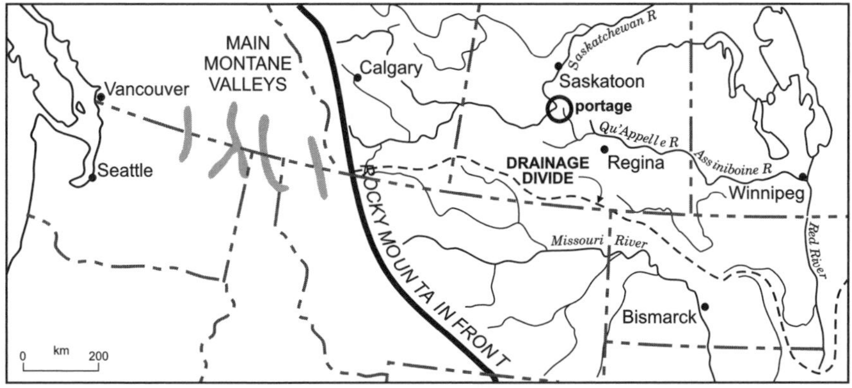

Figure 1. The 49th parallel (A) as revealed in national origins of the population and (B) in the context of terrain and drainage features.

Sources: James P. Allen and Eugene J. Turner, *We the People: An Atlas of America's Ethnic Diversity*, New York: Macmillan, 1987, p. 210; C. A. Dawson, *Group Settlement: Ethnic Communities in Western Canada*, Toronto: Macmillan, 1936, p. iv; and *Goode's World Atlas*, 19th ed., p. 66.

Closer to our topic of land use systems, Hendrik Reitsma considered the 49th parallel from the perspective of agricultural geography some decades ago. He found a number of ways in which the border influenced farming. For example, the ratio between sheep and swine differed markedly from one side to the other. One might have expected sheep to be more numerous on the Canadian side, given the British fondness for mutton and lamb, but the pattern was reversed (Figure 2, A). The explanation lay in a generous governmental wool subsidy in the United States. When that subsidy was subsequently repealed, the border contrast evaporated like a prairie morning fog.[5]

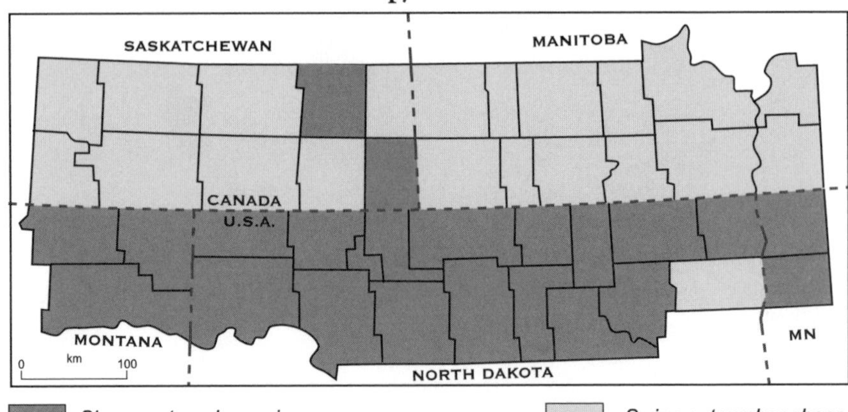

B. Land Use Systems

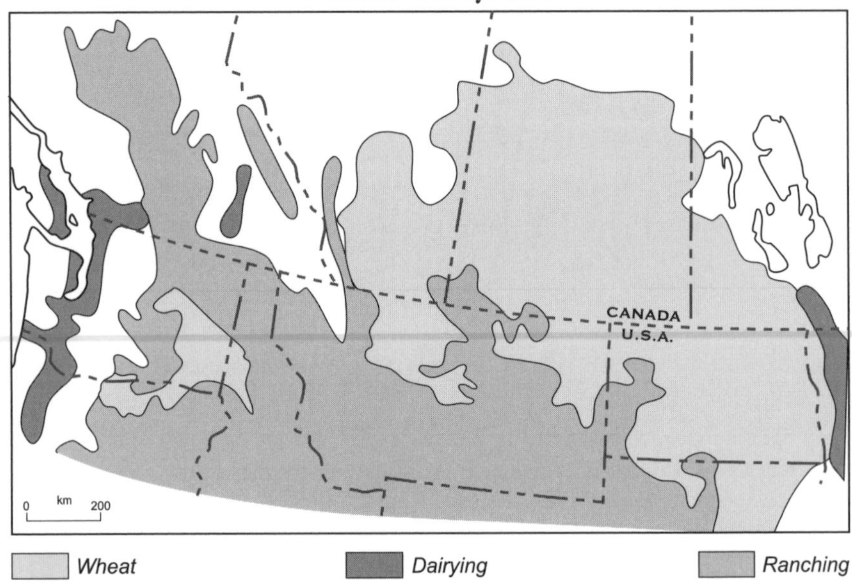

Figure 2. Land use and the 49th parallel. The border is (A) vividly revealed in the sheep/swine ratio but (B) invisible in broadly defined types of agriculture.
Sources: Reitsma, 1971, pp. 220–221; *Goode's World Atlas*, 17th ed., p. 77; and Jordan, *North American Cattle Ranching*, p. 268.

Evidence seems to be accumulating that the border does matter, in diverse cultural and agricultural ways. Perhaps Canadian geographer Simon Evans was correct when he called the international boundary in the West an 'institutional fault line.'[6] Another Canadian geographer, Andrew Clark, assented, suggesting that the 49th parallel, far from being an arbitrary and artificial border, divided two peoples and two separate westward thrusts.[7] As he pointed out, the boundary in the Prairies and Great Plains closely approximates the drainage divide between streams flowing to Hudson Bay and the Gulf of Mexico (Figure 1, B). The Missouri River, from the time of Lewis and Clark, served as an axis of United States expansion, while the Assiniboine–Qu'Appelle–Saskatchewan rivers, linked by a short portage, provided the way west for the fur traders from Montreal and later for the Hudson's Bay Company. These parallel flows later became cast in steel when transcontinental railroads were constructed, with terminals at Minneapolis and Winnipeg, Seattle and Vancouver.

But let us not rush to judgment concerning the border. Contradictory evidence exists. Terrain, as contrasted to drainage systems, invited cross-boundary movements. The vast interior plains, a grassy corridor, beckoned Americans to come northward. Further west, in the mountains, elongated valleys are oriented north–south, as for example the Rocky Mountain Trench, the Kootenay and the Okanagan valleys. These vales also directed human movement across the border, encouraging cultural blending (Figure 1, B).

Evidence that human patterns were influenced by cross-boundary migration and diffusion abounds. No English dialect borders or even isoglosses respect the 49th parallel.[8] A 'moralistic' political ideology seems as deeply rooted in Manitoba and Saskatchewan as in Minnesota or the Dakotas.[9] And, more relevant to the issue of land use systems, virtually every classification of major agricultural types reveal distributions that seem completely free of the influence of the international boundary (Figure 2, B).[10] In the East, dairying laps over the border, in several places, while in the prairies, plains, and mountains, wheat farming and livestock ranching straddle the 49th parallel with impugnity. And so, at last, I come to the topic that provides the focus for our symposium.

I would be the last person to propose that cattle ranching constitutes a monolithic type. In my synthesis of North American cattle ranching, I used the plural word 'frontiers' in the very title of the book to convey the notion of very different systems with diverse roots.[11] In the North American West alone, I discerned three more or less independent types of cattle ranching. The relevant point is that none among the three seemed much affected by the international boundary. My analysis suggested that, insofar as cattle ranching was concerned, the border played no consequential role. The very use of the word 'ranch' internationally implies as much.

A brief overview of my three types is in order. I labelled them the 'Texas,' 'California,' and 'Midwestern' systems. The Texas system of cattle ranching arose as a blending of Hispanic and Anglo–American practices in the subtropical coastal plain of the American South. Characterized by an open-range system, it produced scrub cattle largely of Iberian origin and involved a profound neglect of the livestock, including no provision of winter feed. Its labor force, consisting of southern whites and blacks alike,

managed the semiferal range cattle from horseback, using principally the hemp lasso. A distinctive vocabulary accompanied the Texas system, including words such as 'cowboy,' 'lariat,' 'maverick,' and 'cavvyard.' The Texas system surged northward up the Great Plains in a spectacular manner after 1865, during an unusually mild, wet period, but eventually this subtropical adaptive strategy proved unsuited to cold-winter areas. The Texas system suffered collapse by 1890 in virtually all areas north of the Lone Star State. In any case, the Texans' diffusionary thrust had largely fallen short of the 49th parallel. The Miles City area of eastern Montana and the Little Missouri River Valley of adjacent Dakota Territory became the northermost seats of major Texan influence.

A few Texans did cross the border. Simon Evans said that western Canadian prairies "were occupied briefly by the last survivors of a colorful company of men who had ridden the trails and followed the grass up from Texas".[12] By the late 1870s a few Texans were among the ranchers around Fort Macleod, and a couple even reached the Bow River Valley. A famous African-American cowhand of Texas origin, John Ware, made a reputation for himself in Alberta. Nevertheless, I maintain that the Texans largely fell short of the border, for climatic reasons unrelated to the presence of the 49th parallel boundary.

Some say that Calgary today bears a Texan imprint. Personally, as a Texan myself, I cannot discern one iota of such influence in your lovely city, but if it does exist, then I would seek its origin in the oil industry rather than in ranching.

The 'California system' of cattle ranching developed as a Pacific coastal type with deep roots in the *charro* culture of the western Mexican highlands.[13] It bore much less Anglo-American influence, and its unique vocabulary consisted almost exclusively of corrupted Spanish words—'buckaroo,' 'hackamore,' 'oreanna,' 'major domo,' 'rancherie,' and the like. Its material culture included such distinctive items as the single-cinched Visalia saddle (the Anglo-Texans used a double-cinched type); the rawhide lasso; and the 'Spanish windlass,' a device for pulling mired cattle out of tule marshes (Figure 3). Its Iberian breed of cattle was similar to those raised by the Texans, but they lacked the spectacular horn span.

The California system had more of an impact on Canada than did the Texans. Iberian cattle of Californian origin reached the Nootka Sound settlement on Vancouver Island as early as 1792, and others were brought to Fort Langley on the lower Fraser River by the 1830s. Anglo-Californians, who had adopted the system largely without modifications, marketed cattle in the British Columbia goldfields in the 1850s, and in the following decade some of them established ranches in the province, along the trails they had earlier used to reach the mining markets. In this manner, the Spanish windlass reached the interior plateau of British Columbia, as did the word 'rancherie' to describe the native American quarters on the periphery of towns and villages.

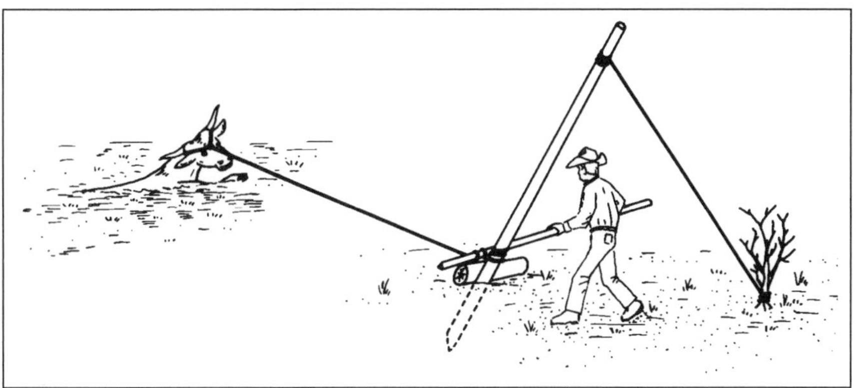

Figure 3. A 'Spanish windlass,' sketched in the ranch country of southern British Columbia. The device represents Californian influence in the Canadian ranching country.
(Redrawn from T. Alex Bulman, *Kamloops Cattlemen*, Sidney, BC: Gray's Publishing, 1972).

Still, the long-term Californian influence north of the border—or anywhere outside of California, for that matter—was negligible. The Californians, like the Texans, pursued a cattle-raising system born in and suited to the tropics or subtropics, to warm lotus-lands. Both systems failed in harsher climes, and we cannot implicate the international boundary in these failures.

The third ranching system came out of the Appalachian Mountains and Midwestern tallgrass prairies. Perfected in states such as Illinois and Iowa, it underwent a successful readaptation to the high valleys and plateaus of the Rocky Mountains in western Montana in the 1850s. This 'Midwestern system' involved the provision of hay as winter feed, the raising of British-derived breeds, a careful tending of thoroughly tame stock, and the fencing of pastures at the earliest possible time.[14] Better suited to the northern climate, it displaced both the Texas and California systems and reigned supreme by 1900.

The Midwestern system of cattle ranching crossed the border with ease, borne by the likes of Jerome and Thaddeus Harper, who were in British Columbia by 1859; Ben Snipes and John Jeffries of Yakima; 'Spokane' Jackson; William Gates of The Dalles; and Dan Drumheller from Walla Walla. The genealogies and even life experiences of such men trace straight back to the American Midwest, as do the life histories of most cowhands who worked for them. As Thomas Weir, who wrote the definitive geographical work on ranching in the interior plateau said, "scratch a British Columbian rancher and you'll find an American expatriate."[15]

If you seek the visible evidence of the Midwestern American ranching culture in Canada, you will find it in such items of material culture as the zig-zagged log pasture fence, whose origins lie back in colonial

Figure 4. Zig-zag log pasture fence, derived from the material culture of the American Midwest and Pennsylvania. This one is in Beaverhead Co., Montana.

(Photo by Terry G. Jordan-Bychkov, 1987).

Figure 5. Three 'Beaverhead' hay stackers, Big Hole, Montana. This invention, achieved by Midwestern ranchers in the Rocky Mountain high valleys, later spread into western Canada. It offers a visible index to Midwestern influence.

(Photo by Terry G. Jordan-Bychkov, 1987).

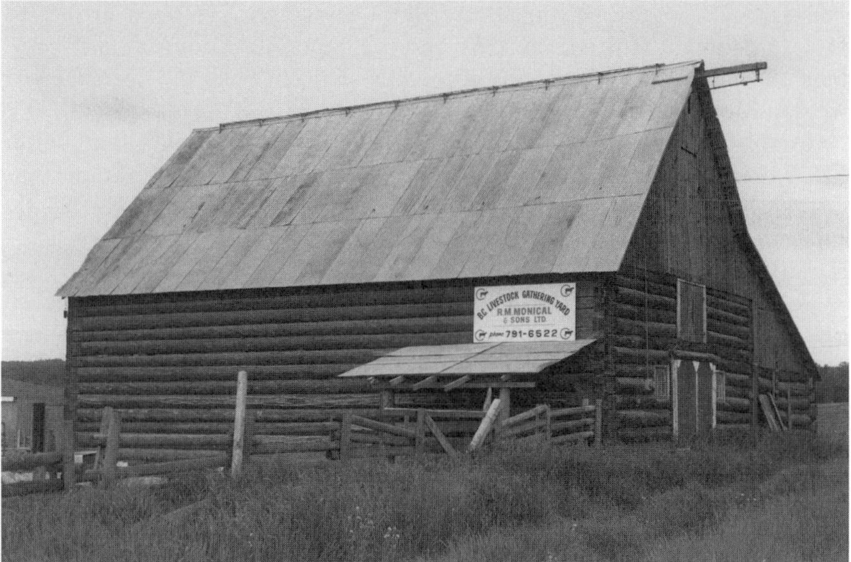

Figure 6. 'Mountain horse barn' near 100 Mile House in the ranching country of the southern interior plateau of British Columbia. Invented most likely in western Montana, the barn provides a visible index of Midwestern American influence in western Canadian cattle ranching. It contains stables for saddle horses, tie-stalls, mangers, box stalls, a tack room, and a huge hayloft. (Photo by Terry G. Jordan-Bychkov, 1990).

Figure 7. Anglo–Canadian carpentry on the Ranchers' Hall from Millarville, Alberta, a structure now at Heritage Park in Calgary. Hewing of the logs only near the end and the dominant use of dovetailed joints is diagnostic of the log-building tradition derived from Ontario and, more remotely, from a British military tradition in North America. This tradition arose independently of the Pennsylvania-based culture complex.
(Photo by Terry G. Jordan-Bychkov, 1987).

Pennsylvania (Figure 4), the 'Beaverslide' haystacker, perfected in the Big Hole, a Montana valley (Figure 5), and the imposing 'mountain horse barn,' built of notched logs and also apparently derived from the mountains of western Montana (Figures 6 and 7).[16]

In spite of the three American intrusions, and especially that of the Midwesterners, was Canadian ranching not in some significant measure distinctive? If so, I cannot detect it, and I certainly did not approach the subject as some sort of chauvinistic American. As a geographer, I am sensitive to and delight in regional cultural differences.

Some have suggested that British influence was stronger among ranchers on the Canadian side of the line, as the national origins map also implies.[17] Even toponyms speak of such influence. Alberta, for example, is dotted with Scottish place names, a nomenclature far more subdued in say, Montana. One reads of a rancher from the North Country of England living in British Columbia and using collie dogs to help herd cattle. Inspecting the log structures at the Bar U Ranch south of Calgary, I discovered that their distinctive carpentry is unquestionably derived from Ontario rather than the American Midwest, as revealed in details such as end-only hewing and the dominant use of dovetailed notches.[18]

In the balance, though, toponyms, notch types or other such details are largely inconsequential, as is the oddity of one Englishman's herder dogs. They do not describe the essential attributes of the ranching system north of the 49th parallel. Instead, both on the Canadian prairies and in the mountains beyond, I discern the shaping influence of the American heartland. Seek your national identity elsewhere, for truly it does exist, and vibrantly. But as far as cattle ranching is concerned, the border does not matter.[19]

Charles M. Russell, Cowboy Culture, and the Canadian Connection

Brian W. Dippie
University of Victoria

Charles M. Russell was inseparable from his portrayal of cowboy culture. He did not stand back from his subject matter, allowing considerations of technique and convention to dictate his depiction of cowboy life either while he was living it in Montana or recording it from memory. Indeed, there was almost never any emotional distance between the man and his art. His heartfelt identification with the life he showed accounts for his enduring reputation as *the* Cowboy Artist on both sides of the international boundary that divides the northern range.

Russell was born in St. Louis in 1864, the third of six children. By all accounts a dreamer as a boy, he chafed at the school room's confinement and often haunted the riverfront where steamboats just arrived from western ports stirred the dime novel fantasies that filled his head. Somewhere out there, far up the Missouri, was a land of romance and adventure. Russell's family was established in business, affluent and secure, and his parents expected that their son would settle down to a successful career in the family firm, a fire brick manufacturing company. But, shortly before his sixteenth birthday, they yielded to his pestering and gave him permission to spend a summer in Montana.[1]

Consequently, in 1880 Charlie Russell first encountered western reality on a sheep ranch in the Judith Basin. His parents had assumed that the experience would knock the fantasies from his head, and they were right in one respect: Russell hated sheep. Montana was another matter. He fell in love with the land and the people and the way of life, and stayed on, drifting about with an older hunter until the spring of 1882. Russell's employment prospects were dim when a chance encounter changed his life forever. He was hired on as a night herder on a month-long cattle drive from Billings to the Judith Basin with responsibility for some forty horses. Luck intervened again when he was retained by the Judith Basin Roundup to fill in for a fired wrangler that spring. Russell had experienced the good fortune that typically befalls a Horatio Alger hero; now it was up to him to prove himself despite his reputation as an amiable but shiftless kid.

In fact, Kid Russell worked out. There were 75 riders on that first roundup, he recalled, and he had charge of 400 horses. He was back for the fall roundup night herding cattle, and over the next 11 years, with time out in 1888 for a lazy summer loafing in Alberta, most every spring and fall he "sung to the horses and cattle."

Russell worked as a puncher only one season, in 1883, and never pretended to be a good roper or rider:

> *the first bronk I forked threw me so high that the boys caught him before I hit the ground an when I lit it jar[r]ed my memory so I will never forget and al tho I have ridden maney years I never reached fame as a broncho buster when riding weavers dip[p]ers sunfishers sky scrapers worn fencers I yoked my stirrups and used all advantages known to the puncher.*

Russell was a good wrangler, however, and he took pride in his record: "worked for the big outfits and always held my job." The wrangler might be low man in the cowboy pecking order, but night herding suited Russell, freeing up his days to observe the other hands at work. And, wrangler or not, the fact remains that Kid Russell was a genuine cowboy. He outfitted himself with some flair, sporting a buckskin jacket like those worn by his boyhood hero, Buffalo Bill Cody. On his first fall roundup he charged boots, gloves, meals, cigarette papers, bridles and a woven sash (he never liked belts) in a store in Utica. He also kept a saloon account and, true to the cowboy type, when he drifted north from the Judith Basin to the open range above the Milk River, he left the store to write off $36.53 in debt. One realizes what a hand-to-mouth, young man's existence cowboying was, with its seasonal employment, modest wages (Russell earned $84 on the fall roundup in 1884) and long winters spent batching with others as poor as himself, scratching for food, drink, and the rest of life's necessities.[2]

Russell, of course, could always bring in a few extra dollars from his art. He had established a local reputation as the eccentric cowboy who loved to draw long before he quit the range for good in 1893. His little watercolor sketch of a starving cow on a snow-blanketed plain, *Waiting for a Chinook*, had even attracted national attention in 1887. (Figure 1) Simple, poignant and powerful, it came to symbolize the bitter winter of 1886–87 and the end of the open range cattle industry. A few commissions followed, and Russell provided the paintings for the first picture book entirely devoted to the cowboy, *Studies of Western Life*, in 1890. Montana's press, which after the success of *Waiting for a Chinook* began faithfully recording his comings and goings and latest accomplishments, routinely urged 'the cowboy artist' to give up the cowboy end of things and realize his destiny as an artist. But as Russell explained to a friend in 1889, "I have tirde [tried] several times to make a living painting but could not mak it stick and had to go back to the

Figure 1. Waiting for a Chinook, Watercolour 1886. Montana Stockgrowers' Association. (Courtesy of the Montana Historical Society, Helcue, Montana, L53.01.01)

range I expect I will have to ride till the end of my days but I would rather be a poor cow puncher than a poor artist." As late as the spring of 1891 he wrote "I still night herd," and his reasons were unchanged. He was "fond" of art, he told a Fort Benton reporter, but there was "not money enough in it."[3]

Change was in the offing, however. While Russell lived out his cowboy fantasies in Montana, he kept in touch with his family in St. Louis, periodically returning home to visit. Unexpected deaths were sobering reminders of life's uncertainty. He lost younger brothers in 1889 and 1891; one had ridden with him in the Judith Basin for two years. He was crowding thirty by 1893. It was no longer enough to drift and play. Another breakthrough came that year when the state of Montana honored him with a display of his paintings in the Montana pavilion at Chicago's World Columbian Exposition, marking the 400th anniversary of Columbus's discovery of America. Such official recognition helped firm Russell's resolve: after returning from the fair, he never cowboyed again. But settling down to an artistic career was hard for a gregarious young man who had friends to visit and wild oats yet to sow.

Russell was barely eking out an existence in the fall of 1895 when he met his wife-to-be, Nancy Cooper. The timing was significant. As Russell's biographer notes, his mother had died that June, creating an 'emotional vacuum' that Nancy filled. Russell was cowboy to the core when it came to sentimentalizing the need for a good woman to guide a man down the path of life. "If the hive was all drones thair d be no huney," he later observed. "Its the lady bee that fills the combe with sweetniss its the same with humans if the world was all he s it would sour and spoil." Marriage in 1896 brought new responsibilities, and a new maturity. The Russells were still just

scraping by when they moved from the little town of Cascade to Great Falls the next year. By the time Charlie died there, in 1926, Nancy's drive and business acumen had long since established him as one of America's most successful artists. But one thing success never changed. To his dying day, Montana's Cowboy Artist remained emotionally more cowboy than artist. The proof was in the painting. [4]

The traditional judgment on Russell was rendered succinctly in 1966: "He was *the* documentary artist of the American West." A well known student of Russell's art elaborated:

> *To the real Westerner, there is a vast satisfaction in the always "rightness" of Russell's paintings. He can appreciate their unimpeachable authenticity, knowing that all important details are accurate. The quill or bead decorations on the clothes of his Indians, for example—whether they were Piegans, Crows, Assiniboine, Crees, or Blackfeet—were designs he had actually seen, knew or remembered.*

Accuracy and authenticity are obsessions that have defined the Western art tradition since George Catlin and Karl Bodmer journeyed up the Missouri River in the early 1830s to preserve a visual record of distant tribes. Certainly Russell, too, wanted to get the details right.[5]

But Russell's concern with *authenticity* has been overemphasized at the expense of his *artistry.* Simply, Russell brought the same powers of observation that he applied to cowboy life to his painting. His world expanded dramatically over the winter of 1903–04 when on the first of several trips to New York City he made the acquaintance of a coterie of established illustrators and observed them in their studios, saying little but watching closely as they posed models, solved compositional problems, mixed their colors, and went about the business of producing professional work for reproduction. He constantly sought to improve as an artist, and his paintings show he did. To insist that Russell was a documentary realist is also to miss the romanticism that defines his art, a romanticism that he was quick to acknowledge. He loved the picture and story part of Western history. Mundane reality never interested him. Accuracy mattered, but it always had a larger purpose: it verified his artistic vision. Thus Russell is best described as a romantic realist. Which brings us to his portrayal of cowboy culture.[6]

When it came to cowboys, Russell was his own expert. He knew what the cowboy of his time and place looked like. "Cowpunchers were mighty particular about their rig, an' in all the camps you'd find a fashion leader," he wrote. Their fashions were one of his own preoccupations. "As a cowboy Charlie Russell was sure strong for cowboy decorations," his friend Con Price recalled. "As I look back on him now, I can see him, seldom with his shirt buttoned in the right button hole, and maybe dirty with part of one

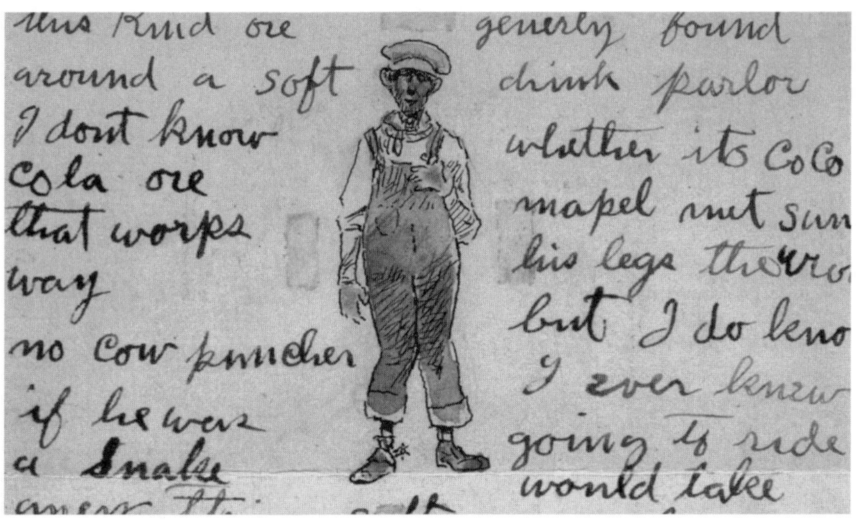

this kind ore generly found
around a soft drink parlor
I dont know whether its CoCo
Cola ore mapel nut sun
that worps his legs the wro
way but I do kno
no cow puncher I ever knew
if he was going to ride
a Snake would take

Figure 2. C. M. Russell to Walt Coburn, November 27, 1924.
(Rockwell Museum, Corning, NY, 80.137F)

sleeve torn off, but his hat, boots, handkerchief and spurs and bridle were the heights of cowboy fashion."[7]

For Russell, the old-time cowboy was the *real* cowboy, and his favorite ploy was to contrast the real with the ersatz. Modern 'bib overall boys,' for example, were not the real thing:

> *these fenced in cow people I see to day are not much good for pictures they ware bib overalls an straw hats I saw one the other day waring a durby an using a snafil bit with ring martengaeles his rope was dun up like a clothes line an he rode a long taled mare he might of been a top cow hand but from looks hed been handyer with a hay fork but a good stacker is what they want to day a man that savyes alfalfa a scim milk puncher dont need no riatta hes swift with a nose bag the rope and hackamore will soon hang beside the bow an quiver a relick of bar barousism [barbarism].*

Beside a caricature of the modern type, Russell wrote in 1924: "I don't know whether its CoCo Cola ore mapel nut sunday that worps his legs the wrong way."

So much for Prohibition improving mankind! "This cococola soke can tell whats the matter with a ford by the nois it makes," he continued, "but he wouldent know that a wet cold horse with a hump in his back is dangerious Shaps spurs and boots and big hat dont make riders neather dos bib overalls and caps make pictures ore storyes." (Figure 2)[8]

This is the kind I saw at the Stampeed at Winnipeg

Friend Bill I guess you think its about time I said something I received your letter last summer and aint lying when I say I was glad to here from you but Bill you know I always was slow an time has made me no swifter

your and my friends have scattered an baring Peete Van I seldom see any of the old boys we used ride with I see old Peet every little while hes blacker an I think has gained about three feet where the flank cinch would come. he still runs cows but dos most of his riding in an automobile. he has an interest in a bank at the town of Geyser

Peet may not have been a financier but we know he was a cow man an when the big heards left the basin he baught a few mighty good cows each of these cows had fower are five calves a year. an Peet was mighty handy with the iron this kind he was realy artistic

but I am glad old Peet or any of my friends got thairs before the dry lander grabed everything

This is the kind we knew

I still make Great Falls my home an have dun well the last fiew years with my work. I spend my summers

Figure 3. C. M. Russell to William R. McDonough, CA. January, 1914.
(Montana Historical Society, Helena, Montana, 80.46.03 A)

Nor was the Hollywood cowboy the genuine article. "This kind I dont know hes not down in natural history," Russell wrote above a sketch of a rootin' tootin' pistol-shootin' cowboy hero. Beside a companion sketch of the cowboy of his day, he wrote:

> *This species is al most extinct but he once ranged from the timber rims in the east to shores of the Pacific from Mexico north to snow*

> *bound land. He knew horses an could tell you what a cow said to her calf the floor of his home was the prarie the sky his roof which often leaked His gift of God was health and he generly chashed in with his boots on he was onley part human but Iv always liked animals.*

This is not to say that Russell disliked Western movies. He admitted to forking over "quite a little coin at them screen round ups." Hollywood cowboys might be "to fancyful to be real," but after watching them at work Russell remarked, "to an old romance loving boy like me its the best thing I v seen in Calif at least they were live men with living horses under them." Romance was one thing, however, pure fabrication another, and Russell's sense of probability was offended by Hollywood nonsense. It clashed with his consistent goal to commemorate the past and a species of cowboy "al most extinct."[9]

Finally, rodeo riders were not the real thing either. A matched set of drawings again made Russell's point. "This is the kind [I] saw at the Stampeed at Winnipeg," he wrote to a cowboy friend in 1914, "This is the kind we knew" (Figure 3). Russell did not deny the rodeo rider's courage or skill. He attended shows at Calgary, Winnipeg, Lethbridge, Saskatoon, Pendleton and all over Montana. But his allegiance was to the West of his youth, and the kind of cowboy—"An old time rim fire man"—he depicted in a sketch which topped a 1913 letter to a bronc-buster from the early 1880s, Bob Stuart. Charlie and Bob had played together in their frisky youths, living "every minute of a twenty four hour day," Bob's aunt recalled, and while they were "worthless" when it came to life's serious business, they "loved everybody and everybody loved them." There were good rides made at the Calgary Stampede, Russell told Stuart, "but Id lik to see one of these up to date twisters ride one of those old time low cantel flat horn shells cow punchers ust to ride." Elsewhere he elaborated this comparison: "The bronc rider always was and always will be a game glory hunter, gritty as a fish egg rolled in sand, but the lives they live to day an the rigs they ride are different." The modern rodeo contestant could specialize; old-timers had to be all-around cowboys. Of course, rodeo horses were also specialists and could outbuck the average cow pony of Russell's day, but the rider's equipment more than compensated. "These modern twisters ride a swell-fork saddle with high horn," Russell observed, and "the cantle is also high an' steep." In contrast, the bronc fighter's saddle in the 1880s

> *was a straight-fork with a cantle that sloped back, an' compared to saddles now, the horn was low. I've seen bronc riders use an old macheer saddle with a Texas tree. It had two cinches an' was called a 'rim-fire.' The horn was low an' flat—so big you*

> *couldn't more'n span it with your hand. The macheer, as it was called, was one piece of leather that fit over the cantle an' horn, makin' a coverin' for the whole rig. This leather was smooth an' so slick it wasn't easy to stay in.*

All bronc twisters might be "glory hunters," but for Russell "an old time rim fire man" was the *real* cowboy.[10]

Russell admitted variations on this northern range prototype. A stay on a large ranch in Mexico early in 1906 duly impressed him. "I used to think the old time [Montana] cow punchers were pretty fancy," he wrote Bob Stuart, "but for pritty these mexicons make them look like hay diggers." He sketched a "Mexican cow boss" and "the common vaquero," and paid tribute to their skills in watercolors done in this period.[11]

Russell also came to respect the California buckaroo. The cowboys who ranged north from California in the old days used

> *centerfire or single-cinch saddles, with high fork an' cantle; packed a 60 or 65 foot rawhide rope, an' swung a big loop. These cow people were generally strong on pretty, usin' plenty of hoss jewelry . . . . Their saddles were full stamped, with from twenty-four to twenty-eight inch eagle-bill tapederos. Their chaparejos were made of fur or hair, either bear, angora goat, or hair sealskin. These fellows were sure fancy, an' called themselves buccaroos, coming from the Spanish word,* vaquero.

In 1919, before his first extended stay in California, Russell admitted: "Long ago I ust to hear them senter fire long reatia Buckaroos tell about Califonia rodaros but at this late day I dident think thair was a cow in Cal that wasent waring a bell." Repeated exposure changed his mind. He was always of the opinion that "it takes a btter man to use a long rop an dally than short one and tie," and in 1926, on his sixth trip to California, he offered this tribute: "These Buckarues are more like the cow punchers of long ago than aney Iv seen they still use senter fire saddels and a raw hide ropers [rope] most of them use raw hide ranes and thair all dally men maby they cant work as fast as tie men but they shure do thair work pritty."[12]

Russell did a few paintings with California settings in his later years, but he never regarded California as home turf. In May 1920, on his return to Great Falls from Pasadena, he extended this advice to cowboy artist Will James: "I was down in Cal this winter and saw som fine back ground for cow pictures rolling country green with patches of poppies and live oak mountian ranges with white peaks that streach away to no where I have never seen this kind of country used in cow pictures Why dont you try it." Russell, in short, elected to stay with what he knew firsthand. The great body of his work on cowboy themes is a testament to that knowledge.[13]

Plate 1. Cowboy camp during the roundup. Oil on canvas, ca.1885–1887 (Amon Cartes Museum, Fort Worth, Texas).

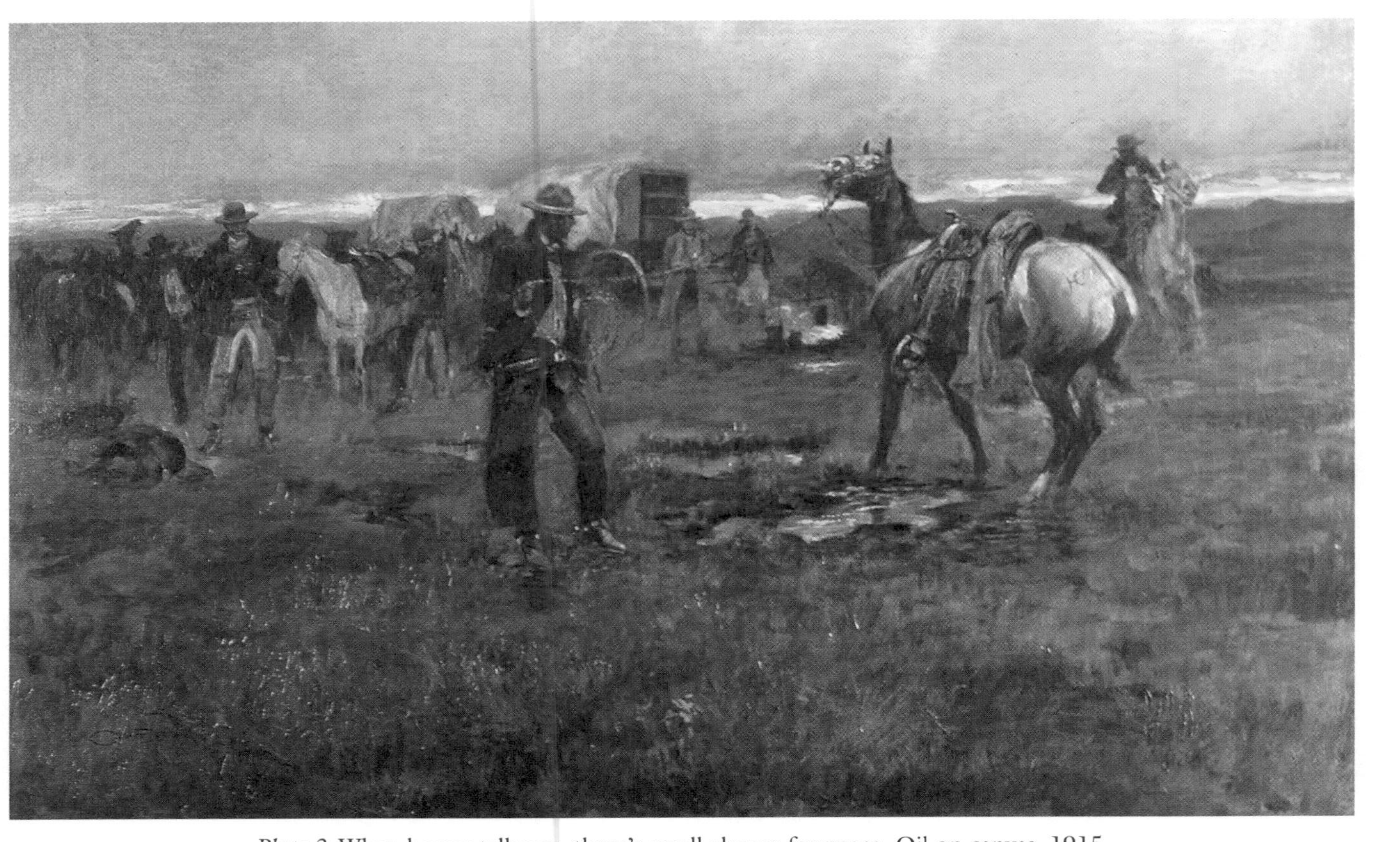

Plate 2. When horses talk war, there's small chance for peace. Oil on canvas, 1915.
(Montana Historical Society, Mackay Collection, Helena, Montana).

Plate 3. One of the rough string. Oil on canvas, 1913. (Glenbow Museum, Calgary, Canada).

Plate 4. Camp Cook's Troubles. Oil on canvas, 1912. (Gilcrease Museum, Tulsa, Oklahoma).

Plate 5. Jerked Down. Oil on canvas, 1907. (Gilcrease Museum, Tulsa, Oklahoma).

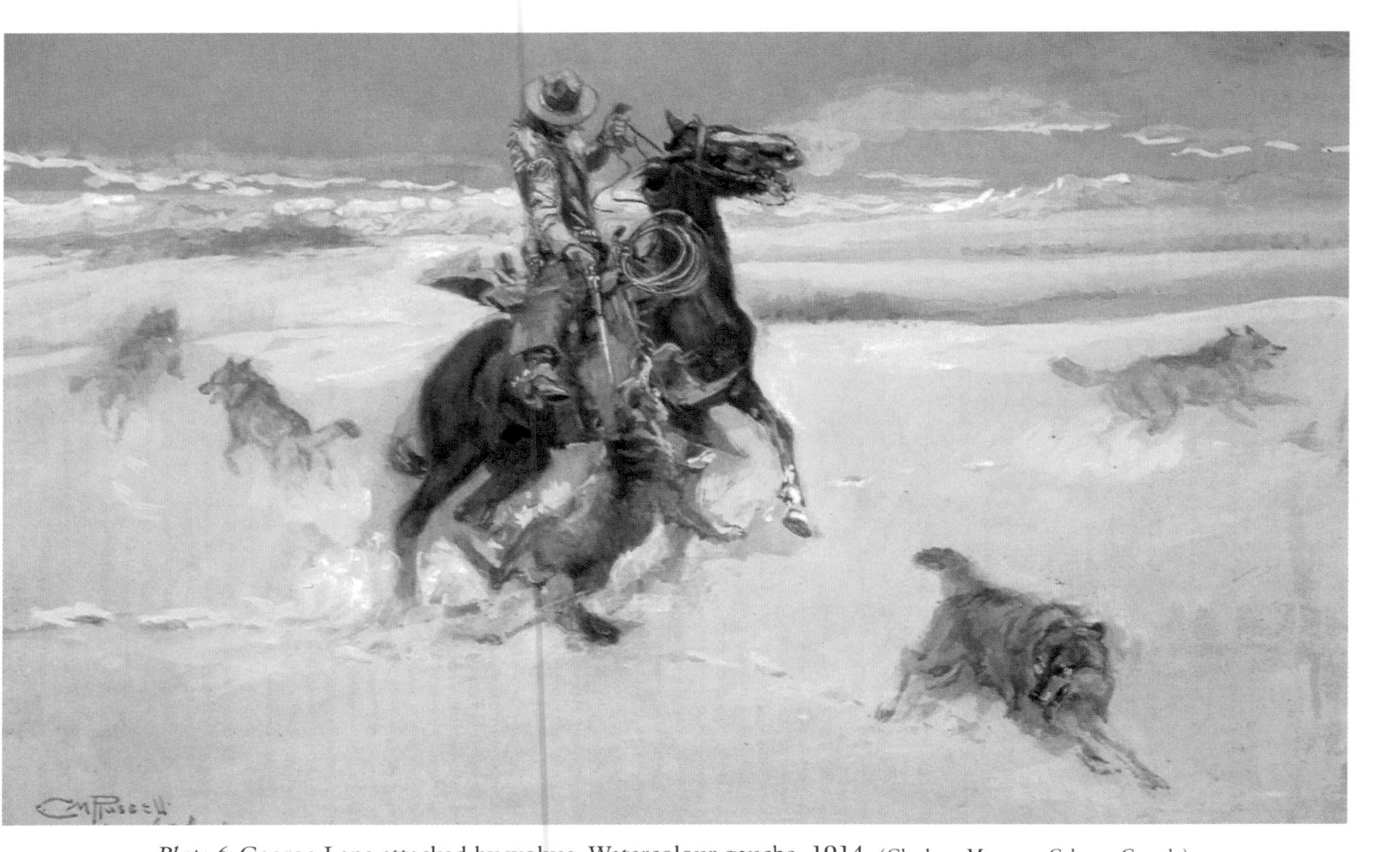

Plate 6. George Lane attacked by wolves. Watercolour gauche, 1914. (Glenbow Museum, Calgary, Canada).

Plate 7. When law dulls the edge of chance. 1915. (Buffalo Bill Historical Center, Cody, Wyoming).

Plate 8. Laugh Kills Lonesome. Oil on canvas, 1925. (Montana Historical Society, Mackay Collection, Helena, Montana).

Russell painted many scenes of cowboy routine (the camp on a rainy morning, riders scattering for the day's work) and cowboy fun (making a tenderfoot dance, racing into town for a drinking spree, animal encounters with rope or pistol, shooting scrapes), but riding and roping were his principal cowboy themes. Concentrating on them facilitates an understanding of Russell's movement from documentarian to memorialist as he refined details of what he had observed into complex, fully realized works of art. By examining his handling of these two themes one can trace both continuity and change in his work as distance and time modified his vision: an increasing distance from the lived experience accompanied by an evolving artistry, and an emotional identity with the subjects portrayed that only intensified over time.

A good starting point is Russell's 1887 oil *Cowboy Camp During the Roundup* depicting the previous year's Judith Basin Roundup camp at Utica, Montana (Plate 1). Its documentary quality is evident in comparing it to photographs of the roundup crew at Utica in 1884. The buildings, the tents, the cook standing in front of the mess tent, and the angle of vision adopted by Russell all parallel the earlier photographs. Moreover, the attention to detail evident here—including the cowboys, so carefully portrayed that participants could still identify each individual in the painting 40 years later—makes *Cowboy Camp* a perfect introduction to several of Russell's later subjects. On the left, for example, is a cowboy trying to gentle a balky horse while his friends look on, relishing his predicament. These elements reappear in the accomplished 1915 oil *When Horses Talk War There's Small Chance for Peace* (Plate 2). (Russell, in a yellow slicker, enjoys the fun as well; indeed, he is frequently a spectator in his cowboy paintings, attesting to his strong identification with the subject at hand). Particularly noteworthy in *Cowboy Camp* are the bucking horses and riders scattered throughout the painting. They represent in rudimentary form a theme never far absent when Russell painted cowboys.[14]

What Russell did in his mature paintings was isolate the particular incidents that crowd *Cowboy Camp,* turning each into an independent work of art. His strong narrative ability ran from prelude to aftermath, though he usually focussed on the action in between. If *When Horses Talk War There's Small Chance for Peace* is considered the prelude, Russell loved to show what happened after that wary rider took his chances and mounted that snuffy bronc. Sometimes he simply showed horse and rider in their ensuing battle for mastery. *Mankiller* (1911) (Figure 4) and *Bucking Bronco* (1917) (Figure 5) are good examples. But take that rider from *Bucking Bronco* and place him in context—a cowcamp in the morning—and a fullblown narrative follows. The horse might carry his rider onto the prairie while the other cowboys relish the contest, as in *One of the Rough String* (1913). (Plate 3). Or the horse might toss his rider about like a rag doll, forcing him to grab for the saddle horn while the bronc takes full control. Then you have a Russell

Figure 4. Mankiller, oil on canvas, 1911.
(Glenbow Museum, Calgary, Canada, CN–59.15.14, PHN 305)

native peoples and eventually made him a painter of the Indian as well as the cowboy. It also added another subject to his repertoire that was distinctively Canadian, the North-West Mounted Police. Russell often crossed into southern Alberta in the period 1906–10 when he co-owned a ranch in the Sweetgrass Hills five miles below the border, and in 1903 he made a probe north all the way to Fort Edmonton, as he styled it, hoping to find a frontier post where fur traders and dog teams were an everyday sight. While touring Montana as agent for the St. Paul-based sportsmens' journal *Western Field and Stream*, William Bleasdell Cameron, a survivor of the 1885 Frog Lake Massacre east of Edmonton, visited the newlywed Russells in Cascade in 1897, signing Charlie up for a series of paintings and drawings at the rate of $15 per oil, $2.50 per pen and ink. The payment might be miniscule, but the exposure was welcome. Another significant Canadian commission came from Charles A. Magrath of Lethbridge, who in 1905 persuaded Russell to paint an unusual history picture, *The Battle of Belly River*, and was pleased enough to buy another oil the next year, *When the Plains Were His*.[16]

Magrath's commission anticipated a remarkable string of Canadian successes for Russell after he agreed to hold his first international one man exhibition in Calgary at the inaugural Stampede in 1912 (see Introduction, Figure 1). Invited by Guy Weadick, the manager of The Stampede (as it was styled), Charlie exhibited a mature body of work, and Nancy found sales most gratifying. She sold 13 of the 20 paintings catalogued, and the Russells were back in Canada the next year for an exhibition at the Winnipeg Stampede (another Guy Weadick extravaganza). Contacts made in Canada led directly to Russell's only exhibition abroad, at the Dore Galleries in London in April 1914. A couple of paintings sold despite the outbreak of war on the continent, but nothing could compare to that first outing in Calgary. Two men accounted for the majority of sales. Sir Henry Mill Pellatt of Toronto bought four oils and a watercolor in Calgary, and subsequently acquired another watercolor—appropriately, a picture of a cowboy on a bucking bronco—to adorn his 'Russell Room.' An Englishman in attendance, A. M. Grenfell, bought three oils and a watercolor. These paintings were later sold to Denzil Newton and, on his death in the Great War, ended up back in Calgary in possession of his brother, Alick. C. Newton. Newton's taste, like Magrath's, ran exclusively to Indian subjects. Indeed, Russell's Indians outsold his cowboys in 1912, influencing the selection of paintings in his subsequent Canadian exhibitions. He made only one direct concession to the Canadian market. After the Calgary Stampede, and for three consecutive years, he painted a Mounted Police subject each year: *Single Handed* (1912), *Whiskey Smugglers Caught with the Goods* (1913), *The Queen's War Hounds* (1914), *When Law Dulls the Edge of Chance* (1915) (Plate 7). In all four paintings he showed the Mounties as imposing symbols of law and order, resplendent in their scarlet tunics, unruffled by circumstances and exhibiting more that a stiff upper lip as they sit their horses ramrod straight, peering sternly down on lesser, dismounted mortals.[17]

Russell had no better patrons than those he met in Alberta. The 'Big Four' who bankrolled The Stampede in 1912—George Lane, A. E. Cross, Pat Burns and A. J. McLean—were cattlemen all, and before The Stampede's dust had settled, Lane commissioned *Camp Cook's Troubles.* Cross was especially attuned to Russell's work. "I always feel that nobody compares with you in drawing animals or men & the beautiful, expressive, western colors of the sky & surroundings," he wrote the artist in 1924. In 1913, Cross could not justify the expense of a Russell painting for himself, but served as an intermediary between Nancy and two potential buyers, The Ranchman's Club in Calgary and the Manitoba Provincial government in Winnipeg. Neither lead panned out, but Nancy was grateful: "You may think these things amount to little but they are of great benefit to us, as Chas is so slightly known in Canada." In fact, the Canadian connection was already becoming electric. William B. Campbell, an Alberta rancher, bought *Pirates of the Plains* at the Winnipeg Stampede in 1913 and the next year commissioned a painting of an Indian burial that finally materialized in 1917 as *Her Heart Is On the Ground.* Campbell was still in the hunt when Russell returned to Canada in 1919 to exhibit at the Victory Stampede in Calgary and a followup event in Saskatoon where the future king, the Prince of Wales, viewed the show and praised Russell's work. Royal interest stimulated sales. Ten of the 24 paintings exhibited in Calgary eventually sold, including an evocative study of mountain men riding into unknown territory, *Carson's Men*, to Campbell. Three of the 'Big Four' who had again bankrolled the Calgary Stampede also came through in grand style. Cross acquired the cowboy painting *One of the Rough String,* while Burns bought one of the Mounted Police subjects on display, *Whiskey Smugglers Caught with the Goods*, and Lane the other two, *The Queen's War Hounds* and *When Law Dulls the Edge of Chance.* He had something special in mind for the latter—indeed, a royal treat.[18]

The Russells had experienced a brush with royalty back in 1912, when the party of the governor-general, the Duke of Connaught, visited Charlie's exhibition and the Russells were introduced to the duke's wife and his daughter, the Princess Patricia. They had hoped for even more in 1919, a chance to meet the Prince of Wales himself. The organizers of Calgary's Victory Stampede had prepared individual invitations for members of the royal party, each embellished with an original Russell pen and ink sketch.[19] But the prince did not reach Calgary until the Victory Stampede concluded. Before he left Canada, however, he was presented with two Russell paintings. He received *When a Left Handshake Is the Safest* on behalf of his uncle, the now-retired Duke of Connaught, while the oil *When Law Dulls the Edge of Chance* was given to him personally by the citizens of High

River in honor of his decision to purchase a ranch—which would be appropriately named the E.P. [Edward, Prince]—next to George Lane's Bar U.[20] Lane, who was instrumental in organizing both presentations, may have been inspired by a set up job the previous year when the citizens of Raymond and Magrath, Alberta, chose the occasion of a big stampede in Lethbridge to 'surprise' rancher Ray Knight with a Russell oil, an action portrait titled *Ray Knight Roping a Steer.* Since Russell had visited Knight in 1917 to sketch the picture's background and had obtained photographs of Knight to work from in capturing his likeness, the surprise was obviously minimal. But the idea of honoring someone with a Russell oil may have stuck in Lane's mind. After the Russells returned home from Canada, Lane visited them in Great Falls to pick up the two paintings for presentation to the prince, proving there is no royalist like an American born one.[21] This much is certain: *When Law Dulls the Edge of Chance* was never hung at the E.P. Ranch. Instead, the Prince of Wales carried it back to England and presented it to the Imperial Institute soon after his return. On 31 May 1920 a secretary to the Prince wrote Russell to thank him for

> *providing such interesting information respecting the painting of yours which was presented to the Prince of Wales while in Canada. We shall now be able to prepare a descriptive label to be shown with the picture, embodying the information which you have so kindly furnished. The picture has been on view here [Imperial Institute] for two months and has attracted considerable attention. Our Canadian Section is now under reorganization, but the picture will afterwards be shown, together with the other presents which his Royal Highness the Prince of Wales has contributed to our Galleries.*

One could not make the point more succinctly. Charles M. Russell's West recognized no border. From the British perspective at least, he was Canada's Cowboy Artist, too.[22]

The Judith Basin "looks like a grave yard," Charlie Russell wrote of his old haunts in 1916, "as most of the men I knew have crossed the range, where I hope theres plenty of cows and horses." In *Laugh Kills Lonesome,* painted in 1925 (Plate 8), the year before he died, Kid Russell steps into the circle of firelight to rejoin those men he had cowboyed with 40 years before. The transition was easy, because while Russell had aged, he had not changed. Two photographs make the point. As he stood with Wallace Stairley in his youth, radiating cowboy pride, so he stood with two younger cowboy artists in 1926, his health long gone, mortality staring him in the face—still radiating cowboy pride (Figures 6, 7). A few months later one of those artists, Charles A. Beil, would lead a riderless horse in Russell's funeral procession. The Campbells and the Lanes sent their condolences to

Figure 6. Charles M. Russell and Wallace Stairley, July 1887.
(Montana Historical Society, Helena, Montana)

Nancy Russell, and A. E. Cross expressed what Russell's loss meant. "You have not only my entire sympathy," he wrote Nancy, "the sympathy of all the old cow men in this country, many of them who knew your husband in years gone by. . . . I always counted him a very old and dear friend and marked his worth so much. It will be a distinct loss, not only to your own

Figure 7. C. M. Russell, Charles A. Beil and Joe De Yong, 1926.
(Colorado Springs Fine Arts Center D.1.41)

community, the United States, but all the world."[23] Russell was buried on 27 October 1926, but for those who dream the cowboy dream, he never died. Charlie Beil, who moved to Banff in 1930 and went on to renown as the sculptor of the Calgary Stampede trophies, explained why:

> *They often talk about different Western scene painters being a second C. M. Russell, but my honest opinion is that there was only one C. M. Russell. There still lingers but one C. M. Russell way down deep in our heart's memory, and there never will be another. He has no equal. Though he now rides the Great Range of the Shadowland beyond, the stirrup of his saddle, on the horse of artistic fame, is too high for any one here to reach.*

Beil's judgment, rendered in 1926, has stood the test of time. Russell's lasting legacy was not merely a vivid documentary record of cowboying on the northern plains, but a visual tribute to what cowboying meant—and still means. That is why, more than a century after he quit the range to take up his art full time, Charles M. Russell remains for so many on both sides of the border *the* Cowboy Artist.[24]

Not an Old Cowhand – Fred Stimson and the Bar U Ranch[1]

Alan B. McCullough
Parks Canada

I AM

The shades of night were falling fast
And the Bar U ranche was reached at last
For the YT boss had a telegram
That knocked from the roost the great I AM
Who said "Goddimit!"

The great I AM did cry and moan
So he lifted his foot and kicked a stone
And dear little somebody made an awful fuss
When she left the ranch with the poor old cuss
Who always said "Goddimit!"

It lifted a load from the cowboys' heart
When they saw the old fellow ready to start,
For he docked their wages on a stormy day,
And when they kicked you would hear him say
"Goddimit!"

The Nitchies will miss their bread and jam
Since they lost their friend the great I AM
For he's gone to the East perhaps to stay,
And no more the cowboys will hear him say
"Goddimit!"

The great I AM is now no more
And old George Lane will take the floor,
He'll tell the cowboys what to do,
And shake them up with a
"Goddamyou!"[2]

Figure 1. 'The great I AM.' Fred Stimson, entrepreneur and businessman, part of the establishment of the Eastern Townships of Quebec. He was acquainted with Senator Matthew Cochrane and the Minister of Agriculture, and had family connections with Sir Hugh Allan. (Glenbow Archives, Calgary, Canada NA-117-1)

Cowboy poetry, whatever its other merits, provides the poet with a concise and sometimes subtle way of commenting on his world. In this case Charlie Millar, a long time bronc rider at the Bar U Ranch, provides a quick and telling sketch of his former boss, Frederick Smith Stimson, aka 'the great I AM' (Figure 1). Stimson was the manager of the Bar U from 1882 to 1902 and one of the leading figures of the golden age of ranching in Alberta. In spite of what are important contributions to the ranching industry he has never entered the first ranks of the pantheon of Alberta's ranching heroes. In public memory, as in Charlie Millar's poem, he remains a bit more of a character actor than one of the heroes.

Ranching—cowboys, roundups, and bucking broncos—forms one of the central images of Alberta. The Calgary Stampede originated as a commemoration of the glory days of ranching. That it has continued to the present is evidence of the continuing fascination which Albertans have for ranching. Individual cowboys and ranchers—John Ware and A. E. Cross, Herb Millar and George Lane—independent, resourceful, forthright—have been adopted as cultural icons by the province.

The iconic nature of ranching certainly influenced the Historic Sites and Monuments Board of Canada when it recommended that ranching was of national historic significance and that it should be commemorated by the acquisition, preservation and interpretation of an historic ranch. The ranch which was ultimately chosen to carry this mythic burden was the Bar U about 60 miles south-west of Calgary on Pekisko Creek. The ranch was chosen in part because it was one of four or five very large ranches which had dominated the first two decades of the ranching era in Alberta and in part because it was the only one of these ranches which had survived largely intact well into the 20th century.

Three men, Fred Stimson, George Lane and Pat Burns, dominated the ranch throughout its long history and ensured its survival. Each man represented a different phase and a different style of ranching.

George Lane learned cowboying in Montana and in 1884 he was hired by Fred Stimson to be the Bar U foreman. Lane's practical skill as a cowboy and knowledge as a stockman are legendary. He left the Bar U in 1889, first to work as a cattle buyer, then to go into ranching on his own account. In 1902 he bought the Bar U in partnership with the Winnipeg firm of cattle buyers, Gordon, Ironside and Fares. He went on to become the biggest rancher as well as the second biggest wheat farmer in Alberta. He was the key member of the 'Big Four' who bankrolled the first Calgary stampede. Toward the end of his life he hobnobbed with the Prince of Wales and helped him establish his E.P. Ranch. He is the model of the cowboy who rose, through his own efforts and abilities, to become a great rancher. When he died in 1925 he was virtually bankrupt.[3]

Pat Burns followed a different route to become the owner of the Bar U. Born in Kirkfield, Ontario in 1855, he homesteaded in Manitoba. He

began buying cattle and then got a contract to supply beef to the crews building the Calgary and Edmonton Railway. He soon became the major buyer of slaughter cattle in Alberta. He built a packing plant in Calgary and established a chain of butcher shops in British Columbia and Alberta. He established his first ranches in the 1890s as winter feeding stations. He acquired a clutch of ranches before the First War, sold them all, and then bought ranches again after he had sold control of his meatpacking business. In 1927 he bought the Bar U from George Lane's estate and ran it as a part of his ranching empire until his death in 1937. Unlike Lane, Burns died wealthy and his firm, Burns Ltd., continued to operate the Bar U until 1950. Like Lane he backed the first Calgary Stampede and he oversaw the E.P. Ranch for the Prince of Wales. He was never a cowboy or a renowned horseman—he was in fact known for his abilities as a pedestrian. He was a shrewd and successful businessman who owned ranches.[4]

Frederick Smith Stimson was central to the organization and operation of the Bar U from 1882 until 1902. Under his management the ranch gained the reputation of being the best run and most profitable large ranch in Alberta. Stimson was also a key figure in the establishment of the ranching industry in Alberta. Although it would be an exaggeration to say he is a forgotten figure in Alberta's history, he is not remembered in the same rank as Lane and Burns. He was, and remains, a bit of an outsider, a man remembered more for his quirks than for his accomplishments. His outsider status offers some clues about the values and attitudes of ranching society.

What I hope to do is to take a look at the 20 years Fred Stimson spent in the Pekisko area and see if I can pull out some threads which throw light on his place in the history of ranching. I am equally interested in how he is remembered in formal history and in popular memory. Much of this will be tentative—Fred Stimson didn't leave memoirs or much in the way of business records or correspondence. His descendents did not stay on in Alberta to write his exploits in local histories. Nor do those pioneers who left accounts of the early years have much to say about him as a rancher or businessman although he is remembered as a storyteller and a character.

Fred Stimson was born in 1842 into a prosperous family in the Eastern Townships of Quebec. His father was a landowner, merchant and money lender in the village of Compton. On his death in 1863 Fred inherited a quarter interest, worth about $25,000, of his estate.[5] Fred took over the family farms and by 1871 he owned 1000 acres, 23 horses and 124 cattle. It seems likely that he was buying feeder cattle and fattening them for sale.[6]

He was an experienced stockman and in 1880–81 he decided to apply this experience to ranching in Alberta. Why? Perhaps he was pushed by hard times. The end of reciprocity, the onset of depression and increasing competition from Ontario and the mid-west put pressure on stock farmers in the Townships in the late 1870s.[7] Perhaps he was pulled by the opportunities presented by the ranching boom which was rolling north

through the American West and would soon cross the Canadian border into the foothills country. As a stockman in the Townships he would have known of the boom. His neighbor, and one of the executors of his father's estate, Senator Matthew Henry Cochrane, was the leading promoter of Canadian ranching. In 1880–81 Cochrane persuaded the Canadian government to establish a system of grazing leases in western Canada which were designed to lure large scale investment in ranching. He planned to invest a half million dollars in putting 8000 cows on a ranch in Alberta.[8]

Stimson was well off but he was not in Cochrane's league and he allied himself with the Allan shipping family of Montreal—probably the wealthiest family in Canada. Together they organized the North West Cattle Company (NWCC) with a capital of $150,000.00.[9] The Allans controlled the company but Stimson was a director and was hired as the resident manager. For the next 20 years he was the man on the spot for the NWCC or the Bar U as it came to be known.

Stimson made his first visit to the west in the summer of 1881 in company with Senator Cochrane and other investors.[10] He made contacts with people in the region, assessed the possibilities of buying cattle and chose a range. On his return he arranged for two leases, totalling 114,000 acres to the west and southwest of Spitzee Crossing (now the town of High River).

He returned West in the spring of 1882. At High River he hired George Emerson to help locate the NWCC lease and Jim Minesinger to build the headquarters buildings. Tom Lynch, an experienced drover, went with Stimson to buy cattle in Montana.[11] They bought 3000 head for about $60,000 in the Lost River region of Idaho.[12] Lynch hired Abe Cotterell as a trail boss and other cowboys, including John Ware and Bill Moodie, and started the herd north. It was a long trip, about 700 miles, and Lynch moved the herd slowly, keeping it in good condition. Apparently Stimson didn't travel with the herd but he was at High River when it reached the ranch on 25 September 1882.

Two days after the herd's arrival a fall storm blew in. It snowed for eight days and the herd drifted south. Stimson "believing all would be lost, took to his bed." Fortunately, his experienced cowboys simply followed the herd south. When the storm finally blew itself out, the cattle were on the Old Man River where they stayed until the following spring.[13] The Bar U suffered minimal losses while the Cochrane ranch, which held its herd on its own range during the winter, lost 3000 head.[14]

Like several other stories about Stimson, the story of the storm does not immediately reflect credit on him. What may be overlooked is that he hired good men and gave them their head; his action did not necessarily make him look good, but it got results.

After the first near disaster, the Bar U led a charmed life. The herd grew rapidly: a visitor in 1884 reported that the ranch had 4500 cattle, 1200 new

calves and had sold 800 steers at $65.00 each.[15] In 1886 it absorbed the the Mount Head Ranch with 1595 head of cattle and a 44,000-acre lease. By 1891 the ranch owned 10,000 cattle, 800 horses, and had 158,000 acres under lease.[16] It was among the three or four largest ranches in Canada and one of the most successful.

As manager of the Bar U, Stimson was active in organizing the ranching community to protect its interests. He was a founding vice-president of the South West Stock Association and "the acknowledged mouth piece of the High River stockmen."[17] His name frequently headed petitions putting the rancher's case to the government.[18] He was one of the backers of the *Calgary Herald and Alberta Livestock Journal* which was organized to counter the pro-farming editorials of the *Fort Macleod Gazette*.[19] Like most leaseholders he supported the Conservatives. In the run-up to the 1896 election he was president of the Calgary District Conservative Association and promised to "fire every man he had that did not vote right."[20]

Often a manager's most difficult task was dealing with owners. The case of managers caught between local conditions and absentee owners is a staple of western tradition. On at least two occasions Stimson found himself at odds with the Allans. When the government announced in 1892 that the grazing leases would be cancelled Stimson wrote Ottawa to say that the NWCC would purchase all of the land to which it was entitled as compensation for the cancellation. He was repudiated by the Montreal-based secretary of the company who wrote to say that no decision had been made and that no one had been authorized to make an application to purchase land.[21] Apparently the Allans were considering winding up the Company.[22]

Certainly the Allans' commitment to the ranch was more tentative than was Stimson's. This became clear in 1902 when, following the death of Andrew Allan, the family sold the ranch to George Lane. Stimson was not consulted about the sale and, if Charlie Millar's poem is to be believed, he was astonished and aggrieved when he was knocked from his perch. Following the sale, the Allans moved to wind up the North West Cattle Company. Stimson thought they had undervalued the ranch and tried to block the liquidation in the courts.[23] When he failed, he left Alberta and moved to Mexico where he lived until his death in 1912.[24]

During the Stimson years the Bar U was primarily a cattle ranch. It, the Quorn, the CC, and several smaller ranches worked together to manage the High River Range which carried about 17,000 cattle and 2100 horses in 1890. The ranches formed the High River Stock Association to represent their interests and organize collective efforts such as the spring roundup.[25] The roundup was the high point of the ranching year. For the owners, it was the one time of the year when a relatively accurate count of the herd and of the calf crop could be made. Socially it brought together dozens of cowboys and provided an opportunity for demonstrations of the skills,

Figure 2. Fred Stimson was never much of a cowboy, but that did not stop him from trying to look the part! Here he poses at Montgomery Ward's store in Chicago, 1882.
(Sheilagh Jameson, *Ranches, Cowboys and Characters*, p. 25)

riding, roping, and cutting out, by which cowboys were judged. The roundup was a working cowboys' experience. Owners and managers of major ranches often visited the roundup but few participated fully in it as working cowboys. Stimson, while he may have been respected as a rancher, was never viewed as a cowboy (Figure 2). Fred Ings, who usually rode with the Bar U wagon, remembered that Fred Stimson only rode in the 1884 roundup and only then because he was meeting his new foreman, and eventual nemisis, George Lane.[26] Lane, although new to the country, was appointed the captain of the roundup in 1885, a testimony both to his ability and to the importance of the Bar U. Stimson made the Bar U his home. Although daily operations on the ranch would have been in the hands of the foreman, Stimson established the atmosphere in which the dozen or so regular hands worked. It is significant that the ranch was able to attract and keep some very good cowboys. The poem, *I AM*, suggests that cowboys had mixed feelings about Stimson. There is wry affection for a representative of an era which was passing; at the same time that there is recognition that he was a hard, profane, employer with a sense of his own importance.

Another story reinforces the impression that Stimson was a hard man. A Bar U cowboy named Mel Zimrose died from a fall. "They were putting him in a box at the Bar U the next morning when old Stimson took a fancy to his boots. 'Damn him, he won't need those where he's going to!' and pulled the boots off."[27] This may be a species of rural myth; it is also part of Stimson's image. The story is in accord with Harold Riley's comment that Stimson had a "penchant for purloining anything that he could lay his hands on."[28]

Ranchers, in Sheilagh Jameson's words placed "greater emphasis on living, or on the art of living, . . . than on the process of making a living."[29] Stimson knew how to live as well as how to make a living. He was an early member of the Ranchmen's Club, an enthusiastic hunter and a popular host; the Bar U was known as a comfortable and hospitable ranch. J. L. Douglas visited the family in 1886 and commented "the ranch really looks like a 'home' which is more than can be said for any of the others I have seen at present; there are nice comfortable chairs, pictures, curtains etc. so it looks very well."[30] Norman Rankin described the Stimson ranch house:

> *Outside, it was a rough log hut, inside a haven of rest and comfort—an Oriental hall of luxury and elegance. Stimson's friends were legion; everyone that knew the Allans and was going west secured a letter of introduction to the genial manager of the Bar U, and so delightful must have been their stay, that when they moved on, back came a present—a token of friendship—at first opportunity. Pottery from Egypt, brasses from India, temple cloths from Japan and China, and the thousand and one*

Figure 3. Fred Stimson was a raconteur and clubman, but he was also an excellent manager and a knowledgeable stockman.

(High River Pioneers, *Leaves from the Medicine Tree*, p. 32)

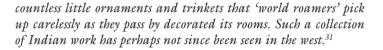

> *countless little ornaments and trinkets that 'world roamers' pick up carelessly as they pass by decorated its rooms. Such a collection of Indian work has perhaps not since been seen in the west.*[31]

Some guests came to him as an authority on ranching; William Van Horne referred a potential British investor to him as the most knowlegeable person on ranching in the area.[32] Others came in semi-official capacity. Lord Stanley, the Governor-General, stayed overnight at the ranch in 1889 and was treated to a wolf hunt.[33]

Stimson's role as a host was enhanced by his ability as a wit and a spinner of yarns (Figure 3). He was, to quote Harold Riley:

> *recognized as the greatest story teller and entertainer in the west. His repertoire of stories was unlimited. He had stories to suit all occasions. He could entertain a drawing room audience of men and women comprising the elite of Montreal's society, with grace, charm and wit, and on the other hand he could keep a gathering of tough and seasoned cowboys and range hands out on the round-ups in roars of laughter with his stories of another type.*[34]

A long and very tall tale which Stimson told in the Alberta Hotel with the intention of deflating two supercilious English visitors, dealt with a trip he had made to England to sell cattle. Stimson had planned to spend some time enjoying himself in London but the Queen heard that he was in England and insisted that he stay at Windsor Castle. Society at the castle was stuffy and to pass the time one evening he taught the Queen and Princess Beatrice to play euchre. Although the Queen enjoyed the game, she retired early, and, disregarding Victorian propriety, left Stimson and Princess Beatrice alone in a pavilion on the grounds. Several hours later when they returned to the castle, they found it locked and shrouded in darkness. Stimson pounded on the door with the butt of his six-shooter, waking the Queen. On learning that it was only "old Fred Stimson from Pekisko" she called down "Just wait for a minute until I put my crown on and then I will come down and let you in."[35] His humour was not to everyone's taste; J. L. Douglas's brother considered the family "A lot of humbugs."[36]

Not only was Stimson a teller of tales, he figured in several. His earliest appearance in the West is in a tale told by Phil Weinard. Weinard met Stimson in Fort Macleod in September of 1882 and agreed to work for him. Weinard recalled their first day's travel:

> *Stimson arrived a little after four [in the afternoon]. . . Leaving town at that time of day led me to believe we were going to stop at some ranch or road-house for the night. But when we crossed Willow Creek about four miles from Macleod, Stimson said we would camp. I thought it strange that a man with 3,000 head of*

> *cattle would camp within sight of town. After supper, which consisted of bacon, crackers and tea, it struck me that I was travelling with a very unusual man. When I started to make my bed, he said in his sing-song way "You-must-put-your-boots-under-your-pillow-or-the-Kit-Fox-will-eat-them."*[37]

Weinard's account gives little indication that Stimson possessed the qualities one would would expect in a man who was to become one of the most successful ranchers in Alberta. It is not, however, unusual in dwelling on Stimson's eccentricities. No stories emphasize his skills as a horseman or even as a shrewd businessman; in this he is quite unlike his successors, George Lane and Pat Burns.

Fred Stimson married his first cousin, Mary Greely Smith, in 1866. They had one child, Bryce. Mary Stimson moved to the ranch in 1885 and although she lived there until 1902 she made little recorded impact on the community.[38] She served as the postmistress at Pekisko from 1886 to 1902 but the few letters which survive in Post Office files are from Fred Stimson.[39] Fred Ings, in a listing of pioneer women in the High River District, makes no mention of her. Billy Holmes, who visited the ranch often, barely recalled her except to say that she spent a lot of time in High River visiting her friends, the Limoges and Robertsons. In the one story he told of her, he confused her with Fred's cousin, Nellie Bowen.[40] Nellie is the "dear little somebody" who "made an awful fuss" when she had to leave the ranch. She lived with the Stimsons for 30 years in Alberta and Mexico and was with Fred Stimson when he died in Montreal in 1912. Mary Stimson had remained in Mexico. In her correspondence Nellie referred to Mary Stimson as "Mrs. Stimson" and to Mr. Stimson as "Fred."[41] Perhaps Mary Stimson was a more formal, less outgoing, personality than Fred. Overall, there is an impression that she did not enjoy life on the ranch; looking back from the end of the 20th century, one wonders if the Stimson marriage was a happy one.

In *I AM* Charlie Millar devotes a verse to Fred Stimson's relationship with aboriginal people. Stimson's place, if any, in the oral tradition of the native people of Alberta is an area which deserves more research. In the 1930s and 1940s Stoney Indians formed a part of the labor force at the Bar U.[42] The Blackfoot probably played a similar role in Stimson's time. At one point a Blackfoot family camped near the Bar U and helped with domestic work on the ranch.[43] Stimson is said to have spoken Blackfoot well and had a reputation for getting on well with the Blackfoot.[44] *I AM* refers to the dispensing of "tea and jam." He had an interest in native culture (Figure 4) and amassed a large collection of beadwork which ultimately found its way into the Royal Ontario Museum.[45]

Fred Stimson made an important contribution to the development of ranching. He brought expertise as a stockman and a manager to the west and helped to establish ranching on a firm footing. He contributed to the

Figure 4. Fred Stimson in Indian regalia. A good friend of native people, he was fascinated by both their material and non-material culture.

(Glenbow Archives, Calgary, Canada NA-2307-33)

social development and traditions of the ranching community. Valuable as these contributions were, they were not sufficient to capture the public imagination and move him to the front ranks of ranching heroes. He remained a stockman and a rancher—he was never categorized as a cowboy, never celebrated for his skill with a lariat or a bronco. He did not participate in the general roundups, much less lead them. Ranching society valued the business skills of the rancher but it celebrated the physical skills, toughness, and practical know-how of the cowboy. It saved its greatest admiration for those, like George Lane, who combined the characteristics of the cowboy and the rancher.

Stimson is best remembered as a wit, a story teller. He is the principal figure in many stories but often the stories have an edge which turns against him. Sometimes he appears as a mild figure of fun—a bit like a remittance man—sometimes as a hard man. Neither character is the stuff of which heroes are made.

Although it is hard to pin down, there is a sense that although Stimson was an important figure in ranching society he was not quite of it. Perhaps his and his family's commitment to ranching society was in doubt. When the ranch was sold in 1902 he left Alberta and never returned. Turning his back on ranching may have ensured that ranching mythology would turn away from him.

George Lane: From Cowboy to Cattle King

Joy Oetelaar
University of Calgary

In the prevailing historical interpretation, Alberta ranching is said to have been distinct from its American counterpart, due to the intrinsically different backgrounds of the elite Eastern Canadians and Britons who formed it. Their wealth, status and political ties assured similar cultural experiences and promoted exclusive relationships. It is further argued that the hegemony of the ranching elite restricted the American influence to a few foremen and cowboys whose duties were limited largely to the physical management of cattle. Moreover, the contrasting 'gentility' and law-abiding nature of Alberta's ranching community caused it to be antagonistic to 'wild and wooly' American cowboys.[1]

Nonetheless, from the beginning, Canadian and British ranch management routinely sought individuals with experience on the western American range, particularly those who had worked in the cattle country of Montana.[2] This study examines the career of one these Americans, George Lane (Figure 1). Lane was one of Alberta's most prominent stockmen from 1902 until his death in 1925, during the so-called 'Golden Age' of Canadian ranching. Soon after his arrival in Alberta, Lane was able to demonstrate his skill as a roundup captain. Nor was it long before he made the transition from being a cowboy employee to becoming a self-employed cattleman. In short order, he married a Canadian woman, became a citizen of the country, and acquired both stock and land. This review of Lane's background and experience will demonstrate that he was well prepared to take advantage of the opportunities presented to him.

The Montana Years

Lane was born 6 March 1856 in Booneville, Indiana to Quakers Joseph William Lane and Julia Pidgeon Lane. While the Pidgeons originally came from Pennsylvania and the Lanes from Kentucky and Virginia, both parents were born in Indiana.

The Lane family moved to Iowa, then Kansas, before Joseph Lane followed the gold rush to Virginia City, Montana. In 1862, 16-year-old George Lane

Figure 1. A formal portrait of George Lane taken in 1920.
(Glenbow Archives, Calgary, Canada NA-3627-30)

joined his father there. Eventually, Joseph and Julia Lane settled on a fruit farm near Boise, Idaho where they lived comfortably until their deaths.[3]

The discovery of gold at Alder Gulch in 1863 initiated the largest placer gold mining in Montana history, attracting some 10,000 people to Virginia City and the surrounding area within a year and a half. This great influx provided another lucrative market to the cattlemen who had already established themselves in the Montana Rockies, where Lane spent his formative years.[4] Although notorious for vigilantes and saloons, contemporary accounts of Virginia City describe a community of 'cultivated women' and 'intelligent society,' whose citizens enjoyed numerous activities, such as good theater, French lessons, and sleigh riding.[5] The clergy, main street merchants, newspaper editors and fraternal groups contributed some balance and stability to the community, while the presence of government officials in the territorial capital led to a considerable degree of social stratification.[6]

Ranchers were also among the territorial elite, and held positions of considerable economic and political influence. Lane worked for some of these men, including prominent stockman, Conrad Kohrs. In the 1880s, promotion of the 'Beef Bonanza' drew eastern and foreign investors to the area, predominantly Englishmen and Scots, whose diverse ethnic, cultural and economic backgrounds provided a cosmopolitan atmosphere to the ranching frontier. Whatever their backgrounds, the majority were thorough businessmen, making deals on the range and in luxurious clubs alike.[7]

The business practices and pastoral methods of the older, established Montana cattlemen were at odds with those who came after the 1880s. Most of the established cattle operations were family businesses or partnerships with local bankers or merchants, some formed to finance single ventures of short duration. In order to adjust resources to meet their land, labor and capital requirements, successful stockmen also needed highly developed entrepreneurial skills. Successful ranchers, therefore, experimented with new operational methods, formed policies with imagination and flexibility, and diversified their operations. Furthermore, individuals who became prosperous without inherited money or corporate assets did so primarily through shrewd trading of various commodities.[8]

Profits also depended upon a reliable, efficient work force. Foremen, for example, required a unique blend of skills, their essential power based "not . . . on any mandate given them by their employers but on positive evidence of their knowledge of the job at hand and the ability to win the confidence and respect of the cowhands."[9] Moreover, despite an enduring romantic portrayal begun by 19th century dime novelists, the working routine of cowboys was fairly monotonous and ranch policies aimed to establish an orderly work force. Consequently, rules of conduct on well-run ranches prohibited lawless and intemperate behavior.[10]

The newcomers, by contrast, were generally hastily formed companies with access to large amounts of capital and their goals were more speculative. Expecting quick profits, they imported low-quality longhorns, ran bigger herds on the range and relied primarily on unfenced pasturage for their stock. Furthermore, they invested minimally in ranch or stock improvements.[11]

Conrad Kohrs, whose career exemplifies the characteristics of the older, established cattlemen, became one of Montana's preeminent stockman and business leaders. After a period of gold mining, Kohrs recognized that providing meat to miners afforded greater opportunities and began buying, selling and butchering beef in the 1860s. He began ranching, placing 1000 head in the Sun River Valley, possibly as early as 1869. Without a personal source of capital, Kohrs financed his expansion through various partnerships and his ability as an entrepreneur. He joined the Wyoming Stock Growers' Association in the early 1870s, and later helped form the Montana association. His attention to maintaining good stock led a contemporary to evaluate him as one of the three most significant contributors to improved breeding in the American West.[12]

In a recent work, historical geographer Terry G. Jordan further elaborates on the distinction between the older, established cattlemen of the Rocky Mountains and those who followed by tracing the development of their cultural/pastoral practices. He maintains that, from the beginning, the Midwestern herding system prevailed in the Rocky Mountains, from Colorado to Alberta and British Columbia. This system contained traits of various cultural groups as herders made their way west and adapted their practices to their new physical settings. A Pennsylvania backwoods culture had made its impress upon the Upland South herders by the time they entered the Kentucky Bluegrass Basin. The movement into the western grasslands established upland herding practices throughout the prairies of Indiana and Illinois and into Missouri, where winter feed was supplemented by wild hay from the wet lands. Beginning in the 1830s, these stockmen moved into Iowa and, in the colder environment, wild-hay production increased substantially.[13]

The Midwestern system was distinguished by attention to the welfare and quality of their livestock, thus making it more labor and capital intensive. Midwesterners winter fed their stock, seasonally moved herds to different pastures, used stock pens, and built pasture fences. They raised mostly shorthorn cattle, bred selectively, imported midwestern stock of British origin and quickly recognized the value of stock associations. These stockmen also grew crops and derived some quantities of milk and butter from their herds.[14]

In the Rocky Mountain ranch country, the Midwestern system was modified to fit the highland environment. Since winter feeding could be required for three to five months, large quantities of hay were critical to success. Although wild hay sufficed initially, by the 1870s and 1880s, timothy, clover and alfalfa production had spread throughout the region. To produce large quantities of hay and to augment the areas of natural flooding, stockmen built irrigation dams and ditches, using methods familiar to the men from Iowa, Illinois and Indiana. Correspondingly, the importance of hay led to early pasture fencing and the use of stock pens, as well as hay stackers, haycribs, mechanical mowers and other implements necessary to haying. The seasonal shifting of pastures became more important and ranchers regularly drove the cattle to the high country in the summer. [15]

The career of Robert Ford, another of Montana's leading stockmen, provides a useful example of the Midwestern tradition and illustrates the close links that developed between Montana and Alberta.[16] Born in Kentucky, he lived in Missouri before moving to northern Montana where he established a large, well-known ranch in the Sun River Valley and the Sweet Grass Hills along the Canadian border. Recognizing the potential market north of the border, Ford drove stock up the Whoop-Up Trail, selling cattle for slaughter to the North-West Mounted Police and Indian agencies. He also supplied cattle to individual ranchers. For example, Alberta's earliest ranchers, John and David McDougall, purchased 100 head of steers and breeding stock from Ford in 1872. From the start, Alberta ranchers and cattle corporations stocked their operations with Montana cattle and horses.[17] Furthermore, a significant portion of the ranch labor force in Alberta consisted of men with experience on Montana ranges. In 1884, the management of the North West Cattle Company and the Cochrane Ranche requested that the president of the Montana Stock Growers' Association, Robert Ford, recommend good men for their foremen positions. George Lane was one of the men selected.

Early Alberta and the Flying E

On the first round-up in 1884, Lane handled his new position with "ease, experience and efficiency."[18] He made such an impression that, the following year, he was elected to the important position of round-up captain and A. E. Cross recalled Lane as "a strict autocrat with all the cowboys (Figure 2). His word was law and no one disputed it."[19] One young Englishman on the roundup confided he could barely say his name.[20] Undoubtedly, Lane's characteristic method of speech—blunt, sparing and direct—added to his authority. However, those who knew him well also uniformly noted the effect his physical qualities had on those around him.[21]

> *A man considerably over six feet tall . . . he moved in a loose-jointed yet positive manner which left no doubt as to the virility and aggressiveness of his nature. Brilliant blue penetrating eyes which concentrated on whoever he at the moment was talking to,*

Figure 2. Willow Creek roundup crew in camp, 1895. Lane had purchased the old Victor Ranch on Willow Creek a few years before. It was called the Flying E because of its brand, and became the Lane family's favorite home. This group included a number of well known High River cowboys. (Left to right:) Ben McDonald, George Winder, Charlie Millar, Charlie Vale, Mike Herman, Charlie Haines, Jim Johnson, George McDonald, Duncan McIntosh (Captain), George Lane, Walter Wake, and two unknown participants. (Glenbow Archives, Calgary, Canada NA-118-3)

> *left an impression of searching behind the words being said to ascertain any deviousness or hidden meaning.*[22]

At a local party, the new man caught the attention of Elizabeth Sexsmith, daughter of one of the first families to settle in High River. With Alvira Sexsmith serving as the bridesmaid and Herb Millar as the best man, Elizabeth Sexsmith and George Lane married one year later. People from all over the district attended a dance at the High River Hotel to celebrate the marriage of 'the radiant little bride' to the tall American boss of the roundup.[23]

While foreman of the Bar U, Lane began building his own herds of cattle and horses, some bought in partnership with his close friend Herb Millar. He and Millar also bought cattle and shipped them to British Columbia, some of the first individuals to enter the coastal market. Lane was also active in the Alberta Stock Growers' Association, one of a dozen men who endeavored to revitalize and strengthen the organization.[24] In the spring of 1889, Lane contracted a serious typhoid infection and, after surgery and a lengthy recovery, left the Bar U.[25]

For a brief period, he held a government contract with Pat Burns to supply beef to the Blood Reserve, before buying the Victor Ranch with partner James N. Rankin in 1891.[26] It was a choice location—a steep cut bank of Willow Creek on the south and rolling hills to the north, with natural springs to supplement the water supply, and abundant natural shelter to shield cattle from cold winter winds. Moreover, the ranch had a good house, two good stables, and corrals and sheds for sheltering and feeding stock.[27] The Lanes would always consider this first ranch, renamed the Flying E, as their 'home place.' In her memoirs, Elizabeth Lane wrote about this period with great fondness. The Lanes enhanced the beautiful foothill setting surrounding the spacious log ranch house with an abundant planting of flowers, making 'a splendid showing.'[28]

Except for two yearly orders for specialty items from the Eaton's catalogue, the family was self-sufficient, producing their own vegetables, fresh beef, and milk and butter. In addition, pike from Willow Creek and a plentiful supply of ducks, prairie chickens and partridge added variety to their diet. Lane had constructed an irrigation system by himself soon after buying the ranch, using only a carpenter's spirit level for surveying a large ditch. He then built a dam on Kuntz's Creek, bringing the water to form a large lake on a hill above the house. The water from this reservoir irrigated the garden and the fields, where Lane planted the first alfalfa in Alberta.[29]

Although their social life revolved primarily around their children, they also visited with Elizabeth Lane's family and their neighbors. While most of the nearby residents were Eastern Canadians, there were exceptions. Lane's old friend, Robert Ford, had recently established a ranch on Willow Creek, just above the Flying E. Natives camped on the ranch and were occasional visitors to the ranch house. In addition, Elizabeth Lane's young brother, Lem, lived and worked on the ranch for three years. The situation was very beneficial to young Sexsmith, allowing him to save money, and take some wages in stock and run them with Lane's herd. By observing and working for his brother-in-law, Sexsmith sharpened his own skills and learned how to operate a ranch. By 1894, he had acquired the nucleus of a small herd of cattle and, with Lane's help in obtaining bank credit, Sexsmith was able to buy his own ranch.[30]

Lane became sole owner of the Flying E in 1896 and continued to improve the ranch over the next 30 years. In 1910, he commissioned a Calgary architectural firm to draw plans for a second house on the ranch. Although not as large as the original house, which remained in use on the site, it was a lovely, well-designed frame home of generous proportions, including a large living room with a great stone fireplace, two main floor bedrooms and two on the upper level. It had the amenities of an urban dwelling, was furnished with ornate late Victorian furniture and easily accommodated distinguished guests. Its design fit well in its surroundings, a verandah on three sides affording comfortable viewing of the foothills.[31]

Lane also added many physical structures to the ranch, increased his holdings and expanded operations. He built a large log barn capable of housing some 40 head of horses, numerous corrals and a well-equipped blacksmith shop. The hog barn was state-of-the art, its distinctive roof design, south facing windows and ventilation systems, ensuring a proper living environment for the animals.[32] An ice-cooled building with the necessary butchering equipment stored meat with a separate, small log building used to prepare pork into hams and bacon. The granary, complete with drive-in aisles and elevating equipment, could store up to 20,000 bushels of grain. The irrigation system had been expanded to provide water for some of the buildings and a two-acre vegetable garden. The larger vegetable garden, and the addition of pigs and chickens to milk cows allowed the ranch to be even more self-sufficient.[33]

By 1925, the ranch held some 22 sections by deed or lease, with an inventory of approximately 600 head of cattle and 200 horses. Feeding these herds in severe winters required stacking 500 tons of hay, and growing and stacking up to 200 tons of oats, rye, barley. All the necessary farm equipment to seed, harvest and thresh these grains was on the ranch. This labor-intensive operation required a farm foreman and farm crew, a full-time blacksmith, a book-keeper, and, of course, riders and a manager.[34]

The Formative Years: Partnerships, Expansion, and Diversification

As early as 1894, Lane and partners A. V. Newsom and J. G. Templeton applied for a charter to form The Willow Creek Cattle Company, a general ranching and trading business dealing in horses, cattle, sheep and swine. Sheep production had been a small but healthy element of the Alberta economy for some time, and some cattle and horse ranchers were adding sheep to their stock, including veteran cattleman E. H. Maunsell and the Conrad Brothers. Lane also began exporting cattle on his own, became a cattle purchaser for J. T. Gordon, and later shipped cattle for the firm of Gordon & Ironsides, the largest purchaser of western range cattle for export to Great Britain.[35]

Although an accomplished cattleman, Lane was also an experienced horseman and farmer. He had spent his youngest days working on his parents' farm and grew up in Iowa and Kansas, agriculturally diverse areas which supported cattle, horses, mixed-farming and grain-growing. Lane was quite aware, therefore, of the requirements of these agricultural sectors and realized that, as farming in Alberta continued to grow and expand, so would the need for good work horses. Pragmatically then, he began breeding purebred horses to supply that need.

Lane's experience on the ranges of Montana had acquainted him with breeders known for their quality horses, the Percheron in particular. In 1898, with financial backing from W. H. Fares, Lane bought the entire stud of 'Diamond O' purebred Percheron stallions and 1200 grade mares from the Mauldin horse ranch at Dillon, Montana. A general economic downturn and panic among horse breeders over the popularity of mechanized vehicles caused James Mauldin to sell the purebred Percherons for twenty dollars a head, a fraction of their book price. In short order, Lane increased his herd, purchasing Percherons from the Riverside Ranch in Mandan, North Dakota and, with partner Herb Millar, he bought other Montana horses. To accommodate his horses, he purchased a second ranch, the Y T, east of Stavely on the Little Bow River.[36]

Lane's background and experience allowed him to develop, improve and expand quickly with few miscalculations. Making sound decisions was particularly crucial for Lane who lacked access to large amounts of capital. In a study of A. E. Cross, for example, Henry Klassen focuses upon the entrepreneurial aspects of his career. Cross came from a wealthy Montreal family who supported his education through business, agricultural and veterinary colleges in Ontario. When Cross graduated as a veterinary surgeon, he was offered the position of assistant manager, bookkeeper and veterinary surgeon for the Cochrane Ranche. After leaving this position, Cross established the A7 ranch, in partnership with his brothers, after leaving the Cochrane. Unfortunately, the location was a poor one, requiring Cross to rebuild the A7 in the foothills a year later. At the new location, his method was one of 'trial and error.'[37] Klassen argues that Cross's ability as an entrepreneur transformed his experiences into a successful operation. What is included, but not emphasized, in this study is that, for both his cattle and brewing businesses, A. E. Cross's learning process was subsidized by the steady influx of large financial investments from his father, Judge Alexander S. Cross.[38]

In contrast, George Lane was not formally educated and he gained his knowledge of ranching from observation and work experience. Lane's family was clearly not wealthy and, although Joseph Lane likely made a comfortable living at farming, his various moves, including a time in Montana gold country, would suggest he hoped for improved fortune. Lane began earning a living early, presumably to augment the family income. After receiving his pay from the United States Cavalry, for example, Lane turned the entire amount over to his mother.[39] Since Lane could not turn to his family for financial support, he relied on an array of other sources, including small investments, co-ownerships of stock, short-term partnerships, and the profits from trading and exporting stock. Lane's entrepreneurial skill, therefore, was critical to success, with little room for trial and error.

The individuals Lane chose as his closest associates were equally important. At first glance, Herb Millar, J. T. Gordon and Robert Ironside appear to be quite dissimilar. Yet, upon closer inspection, some significant commonalities emerge. Soon after the North West Cattle Company was

established in 1881, shareholder and manager Fred Stimson went to Chicago, bought 21 Shorthorn bulls, and hired Herb Millar to bring the bulls to Alberta. Millar, born on a small Illinois farm near Chicago Heights, had spent his spare time as a young man around the Chicago Stock Yards. When he arrived, Millar was hired to work on the Bar U as a cowboy and remained employed on the ranch by its different owners for over fifty years. Owners, managers and ranch hands alike highly valued his ability and judgement which contributed significantly to the Bar U's success.[40]

The partnership of J. T. Gordon and Robert Ironside underwent various transformations initially, including periods when they operated separately. Both men moved to Winnipeg from Ontario, Gordon in 1878 and Ironside in 1882. Gordon came from an Irish farming family, while Ironside was the son of a Scottish millwright. Gordon was employed for three years by a local lumber company before beginning his own lumber, wheat and cattle business. Ironside sold farm implements for a period of time, before entering into the grain business. The partnership began dealing in lumber, wheat and cattle but soon expanded into meat-packing and cattle exporting. W. H. Fares, a cattle buyer in Alberta, was later admitted as a third partner. In the early 1890s Ironside moved to Montreal where he looked after the firm's business in the eastern provinces until his death on 10 October 1910.[41]

It becomes apparent that, although Millar, Gordon and Ironside concentrated on the cattle business and subsidiary activities for the better part of their careers, their roots were also in the farming sector. Ironside apparently did not farm himself but, through regular contact with local farmers, he learned a great deal about the grain business. He also identified particular problems and provided a solution to at least one by erecting the first local grain elevator with a capacity of 40,000 bushels. It is significant that these men and Lane did not view the grain and cattle economies as separate or, as necessarily competing, agricultural sectors. Rather, the prior experience of all four men made them aware of the essential connection between growing grain and raising cattle. Consequently, haying and growing grains for winter feeding was a basic component of their joint ventures. Moreover, they had a good understanding of the importance of well-fed, fat cattle in the export business from their experiences in the Chicago stock market and that of Winnipeg, the 'Chicago of the North.' Indeed, the economic strength and growth of these prairie cities was based upon their dominance as distribution, grain and stock centers.

It is not surprising that, soon after arriving in Alberta, Lane and Millar had formed a business and personal relationship based on their shared midwestern heritage. Nor is it surprising that Lane had turned to J. T. Gordon to further his aspirations, even though other potential sources were closer at hand. In 1902, Lane brought his aspirations together with the strength of these relationships and became the principal owner of one of the jewels of Alberta ranching, the Bar U Ranch. When Lane purchased the Bar U in conjunction with Gordon, Ironside & Fares, it was the largest ranch sale of its time, the transaction including 19,000 acres owned outright, 3090 head of cattle and 500 horses at a price of nearly a quarter of a million in cash. Although the Winnipeg firm later purchased a ranch on the south Saskatchewan and an extensive one in Mexico, the Bar U was its first. Millar had left his position as Bar U foreman earlier to work with Lane and returned to the job when Lane bought the ranch.[42]

The following decade was a difficult one for Alberta cattlemen. A general deterioration in the quality and value of range stock which began years earlier climaxed in 1902.[43] While the quality of their stock was less problematic after 1905, cattlemen faced other serious problems. Eradication of mange became an expensive and time-consuming process which took years to complete. The hard winter of 1906–07 resulted in grave losses of cattle, leaving many ranchers discouraged and searching for new strategies, or leaving the business. By 1911, because of the massive sell-off of breeding stock, there was a real shortage of cattle, and in many districts the local market could not be supplied.[44] In addition to these specific problems, the ranchers faced the steady encroachment of homesteaders onto their range lands, and a Liberal government which favored the farmers over the cattlemen.

The cattle business in Alberta had been founded and sustained, in large part, because of the ties between the large cattle companies and the Conservative party. After the Liberal victory in 1896, those ties were frayed, if not severed. The Alberta Stock Growers' Association put increasing settlement and crowded ranges at the top of its agenda in 1903 and 1905, during which time Lane served as second vice-president and vice-president respectively. The association petitioned the government at each meeting for the right to purchase grazing leases or have closed leases for a specified period of years. In addition, the association asked for certain districts to be designated unfit for settlement and reserved for ranching. In each case, their efforts were refused unceremoniously.[45] After the 1903 petition failed to win any consideration, Lane traveled to Ottawa to present the stockmen's case personally.

In a June 1st, 1904 statement to the Commissioner of Dominion Lands, J. W. Greenway, Lane asked for the reservation of large portions of the eastern slope of the foothills for grazing, an area traditionally used as the summer range. While he noted that prohibiting the lease or sale of large tracts of land in areas reasonably considered fit for farming might have validity, arable land in the high, rough foothills was minimal. Without closed leases in this area, cattle ranching in the region would be destroyed. Lane urged that small ranchers in the district be allowed first selection of land with larger stockmen choosing from the remainder.[46] Three days later, Alberta MP Frank Oliver went on record to the Minister of the Interior, Clifford Sifton, supporting Lane's proposal. Oliver's letter of nearly five

pages is emphatic and unequivocal, his only quibble being his preference for selling the land outright to the parties rather than leasing.[47]

Apparently, Oliver had time to reconsider and amend his view, for when he became Minister of the Interior in April 1905, he immediately ordered a review of all legislation concerning grazing leases and began to chip away at the ranchers' domain. However, under the previous administration, new lease regulations had been implemented allowing both open and closed leases, and six closed leases were granted under these regulations. Half of these leases had been given to cattle companies with significant Liberal supporters, including George Lane's. In a political atmosphere which, for decades, had rewarded large Conservative cattlemen with similar favors, it is interesting that both contemporary and retrospective observers viewed Liberal favoritism with cynicism.[48] Nevertheless, at a time when other large lease holders faced serious difficulties from changing government policies and encroachment by homesteaders, Lane kept the Bar U intact. His acquisition of a closed lease covering 47,000 acres of winter range, spreading north and west from the ranch headquarters, was augmented by the purchase of key quarter sections to round out the deeded land on which hay and crops were grown. Lane's midwestern experience, moreover, contributed to growth and development on the Bar U. His early implementation of extensive irrigation and growing large amounts of feed grains further expanded the winter feeding of stock.[49] His use of milk cows, hogs and other produce set him apart from other large cattlemen at the time.[50] He was the only prominent cattleman to publicly advocate mixed farming as being necessary to Alberta's development.[51]

His Montana experience was also reflected in the way he ran the Bar U. Lane continued to use the same methods which had served him so well as foreman; that is, through positive evidence of his knowledge of the job at hand. When he told his employees what to do, they knew full well that he had done the job himself many times. On the rare occasion that a cowboy failed to perceive this fact, Lane was not amused and demonstrated the task vigorously and with less than good humor.[52] While his men may not have always found him amiable, they did respect him. In addition, Lane remained personally involved as owner. When most large-scale cattlemen directed their business entirely from Calgary, Lane was not content to do so.[53] Even after his operations expanded enormously, he had the unnerving habit of showing up to observe how a particular job was being done, much to the discomfort of any employee performing poorly.[54] Although he demanded a high level of performance from his employees, he administered policies in a fair manner, with no arbitrariness. Moreover, since the ranch was well-run with a high premium placed on efficiency and skill, the Bar U became the training ground for Alberta's cowboys.[55]

At one time or another, the best of Alberta's cowboys, like Herb and Charlie Millar, Bert Pierson, Johnny Franklin, and Bert Wilder, worked for

Lane and many became ranch owners after leaving the Bar U.[56] Charles McKinnon, for example, was a native of Ontario who came to Alberta in 1889. He began his employment with the Bar U in 1892 where he remained for fifteen years. He left to establish the L. K. Ranch with Alex Nesbitt in 1907.[57] Other former employees are less well-known. Roy Clines, for example, grew up in Missouri and worked in Idaho for a year before joining the Bar U in 1915. He worked for Lane for many years, becoming his foreman at the ranch in 1922. Clines married, left the Bar U and bought two sections of land from Lane which he farmed and ranched for some 30 years.[58] Ezekiel Stone Roberts, a native of New Brunswick, worked on the Bar U for 19 years before leaving in 1909 to begin his own cattle business. In 1922, Roberts worked for George Lane again as summer range rider, the last year the Bar U had cattle on the Bassano land.[59]

Through his attention to breeding, Lane continued to be highly successful in the cattle business. His October 1912 shipment of fat, well-formed, and well-finished cattle broke all records previously held by western cattle on the Chicago market. Although within a few short years, the list of Alberta cattlemen shipping to Chicago read like a who's who of ranching, in 1912 Calgary cattlemen speculated publicly on how much Lane would lose on the venture. When it was announced that, after deducting freight, duty and expenses on route, Lane still made a larger profit than possible on the British, Winnipeg or home markets, the same cattlemen were still sufficiently nettled to issue a rejoinder in print.[60] Such differences aside, Lane was elected as president of the Alberta Stock Growers' Association the following year. When the association met serious funding and membership problems in 1919, he was the driving force behind the establishment of its successor, the Cattlemen's Protective Association. Moreover, he continued to rank prominently as a breeder, his cattle topping the Chicago market again in 1916.[61]

During this period of time, Lane further improved and expanded his horse and grain-growing operations. His show team of purebred Percherons brought him international recognition as a horse breeder and, in 1913, Lane bought the Namaka farm east of Calgary to develop breeding on an even larger scale.[62] An active promoter of good horse breeding, he helped form the Canadian Percheron Society in 1907, serving twice as its president, and provided leadership for the Alberta Horsebreeders' Association. Lane also began growing grain on a large-scale. In 1911, he plowed 1500 acres in the Bar U flats for the first time in its history and seeded winter wheat. Six years later, Lane and C. S. Noble were the largest grain growers in Alberta. Lane believed that mixed farming was an issue of great importance to Alberta's development and became an increasingly vocal supporter.[63]

Lane as a Public Figure

The role of boosterism has been examined in numerous studies on Western expansion in North America. More often than not, frontier boosters are characterized primarily by their considerable rhetorical talents and salesmanship skills. Canadian urban historian Alan J. Artibise has argued, however, that more than these characteristics, boosterism was a unique interaction between the "hopes, beliefs, energy, community spirit, initiative and adaptability"[64] of individuals and groups, and their economic, technological and political environment. The decisions made and actions taken by boosters to build up their communities significantly influenced the rate and pattern of western urban development.

By 1912, George Lane had become an unabashed Alberta booster, using his considerable reputation as a cattleman, horse breeder and farmer to promote the agricultural and livestock potential of the region throughout Canada, the United States and abroad. In 1912, for example, he saw the Calgary Stampede as the perfect vehicle to advertise Alberta as a livestock country and to encourage wealthy stockmen to locate in the area. Moreover, he saw the event as the best way to show the "aggressiveness and modernity of the west," while also celebrating its frontier past.[65] H. C. McMullen, general livestock agent of the CPR, and Guy Weadick first proposed the idea to Calgary Exhibition management and were flatly rejected. They then outlined their plan to Lane who arranged a meeting with Pat Burns and A. E. Cross and, later, A. J. McLean.[66]

Lane was particularly active in the community of High River where he built one of the town's first business blocks and was a member of the executive board which organized a local Agricultural Society and Exhibition in 1909. High River sent Lane to Ottawa as one of three official envoys to secure a second railway in 1911. Six months later, the Canadian Northern Railway added the town to its line.[67] Lane's most notable contribution, however, was his role in the establishment of the E.P. Ranch. Regionally and nationally, his work and enterprise were credited for making the purchase a reality. Moreover, local citizens and national observers recognized the potential benefits to Alberta and Canada from having the Prince as a Canadian rancher, especially as an inducement to other wealthy Englishmen to follow suit.[68] Although the Prince of Wales was the most celebrated of Lane's guests at the Bar U (Figure 3), many other dignitaries made publicized visits which further encouraged national and foreign investment in Alberta ranch country.[69]

Lane and other Alberta businessmen became increasingly aware that investment without control over the region's modes of production did little to further development. The high price of flour ignited a local backlash against manufacturers, perceived as exploiting Westerners, and the call was made for the establishment of a local mill.[70] Lane and others formed the

Figure 3. The Prince of Wales at the Bar U Ranch house during his visit in 1919. People in the foreground, left to right: Professor William Carlyle (Lane's manager who became manager of the E.P. Ranch), Edward Prince of Wales and George Lane. (Glenbow Archives, Calgary, Canada, NB-16-144)

Alberta Flour Mills in 1915, Lane serving as a stockholder and a member of the board of directors.[71] Despite a vigorous financial and public campaign and the injection of large loans from stockholders Lane and William Pearce, the company sold its assets to Spillers Ltd. of England in 1925.[72]

Lane's outspoken criticism of federal policies governing regional issues had begun during the 1911 campaign for reciprocity. In a letter to Frank Oliver, published by the *High River Times*, Lane advised the honorable minister to listen to the 'mass of people' who were in favor of reciprocity rather than to the manufacturers and corporations.[73] Indeed, the common Liberal indictment of the Conservative Party was to associate it with Eastern banking and financial interests. Although reciprocity failed federally, its regional popularity proved disastrous to Alberta Conservatives.[74]

In April 1913, Lane was nominated as the Liberal candidate for Bow Valley. In his acceptance speech, Lane said he did not believe the district people could be swayed by big money and, if they could be, he did not want the office.[75] Initially, the Conservatives treated Lane's candidacy with derision; R. B. Bennett called him a joke as a public figure who had money but no brains. However, the voters appeared to be taking Lane seriously, and the Calgary paper carried a number of sensational articles designed to discredit him.[76] After the polls were in, the *Herald* had to report that the

Bow Valley had gone 'sweepingly' for Lane. Even the Tory stronghold of Bassano turning in a 'crushing' Lane victory.[77] Lane's tenure as Member of Parliament was short-lived, however. Three days after the election, Lane offered his seat to C. R. Mitchell, the only minister to be defeated. After consulting his constituency, Lane resigned his seat in Mitchell's favor.[78]

At the Liberal convention in February 1915, however, Lane was unanimously elected as a candidate for the next federal election. During the next two years, the war in Europe created unprecedented upheaval in traditional party politics as candidates realigned themselves in relation to the proposed Union government. As late as 8 November 1917, just weeks before the December election, the Conservative candidate for Bow River announced he was prepared to resign his candidacy in Lane's favor and work for his election if Lane ran as 'a win-the-war' candidate. As the local press noted, since Lane had already signified his approval of the Union government, his election was virtually settled.[79] As Liberal Unionists gathered for their convention on 17 November, victory across the board appeared assured. In a surprising move, however, Lane sent a written communication withdrawing his name. In a statement read to the convention, Lane said he had always been a believer in Liberal principles and, after serious consideration, he had been persuaded by his many friends in 1914 to enter the federal arena. However, he would not be a party to the recent political dissension in the Bow River district and would seek no place or position.[80]

Concluding Remarks

Although the standard perspective of Alberta ranching claims successful Americans were anomalies, a closer examination of George Lane and his times reveals that a number of assumptions on which this view is based require revision. Although this perspective has provided a useful political framework for ranching history, it unduly emphasizes socio-cultural behavior and provides far too little attention to cultural praxis. While the Alberta cattlemen were the social elite for a time, the essential characteristics of their elitism were not unique to Alberta. Ranching that emerged in the American Midwest and later expanded into the northwestern states and Canada was led by powerful, high-profile stockmen from diverse, cosmopolitan backgrounds, with a strong component of Scots and Englishmen. The conventional perspective places great emphasis on the social milieu and its 'outward manifestations,' such as well-kept and refined ranch homes where the elite hired cooks and governesses, played polo and hosted genteel social events, and made deals in exclusive urban settings. Moreover, the evidence of the law-abiding nature of Alberta ranching society rests too frequently on the cultural activities of its members, the presumption apparently being that well-tailored cattlemen, by definition, refrained from illegal activities.[81] It has been demonstrated that George Lane's background and experience enabled him to move and operate within the Alberta ranching elite because the two were so similar. But it was Lane's competence and judgment which made him so influential, not his social gifts. In many ways he seems to epitomize many of the characteristics of Jordan-Bychkov's Midwestern ranching tradition, which served equally well on both sides of the Alberta–Montana border.

Tenderfoot to Rider: Learning 'Cowboying' on the Canadian Ranching Frontier during the 1880s

Simon M. Evans
Memorial University

Preface

Robert W. Newbolt was just the kind of young Briton, privileged, well to do, and unconsciously aware of his own superiority, that was the favorite butt of westerners' jokes.[1] He was the stuff of which the stereotypical 'dude' was made. Born into an army family and educated at the prestigious Uppingham public school, his plans to follow his father into the military were rudely shattered when he failed the medical due to a sporting injury. Instead of heading off to Sandhurst, eighteen-year-old Bob found himself crossing the Atlantic to join Major General Strange at the Military Colonization Company Ranch, a colonization project in the North-West Territories of Canada for 'men of means and good character.'[2]

In his cabin trunk was a complete set of English riding regalia, the best and most up to date that money could buy. Fortunately perhaps, General Strange met Bob at Kingston and sensibly forbad him to take his prized riding outfit any further west!

The long trail from the Lemhi Valley, Idaho, to the ranch on the Bow River was to be Bob's 'Damascus Road.' He started the two-month cattle drive a complete tenderfoot, and emerged as a trusted member of a trail outfit. Initially he was given the task of driving the wagon behind the cook. Years later he recalled:

> *I, being a 'green horn', of course they took all sorts of advantages of me, along with driving the wagon all day, I was put 'night herding' at night and all night at that. I did not catch on for quite a while that the other riders were being relieved at midnight, because meeting them in the dark I would not know the difference . . . . So far, on this trailing and night herding, I was dressed in my English clothing, flannels, puttees, bowler hat*

Figure 1. Bob Newbolt in Montreal on his way west. His loud check coat, unremarkable in the English countryside, label him a stereotypical 'dude' in western Canada. (Glenbow Archives, Calgary, Canada NA-1046-5)

> *and all [Figure 1]. These garments were far from suitable for such use, so I outfitted myself at Deer Lodge with a complete western cowboy outfit, except only for a 'six shooter', something I never did carry or use. After acquiring this new outfit, which of course included a cowboy hat, I put my beloved bowler in the wagon where I thought it would be safe, but the riders found it and soon riddled it with bullets.*[3]

Bob was given an old white horse to ride, the only one considered safe enough for such a greenhorn. However, he had ridden to hounds in England, and discretely taught his mount how to jump any obstacles in their way. When some cattle got stuck on the wrong side of a homesteader's rail fence, Bob and his mount jumped neatly over and retrieved them. Tom Lynch was so impressed that he gave Newbolt a chance to choose a mount from the remuda. Of course, the boys chose a well-known bucking horse for this initiation rite, and Bob was promptly 'piled' three times. He completed the story:

> *Then a Mexican chap showed me how to hobble my stirrups and also to hold one rein tighter than the other to keep the horse bucking in a circle. Then I rode him to a stand still.*[4]

As week succeeded week and the leisurely drive continued, Newbolt absorbed new skills:

> *I was developing into a pretty fair cow-hand and the boys were beginning to treat me with a good deal more respect than was the case at the start of the trip. I was enjoying the experience immensely and had developed a love for the great wide-open spaces.*[5]

It was a measure of his new abilities that Bob was chosen to ride ahead of the herd from Fort Macleod to the ranch on the Bow to tell General Strange of their progress.

This reminiscence is but one example of the way in which a young man adapted to the ways of the ranching frontier (Figure 2). As one reads the letters and diaries of others who came to Alberta one cannot help but be impressed with the speed of their transformation from greenhorn to seasoned rider. This paper will focus on the manner in which they learned their new trade.

The Context

The 1990s have witnessed a number of significant additions to the scholarly literature on ranching.[6] In particular, Terry G. Jordan has provided a broad continental context which challenges us to review old dogma and to look at the establishment of ranching in western Canada in new ways. In *North*

Figure 2. Bob Newbolt transformed into a 'rider', on his own place two years later. Like many young immigrants he was both highly motivated and pre-adapted to learn the skills he needed to succeed as a rancher. (Glenbow Archives, Calgary, Canada NA-1046-18)

American Cattle Ranching Frontiers he traces the origins of North American pastoral traditions not to a single hearth but to a variety of source regions along the Atlantic fringe: Andalusian and Mesetan in Spain; Upland British; and in Africa, Sahelian and Sudanese. Traits from these varied sources first gained a trans–Atlantic bridgehead in the Antilles, and they mixed and melded there before becoming established on the continental mass of the new world. From the early beginnings in the 17th century, there was not one cattle rearing tradition but several, not one ranching frontier, but many. From these varied coastal enclaves, Jordan tells of the emergence and expansion of three Anglo–American cattle ranching systems, Texan, Californian, and Midwestern. Using the evidence of material culture as well as an impressive array of archival documentation, he chronicles the diffusion of cattle culture and traces the roots from which each advance took place. Traditions met and fused as the three related but distinct pastoral traditions collided and competed for territory. When his complex and detailed exposition is completed, it becomes clear that Jordan is proposing a radically revisionist hypothesis which downplays the contributions of the Hispanic traits which shaped both the Texan and the Californian traditions. The title of his penultimate chapter tells it all, "The Midwest Triumphant." He suggests that increasing intensity of pastoral activity, greater inputs of labor and capital, haying, fencing, and irrigation, represent the take-over of

Midwestern stock farming traditions, and the disappearance of the extensive ways of the Hispanic open range and trail driving days. Yet perhaps even this is to oversimplify. Jordan qualifies his conclusions:

> *The outcome of this contest for the last frontier was by no means simple. While the midwesterners should be judged the winners, conquering even the strongholds of their rivals, the mixing and borrowing and tinkering went on to the very end . . . nothing approaching cultural homogenization was ever achieved in the ranching west, even to the present day.*[7]

Where does the emerging cattle industry of the Alberta foothills fit into this continental context? More than twenty years ago, David H. Breen challenged the assumption that the Canadian ranching frontier was a straight forward case of technical and land-use diffusion from the United States. He demonstrated that the role of the Canadian federal government, and its agencies in the west, insured that ranching in Canada developed in a very different institutional environment from that of neighboring Montana or the Dakotas.[8] Nevertheless, this 'institutional fault line' was permeable. New pastoral enterprises in the Dominion required personnel, cattle, capital and technology, and those who aspired to be 'cattle kings' were prepared to look far and wide to satisfy their demands. There were three available sources for these vital inputs: eastern Canada, the United States, and Great Britain. Each of these regions contributed something to the transformation of the young immigrants who were drawn to western Canada by their hopes of becoming cowboys. This paper seeks to explore the way in which such newcomers learned the necessary skills. Who taught them? And in turn where had their 'teachers' served their apprenticeship? My focus is on the working life of newcomers as they struggled to master the elements of 'cowboying.'

In a previous paper, I used the nominal returns of the Canadian census to explore some characteristics of the range labor force.[9] 'Place of birth data' was used to weigh the relative importance of Canadians, British and Americans among those who worked on the range. This gave a somewhat spurious precision to what I knew to be a complex reality. For example, there were individual Canadians who had spent years in the United States before returning to Canada. There were also cases of young Americans who arrived in Canada as teenagers and learned their skills on the Canadian range. As far as the diffusion of technology was concerned, the place of birth was surely far less relevant than the place of apprenticeship. However, in order to reach conclusions as to origins, one is forced to look at life stories in some detail. This paper is based on biographical material, letters, diaries, reminiscences and contemporary newspaper accounts. In a relatively short paper only a few cases can be explored in any detail, and this means that any generalizations may seem to be based on *ad hominem* arguments. I

have done my best to balance this danger by making reference to the larger sample of cases which were considered in the original work.[10]

Migration involves transformation. All that is familiar is left behind and the process of becoming familiar with a new physical, social and work environment begins. In some situations the path toward assimilation is pursued grudgingly and reluctantly. In the case of many of the young men who aspired to be riders or ranchers in the Alberta foothills this adaptive journey was embraced joyfully and the transformation was often miraculously quick. Habits of dress and speech, attitude and behavior, were relinquished almost over night. The 'new and naked land' was explored and its seasons evaluated; the unexpected gift of a mid-winter chinook was experienced for the first time.[11] An attempt will be made to examine this process of adaption which transformed young men from eastern Canada, Great Britain and the United States into Albertans.

Greenhorns had to learn new skills from experienced rangemen. However adaptable they were, and however motivated to succeed, they had to be shown what to do and how to do it. They did not lack instructors. From the mid–1870s onwards, small scale ranching enterprises had begun to appear in the foothills, especially along the Oldman River west of Fort Macleod.[12] Bunches of cattle were trailed across the line from Montana both to fulfil government contracts and to stock homesteads and small ranches. After 1875, these movements became more or less regular in occurrence. Ox-trains and coaches maintained a seasonal service between Fort Calgary, Fort Macleod, and Fort Benton.[13] Men who had been involved in trading with the Indians of the plains, and in the collection and transportation of buffalo robes, changed the focus of their activities somewhat as the flow of robes dried up and the 'beef bonanza' began to gather momentum. These 'plainsmen' constituted an important pool of skilled labor on which prospective ranchers could draw.

The Canadian government, in pursuit of its National Policy, established lease regulations which propelled the range cattle industry to take off from these small scale local beginnings. In 1881 there were only 9000 head of cattle in the North-West Territories, five years later there were 100,000.[14] A flood of risk capital from eastern Canada and Great Britain underwrote the establishment of ranches both great and small.[15]

The major investors, almost all of them men with deep knowledge of stock rearing 'back east,' did their best to insure that their leases were stocked with the best available cattle, they also made vigorous efforts to protect their enormous investments by searching out and recruiting experienced rangemen to run their ranches. The American cowboys, who filled these positions as foremen and managers, played a crucial role in the successful expansion of ranching in Canada during the 1880s. Young newcomers lived and worked alongside both plainsmen and professional cowboys, and from them acquired both the practical skills and the vital 'cow sense' which were the foundations of their new lives.

The aim of this paper is: (1) to describe the way in which young men from a variety of backgrounds adapted to range life; (2) to assess the role played by their 'teachers' in this process, and to evaluate where these men had learned their trade; and finally (3) to relate these findings to a more general continent-wide interpretation of cattle ranching frontiers.

The Newcomers: Origins and Transformations

Ted Hills, like Bob Newbolt, was born into a British service family. He too was sent to Uppingham School for his education.[16] As he was the eldest of ten children, he was encouraged to fend for himself as soon as his schooling was over. He came to Canada, and spent the summer of 1884 with a survey crew in the Fort Carlton area of Assiniboia. He wintered with an Englishman and his son on Fish Creek outside Calgary, and as soon as the snow began to melt in the spring of 1885, young Hills started to look for a job as a rider. Throughout this exciting transition in his life, Hills was a faithful correspondent with his parents. Some 50 of his letters, dated from April 1883 to October 1885, have survived, and provide a vivid account of Ted's initiation into the ways of the range.[17]

Hills had a somewhat egotistical attitude to the Riel Rebellion, for he felt that it would improve his chances of finding employment substantially. In April 1885, he wrote:

> *This little rebellion that is going on here is a splendid thing for the country and is leaving a lot of money in it. Teams are getting $8.00 a day and man and horses found in everything . . . as so many are out of the country men are very scarce on the range so that I may be able to drop on something.*[18]

He was right, for he was taken on by Fred Stimson to join the Bar U wagon for the spring roundup. Hills was given the job of horse wrangler, looking after the remuda of spare horses.[19] It was a responsible job, for the mobility of the whole outfit depended on its horses. Hills was well prepared for his task because he had been around horses all his life, and had been responsible for the horses of the survey team the previous summer.[20] Ted managed to scratch a hurried note to his parents after a couple of weeks on the roundup, and described a typical day:

> *I have not had a chance since last writing to you of mailing a letter. But I hope that we may soon have a chance to post a letter. I am taking advantage of a fine day, the horses are grazing quietly, and having a horse that does not try to run away, I am able to lie down on the grass and write this . . . Since I last wrote to*

> *you we have been turning out at 3 a.m. everyday, and as I don't take the horses in until 8 p.m., my hours are rather long. The night herder brings the horses in every morning shortly after 3, and we have to form a temporary corral with the waggons forming one side and ropes tied to the wheels make the third side, while the men stand at the side and rope the saddle horses that are wanted for the morning. At noon I corral them in the same way and the afternoon ones are caught. There always used to be a lot of delay, due to there being such a wild lot of saddle horses, one or two fellows used to get spilt every morning. There has only been one bad fall.*[21]

The next few letters tell of hail storms, which stampeded the horse herd, of rattle snakes, and dangerous river crossings. It is somewhat surprising that Hills makes no reference to acquiring specific skills. All the hands needed to have some proficiency with a rope, and it is hard to believe that Hills did not look for opportunities to learn the basic techniques, and to practice them during the long monotonous days he spent on watch.[22] One letter does hint at the manner in which a receptive young man could learn his craft. Hills wrote:

> *I have just forded the Oldman's River with Nigger John [John Ware] who showed me the ford. It is a bad river to cross and most people cross by the scow, but we thought that a dollar saved was a dollar gained, that being the modest sum that they ask to ferry a saddle horse over.*[23]

One can imagine the famous cowboy, the veteran of hundreds of tricky river crossings, pointing out the dangerous holes and quick-sands to the young Englishman, and showing him the safest way across.

Hills was to spend the next twenty years in the foothills. He worked for the CC Ranch, the Skrine brothers, the A7, and was a regular at the roundup on the Willow Creek or Bar U wagons. When he got married, Hills homesteaded on the middle fork of the Highwood River and established the Echo Glen Ranch. In 1908, he and his wife returned to England, and then moved on to Kenya where they ran a coffee plantation. A near neighbor was H. B. Alexander, who had owned the Two Dot Ranch. Hills never forgot his time in Alberta, and when he finally retired to Sussex, he used to spend the occasional summer night up on the bare downlands under the stars, because, he said, it reminded him of the roundups in the foothills.[24]

Many other young Englishmen left accounts of their experiences on the Canadian range.[25] For example, the Church brothers who established the Hadley Ranch and specialized in gentling horse in the English manner;[26] Claude Gardiner in his lonely and isolated line cabin during his first winter in the Pincher Creek district;[27] and H. M. Hatfield, with his packs of wolf hounds

MONTREAL DAILY STAR – FRIDAY, NOVEMBER 13, 1901.

BOWIE KNIVES

TRINKETS TO PACIFY THE SAVAGE INDIANS

SNOW SHOES AXES ETC.

BLANKETS

REVOLVERS

'PON ME WORD, I FEEL QUITE LOST YOU KNOW, WITHOUT ME TOP HAT BOXES, EVENING DWESS CASES AND TWOUSER STWECHERS, BUT I WON'T NEED THEM AT ALL IN CAWNADA DON'TCHER KNOW.

RIFLES AND GUNS

AMMUNITION

BLANKETS

HEAVY CLOTHING

FURS

ASSORTED PIPES

THE ENGLISHMAN IN CANADA—8.

He Goes on Board.

Figure 3. The way the west saw privileged English immigrants! (From A. G. Racey's 18-part cartoon series published in the *Montreal Star*. Autumn 1901).

(Glenbow Archives, Calgary, Canada, NA-3683-3)

and coyote hounds, railing day after day in his diary at the bitter weather which was killing his cattle.[28]

By no means were all aspiring cowboys privileged immigrants (Figure 3) from Britain. There were at least as many young men from eastern Canada, and a good number from the United States, who learned their skills in the foothills and emerged as foremen, managers, ranchers and exemplars of range skills in competitive events.[29] One thinks of Fred and Walter Ings, Frank White, James Hargrave, Walter Ross, A. E. Cross, and a host of others. Lachlin McKinnon came from as humble origins as any and founded a ranching dynasty.[30] Brought up by poor Scottish parents in Grey County, Ontario, he made his way west in 1886 and started as chore boy on the Military Colonization Company Ranch. His particular task was to help Major-General Strange who had been badly injured in an accident. McKinnon learned fast and benefited from his friendship with Roy Cowan, the experienced cowboy who had been hired to 'tutor' the young shareholders in the enterprise. Lachlin himself survived a harrowing series of riding accidents, and built a reputation as a solid and reliable hand. He was employed for some years as foreman of the Canadian Coal and Colonization Company's 76 Ranch. During the 1890s McKinnon got married and homesteaded on the Bow River close to Bob Newbolt.

Mike Herman and Charlie Millar both came to Alberta in their teens, Mike with a trail herd from Montana, while Charlie followed his brother Herb to the Bar U Ranch from the Chicago area. Both young men spent their working lives around cattle and made names for themselves as highly skilled cowboys, Millar being noted for his riding and Herman for his roping expertise.[31] However, if one had to choose a single figure to exemplify this group of 'local heroes,' the natural choice would be Herb Millar, because of the tremendous influence he exerted on others and the prominent position which he carved for himself in the councils of cattlemen.[32] Of the many compliments savored by Herb Millar on his 80th birthday, probably none gave him more satisfaction than that written by Harold Riley who mentioned that many well known figures,

> *who subsequently became ranch owners or expert riders, ropers and general all-round ranch hands were in a sense 'pupils at the Herb Millar school.' Under his watchful eye they rode the range with him as their boss. From him they learned many valuable lessons in the art of handling livestock and ranch management.*[33]

Millar was among the first employees of the Bar U Ranch and worked there, off and on, for more than 50 years. He was a tough taciturn man who had mastered all the varied skills of a cowboy, indeed, many acclaimed him as being the prettiest rider they had ever seen break an outlaw horse. In addition to these practical gifts, Herb's council on all matters related to stock and grass were highly valued by his employers, men like Fred Stimson, George Lane, and Pat Burns. Like any good 'non-commissioned officer' his influence was felt down in the ranks and up in the corridors of power. It is therefore important to establish that Millar learned his skills on the Canadian range, although he was born in the United States.

Millar was an Illinois farm boy. He was hired in 1881 by Fred Stimson to care for twenty one purebred Shorthorn bulls which had been purchased for the newly formed North West Cattle Company. The arrangement was that the nineteen-year-old Millar would feed the stock over the winter at the Chicago stock yards and then bring them up to Alberta in the spring. This journey was quite an undertaking, for it involved travel by rail to Bismark, North Dakota; thence by stern wheeler up the Missouri to Fort Benton; and finally up the Whoop-Up Trail to High River. Millar had admitted to Stimson when he 'boned' him for a job, that although he had grown up around stock, he had no experience of ranching. Stimson, who was heading west for the first time himself, and had no experience either, assured him that he would soon learn! And learn he did. His first winter in Alberta was spent with Jim Minesinger, Cal Morton, George Emerson and Phil Weinard, constructing the first buildings at the ranch headquarters. Being the youngest, Herb was assigned the duties of cook, for which he proved to have little aptitude. He did much better at learning cowboying and it did not take him long to become a seasoned ranch hand. Slimly built but very wiry, he proved to be a natural rider, and was soon responsible for managing the 'rough string,' and providing the Bar U cowboys with range broken horses. He was Fred Stimson's choice to succeed Everett (Ebb) Johnson as foreman when Ebb left the big ranch. When he arrived in Alberta, Millar was as much of a 'greenhorn' as was Ted Hills, but he became one of the most respected rangemen in Canada.

These three young men, Hills from Britain, MacKinnon from eastern Canada, and Millar from the United States, brought different life experiences to the Canadian range, but shared in common the speed and completeness with which they adapted. It is important to place their experiences against the more general context of the Great Plains. The speed with which greenhorns became useful cowboys has been stressed. Was this transformation in any way exceptional? The answer must be a resounding no. The majority of riders who followed the herds north from Texas made only a single trip.[34] Many of them were lured westward by the mystique of the ranching frontier, promoted by dime novels, posters and western shows. They included college graduates, mid-western farm boys, recent immigrants, and refugees from the industrial towns of the east. They learned what they had to know during a few hectic weeks, made a contribution to the success of the drive, and then most of them passed on to find other occupations. The story—like Bob Newbolt's—of a young Englishman transformed from 'dude' to rider during the course of a long cattle drive is part of the mythology of the ranching

frontier.[35] There were far more Britons in the western United States during the 1880s than there were in the foothills country; they were just spread more thinly. Fred Ings' comments about his apprenticeship on the range applied equally well on both sides of the line. "We were young and learned quickly, we had to, as it was essential that we knew these things well."[36] This transformation from greenhorn to rider was facilitated by the contribution of a variety of informal 'instructors' who taught by example.

The Plainsmen: Continuity and Adaption

It has often been said that the back bone of every army is its non-commissioned officers, and at the heart of any efficient and happy ship is a group of dedicated petty-officers. These are the men who are in constant contact with the young recruits and oversee their every move: the drill instructors and platoon sergeants who private soldiers hate and at the same time try to emulate! The 'newcomers' we have discussed may impress us with their unexpected hardihood and adaptability, but they were clearly incapable of managing a multi-million dollar business. They needed to be shown what to do. In particular, those who hoped to become ranchers in their own right, had to learn something far more important than the ability to stay in the saddle or even throw an accurate loop, they had to develop 'cow-sense.'[37] This they learned on the job, by observation, discussion, and by being 'cussed out' when they made mistakes.

Many of the men who emerged as leaders of the first generation of Canadian cattlemen during the 1880s had experienced the last wild free days of the fur trade era. They had wandered westward to the Montana gold fields in the 1860s, had lived among the Indians of the plains, had driven bull-trains loaded with trade goods to isolated forts, and had spent time in the employ of the rival trading giants, the Hudson's Bay Company and the I.G. Baker Company. They were frontiersmen rather than cattlemen, but their general experience enabled them to adapt quickly. Their contribution was crucial for they were the trail herders who brought the first herds from Montana, the captains of the early roundups and the charter members of the cattlemen's associations.

George Emerson was perhaps the archetype. Born and raised in Danville, Quebec, he left Canada as a young man and homesteaded in Council Bluffs, Iowa.[38] The gold rush attracted him to Virginia City, Montana, in 1865, and from there he wandered north to prospect along the North Saskatchewan River. He spoke Cree and Blackfoot fluently and did some free trading with the Indians before going to work for the Hudson's Bay Company as a freighter.[39]

When the North-West Mounted Police established forts at Macleod and Calgary, Emerson formed a partnership with Tom Lynch and started

Figure 4. The 'non-commissioned officers' of the range: a group of foremen and managers pose during roundup. The roundup was the culmination of the year on the range and taking part was regarded as something of an honor. These formal photographs remind me of those taken of hockey and football teams today. (Left to right): Jack Glendenning, Burns NL; Howell Harris, Circle; George Ross, Mosquito Creek Pool; Walter Watt, Oxley; J. H. '7U' Brown, Bar U. (Standing): Jim Fuller, Circle; Lou Murray, Walrond; and Charlie McKinnon, Bar U.

(Glenbow Archives, Calgary, Canada, NA-748-43)

trailing small herds of cattle from Montana to be sold to police officers. This proved successful for a year or two, and then in 1879, the partners brought in 1000 head of cattle for themselves, and planned to range them north of the Highwood River. From an initial base close to the present site of High River, Emerson moved his ranch headquarters to Pekisko Creek and maintained a successful ranch there, a few miles upstream from the Bar U, for twenty-two years. He was a tough and crusty old bachelor, but welcomed all comers to his house. Young cowboys were drawn to him both because of his mastery of range lore and his colorful story telling. Charlie Douglas visited him whenever he had a chance, and young Mike Herman, one of the finest ropers the foothills produced, stayed with him off and on for some years after accompanying Lynch and Emerson up from Montana with a herd.[40] In retrospect Emerson has been called 'the grand old man of the Canadian range,' and the high esteem in which he was held is reflected in the fact that he was elected to be vice-president of the fledgling stock association of 1887.[41]

Howell Harris (Figure 4) was another legendary figure of the Canadian range, and his long career spanned a period from the Montana gold rush until just before the First World War.[42] He too was born in Missouri, and was drawn west by the scent of gold. The late 1860s found him freighting for the I. G. Baker Company. In 1871, he pushed his ox-train northward to the Highwood and established a trading fort close to the Medicine Tree.[43] This venture was only partially successful, and Harris withdrew to Fort Benton the following year. He went to work for the Conrad brothers as a trail driver and foreman. His younger brother John Harris was a partner with the Conrads in a cattle company which was eventually reorganized and expanded to become the Benton and St. Louis Cattle Company, with John as the general manager. In 1886, when Howell Harris was 40 years old, he was sent across the line with 5000 head of cattle to manage the company's Canadian ranch. This outfit had had a presence on the Canadian range for a decade, but had only recently acquired a formal lease to a swathe of prime grass between the Bow and the Little Bow rivers. Harris' reputation as a capable cattleman and a respected leader of men is reflected in the fact that he was elected as captain of the 1886 roundup, the same year that he came to Canada.[44] For 25 years he guided the fortunes of the Canadian 'Circle outfit,' a U.S. owned ranch which by any measure was the equal of the Cochrane, the North West Cattle Company, the Oxley or the Quorn.

If a screen writer had the temerity to base a script on the life of Phil Weinard (Figure 5), it would probably be rejected as being unbelievable![45] His family came from Bitburg in Prussia and emigrated to Minneapolis in 1872. As a child Phil frequented nearby Indian camps and quickly learned both Sioux and the universal sign language of the Plains Indians. When he was fifteen he ran away from home and worked on river boats on the upper Missouri, freighting overland with bull teams during the winter. A chance meeting with Fred Stimson on the stage coach north from Fort Macleod, coupled with a storm that forced him to break his journey at High River, led to Weinard being engaged to put up the first buildings for the North-West Cattle Company along Pekisko Creek in 1882. His skill with an axe was also put to good use at the Quorn Ranch a year or two later.[46] After his run-away marriage to Mary Ferris in 1888, he was foreman of the Bar S Ranch for Walter Skrine for some years before establishing his own River Bend Ranch on the Highwood. Phil Weinard's lean face, swarthy complexion and piercing eyes can be seen in many early roundup pictures; he could put his hand to anything from roping and trail-herding, to bar tending and singing!

None of these frontiersmen had been brought up on a ranch, nor had any of them spent any length of time in Texas or the range country to the south. They picked up the skills of the northern range because, with the advent of the beef bonanza during the 1870s, that became the obvious way to make a living. Their influence on the growing Canadian cattle industry was enormous. As has been mentioned, they were roundup captains and found-

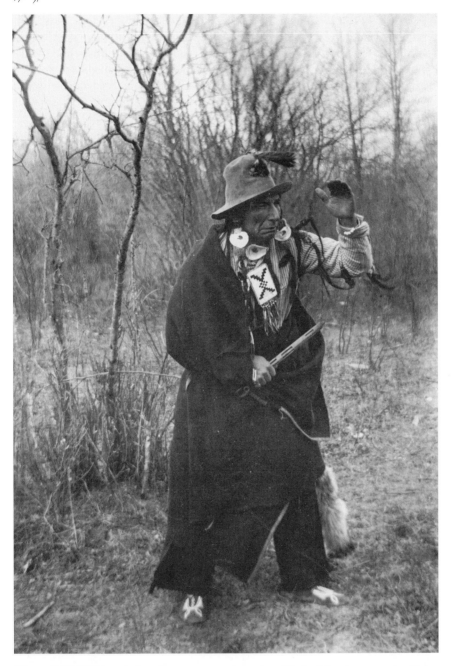

Figure 5. Phil Weinard, frontiersman turned rancher. He had lived among the Plains Indians, and had been a bull-whacker and trader before he started cowboying. He was also an expert axeman, and could turn his hand to anything. In this photograph he is dressed as an Indian. (Glenbow Archives, Calgary, Canada, NA-2711-1)

ing members of stock associations. They passed on their 'cow sense' to a whole generation of young riders. They were practical men who prided themselves on their ability to get the job done. They had little time for the attitude of the Texas cowboy who would do no work unless it could be done from the saddle, for they knew too well the value of wild hay stacks during the late spring on the northern range.

The Professionals: Foremen and Managers

The great Canadian corporate ranches which were established from 1881 onwards represented huge investments of risk capital from eastern Canada and Great Britain.[47] Not surprisingly the owners and shareholders were anxious to seek out men of experience and skill to be responsible for the day to day handling of the stock and management of the labor force.[48] In some cases it was possible to persuade the 'trail bosses' who had driven in the foundation herds to stay on for a while to look after things, but conscious steps had to be taken to fill these vital positions. On their long rides into Montana and Idaho in search of good stock at reasonable prices, men like Stimson, McEachran, Craig and the younger Cochranes, kept their eyes open for likely employees. In a more formal sense, would be 'cattle kings' like Senator Cochrane and Sir Andrew Allan, corresponded with Robert Ford, the president of the Sun River Stock Association of Montana, and asked for his help in locating foremen to manage their new undertakings.[49] These initiatives were largely successful. Almost all of the foremen employed on the 'Big Four' corporate ranches during the 1880s were experienced American cowboys. At the Bar U, Tom Lynch, who drove in the first herd, stayed until 1884, when he was replaced by George Lane until 1889, when Everett (Ebb) Johnson took over. The first foreman of the Cochrane outfit, W. D. Kerfoot, was joined by Ca Sous (Jesus Lavarro), and in 1884, Jim Dunlap became the 'ram rod' of the southern lease until his untimely death in 1887. Thereafter manager W. F. Cochrane looked after things for himself. At the Walrond, G. W. (Doc) Frields acted as McEachran's right hand-man in getting the outfit established. He was appointed 'local manager' in 1884 and James (Pat) Patterson took over as foreman. Only the Oxley Ranche seems to have lacked 'non-commissioned officers' who, by their contribution and personality, had their names recorded in the archives of the range. Of course, John Craig the manager was a practical stockman of experience and competence, but his time-consuming battles with his major sponsor over money matters, must have meant long absences from the ranch.[50] When Stanley Pinhorn took over management of the Oxley in 1885, he persuaded Jim Patterson to come over from the Walrond to help him. Of course, these men who occupied the plum supervisory positions in the rapidly expanding Canadian cattle industry, were but a few of the competent American cowboys deployed throughout the North West. In 1891, one out of six men working on the Canadian range was born in the United States.[51] In retrospect, the contribution made by these men can hardly be overestimated.

No American cowboy brought more skill and experience with him to Alberta than did George Lane. Although he was born in the midwestern United States, George followed his father to the gold mines along Alder Gulch, Montana, when he was 16.[52] Two years later he started working for the United States army, first as a stable boy, later as dispatch rider and scout.[53] Thereafter Lane worked at several of the biggest and most famous ranches in Montana. At various times he worked for Granville Stuart and Conrad Kohrs as well as for the Conrad brothers of the I. G. Baker Company. These men were leading cattle breeders, and had already improved their 'westerns' with imported bulls. They were fencing their hay pastures and experimenting with irrigation.[54] Lane developed an enviable reputation as a fearless rider, a crack shot and a roper of legendary skill, and he combined these attributes with exceptional leadership qualities and organizational abilities. When Senator Cochrane and Sir Andrew Allan wrote to Robert Ford for help in finding an experienced stockman, Lane was a natural choice.[55] It was not long before he was a respected figure on the Alberta range, and when the wagons came together for the general roundup of 1885, Lane was elected captain, which, as young Ted Hills wrote home, was quite an honor.

He was not so impressed with Lane's brusque manner!

> *Lane was elected Captain, which is rather an important office as he has control of all the different outfits and gives directions as to how the country is to be worked . . . The first part of the time I used to share a tent with Lane and Paul. Paul was a very nice sort of fellow but I can scarcely say the same of Lane. The tent was a wretchedly leaky one overhead and had no fourth side to it at all.*[56]

Everett (Ebb) Johnson had also gained his experience on the northern ranges. He was born in Virginia in 1860, and grew up in Minnesota. At fifteen he started working on the stage coach run to the Black Hills, and moved on from there to Wyoming. At 19 he was one of three foremen managing the herds of the Powder River Cattle Company, and was elected captain of the Johnson County roundup.[57] When Moreton Frewen sought to move his herd northward from the dry and overcrowded range in Wyoming he sent Johnson ahead to pick out a lease in Alberta. Ebb was able to find a block of fine grazing along Mosquito Creek, and the 76 outfit moved there during the fall of 1886. A year or two later, Scotsman D. H. Andrews who had employed Johnson in Wyoming, recommended him to

the North West Cattle Company in the following glowing terms: "a first rate cowman, in fact I think about the best all round cowman in this country, and he is very good with young horses."[58] So he came to the Bar U as foreman to replace George Lane, who had been stricken with a bout of typhoid. There he met Mary Bigland, a registered nurse who had been helping the manager's wife, Mary Stimson, recover from scarlet fever. They were married in November 1891, and Ebb's friend from Wyoming, Harry Longbaugh—alias The Sundance Kid—was best man at the wedding.[59]

William Kerfoot was another Virginian, the son of a cavalry captain in General Lee's army.[60] Like many Confederates, he moved to Montana and established a small ranch. However, he was caught up in the acrimony between cattlemen and sheep herders, and his property was burned. When James Cochrane, who was in Montana buying cattle, offered him a job as foreman of the Cochrane Ranche, Kerfoot jumped at the opportunity. Kerfoot has sometimes been blamed for the losses sustained during a fierce early snow storm to a herd of cattle recently purchased from Poindexter and Orr. But this disaster was, in fact, the last blow delivered by Colonel James Walker, whose rigidity and poor judgement had led the company to the brink of bankruptcy. A careful reading of Frank White's diary depicts Kerfoot as a knowledgeable, loyal and humane man.[61] He was responsible for gathering the company's cattle from their extensive Bow River range and organizing the trail arrangements to their new leases on the Belly River. Then he went to Montana and brought back 8000 sheep for the reconstituted British American Ranch Company. It was entirely in keeping with his exemplary character that he was sacked for refusing to get rid of a shepherd who, he felt, had acted bravely in the company's best interests. He sued for wrongful dismissal and won his case. Later he told his son that he did not look back at his years with the company with any great pleasure as it was run from eastern Canada, and "the company seemed to have the happy knack of getting together a lot of good men and then ignoring their recommendations, usually with heavy loss to themselves."[62]

A review of the biographies of these cattlemen and others reveals that almost all of them were from the northern ranges—from Montana, Wyoming, and Idaho. As a group they shared a lot of characteristics with the 'plainsmen' already discussed. They were not from Texas or New Mexico, and—while much of their material and nonmaterial culture may have derived from Texas and ultimately from Spain—their attitudes, expectations and management techniques were different. The herds they drove northward into Alberta were 'westerns,' they showed their Shorthorn and Durham ancestry and a generation or more of improvement from the attentions of purebred bulls.[63] These cattle, which impressed Lord Lathom so much, differed radically from the rangy longhorns which had moved up the Chisholm Trail during the 1870s.[64] So too, the dusty trail bosses in charge of the incoming herds had served their apprenticeship on northern ranches where more careful and intensive methods of raising cattle were rapidly gaining acceptance. Unlike their counterparts from Texas, they were by no means unfamiliar with wild hay stacks, fenced bottom lands, and the winter feeding of imported stock and weak calves.

Revisiting the context

How do our observations of the ways in which young men learned new skills in the Alberta foothills during the 1880s, and our brief profiles of some of their instructors, accord with Jordan's continent-wide model? Certainly, the origins of the American cowboys who became foremen on major Canadian ranches endorse his thesis. Almost all of them had spent their working lives on the northern ranges, and they had all been exposed to more careful and intensive pastoral methods associated with the Midwestern tradition. The plainsmen too had adapted to the ways of the border country, although their attitudes and experience was also influenced by their occasional forays into British Columbia and Idaho, where they would have been in contact with a modified Californian ranching tradition. And what of the newcomers? Although they were completely unfamiliar with range lore, nevertheless, they brought some previous life experience with them. Englishmen like Hills and Newbolt had been brought up around horses, and had spent many of their happiest childhood hours in the stables and paddocks of their homes. They brought across the Atlantic in their 'cultural baggage' elements of the British pastoral tradition. MacKinnon, in eastern Canada, and Millar, in the heart of the Midwest, had been introduced to the endless round of farm chores as soon as they were strong enough, and these early experiences influenced their attitudes to stock rearing. This paper has not explored the attitudes and perceptions of the 'staff officers' of the Canadian range, but it is a matter of record that managers and entrepreneurs like Cochrane, Stimson, McEachran and Craig were all prominent cattle breeders in eastern Canada.[65] Further work on these men and on those who established family ranches within the foothills may well demonstrate that southern Alberta during the 1880s represented the finest flowering of Jordan's Midwestern tradition.

Finally, by way of postscript, one must emphasize that Jordan's model is of particular utility in interpreting the situation only during the 1880s. Things changed rapidly around the turn of the century. There was an influx of big ranches into the Canadian shortgrass prairie direct from Texas, and they brought with them both their riders, their cattle, and their traditions.[66] Moreover, a man like George Lane, who in some ways represented the Midwestern tradition, undertook a regime of winter feeding and 'breeding up' his stock at his Bar U ranch, while at the same time he threw thousands of head of pilgrim stock onto the remaining blocks of open range along the Red Deer River, in a gamble with the weather and the market.[67] He even

went to Mexico to buy young stock. Meanwhile the canny Irishman, Pat Burns, was already experimenting with large scale feed lots some 50 years before his time. Even within the Canadian ranching country there was a broad spectrum of goals and strategies; our conclusions must be carefully qualified as to both time and place.

The Untamed Canadian Ranching Frontier, 1874-1914

Warren M. Elofson
University of Calgary

The purpose of this article is to demonstrate that ranching society on the Canadian prairies in the late 19th and early 20th centuries displayed considerable disrespect for legal authority. To make this argument is to go directly contrary to one of the most enduring and cherished myths about the West and its symbol of law and order, the North-West Mounted Police. In 1874, we are told, government leaders in Ottawa recognized that Ontario farm families were about to venture into the western hinterland. To ensure a peaceful transfer of land from the Indians to the white settlers, and to avoid the range wars and other chaotic circumstances south of the border, a fine selection of young men was sent out in advance of the migration. They built police posts and began making regular patrols and then, as settlement ensued, their forces and facilities "were constantly increased to keep pace." By 1889 "a vast surveillance network thoroughly covered" the frontier. Five divisions served the cattlemen in southern Alberta and Assiniboia—D and H headquartered at Macleod, K at Lethbridge, A at Maple Creek, and E at Calgary.[1] These exerted such a pervasive influence that racial friction was reduced to a minimum, new towns became centers of tranquility and rustlers, along with the whisky traders, were either arrested or chased back to the United States.

It should be acknowledged that over time, modest revision of this view has also occurred as some historians have provided specific examples of criminal activity on the cattle frontier. Stanley Hanson has uncovered extensive rustling in the Wood Mountain area although he insists that ultimately the enforcement techniques of the Mounties along with the law-abiding character of the pioneers won out.[2] Thomas Thorner has shown that around Calgary, property crimes, liquor offences, prostitution and gambling flourished in the final decades of the 19th century while crimes of "extreme violence against persons were few."[3] More recently Louis Knafla has drawn our attention to the Dubois brothers who were involved in rustling and intimidation over an immense area stretching from their spread at Stettler all the way to Montana.[4] And Hugh A. Dempsey has provided

Figure 1. Cowboy cavalry during the Riel Rebellion, 1885. One of the reasons the government of Sir John A. Macdonald had promoted large scale ranching in the North West Territories was the perception that the armed and highly mobile cowboys would be able to act as cavalry to back up the police if an emergency arose. This expectation was realized by the formation of the Rocky Mountain Rangers. This sketch by J. D. White accompanied an article by John Higinbotham, the Fort Macleod druggist, in the *Canadian Pictorial and Illustrated War News*, 20 June 1885. White included his store, The Rockies Paintshop in the picture although it was on Stephen Avenue in Calgary, and the Rangers never came to Calgary. [See Gordon E. Tolton, The Rocky Mountain Rangers, Lethbridge Historical Society, 1994]. Lorain Lounsberry has pointed out that the composition of White's sketch corresponds very closely with two engravings which appeared in the American magazine *Harper's Weekly* during the next few years. The first, *Painting the Town Red*, by Rufus F. Zogbaum (1886), and the second *Cowboys Coming to Town for Christmas*, by Frederic Remington (1889). Both these illustrations show a group of cowboys galloping down a street framed by stores and onlookers. (Glenbow Archives, Calgary, Canada, NA-1353-24)

numerous descriptions of thieves and outlaws in his exciting monograph, *The Golden Age of the Canadian Cowboy.* He concludes that while lawlessness and violence were not as prevalent here as they were south of the border, the Canadian West itself was not "entirely docile."[5] (Figure 1)

Still, the myth of the orderly society has for the most part remained in tact. Museum curators continue to describe early ranchers simply as "a very law-abiding" people[6] and, on the advice of scholars, at least one journalist has gone so far as to label the frontier "the Tame West."[7] Calgary, that journalist claims "was hardly the rootin' tootin' rodeo that some would have us believe in." It was genteel at the top and deeply respectful of the law at every level. Much of this image is also assumed in the latest, and otherwise very informative, study of the North-West Mounted Police.[8] Originally it seems to have been developed primarily because writers were anxious to identify what made us unique and, equally important—different from the Americans.[9] Its major shortcoming is that it substantively underrates the degree to which the frontier setting hindered the Mounties in their attempts to impose the rule of law.[10] Their strength, based on numbers of men stationed within the five divisions, fluctuated as follows: in 1873 it was 300; 1885, 1000 because of the Riel Rebellion; 1895, 750; 1898, 500; and 1901, 450.[11] At the turn of the century, in 'organized' areas of the North West Territories, this was equivalent, according to the estimates of the police themselves, to about 1 officer for every 500 square miles and for every 350 people.[12]

Moreover, roads were non-existent or very poor and travel was by horseback and unsupported by two-way radios or even a satisfactory telephone system. No one working under these conditions could do a proper job of keeping crime under control. Professor Breen has pointed out that extensive networks of regular patrols were instigated to prevent rustling. One has serious doubts, however, about how effective they could possibly have been. For one officer just to ride around 500 square miles (approximately 120 miles) on horseback at five miles per hour would have taken 24 hours or three days working eight hours per day. After such a patrol the officer might have some idea of the periphery of his area but absolutely none of the interior which, after all, would stretch the equivalent of 10 miles across and 50 miles long.

Another thing that has to be realized about the frontier is that it had virtually no facilities for servicing the basic needs of the general population. This meant that the policemen had constantly to carry an inordinately heavy load to ensure the survival, first, of both themselves and their mounts and, second, of the civilian population. To comprehend the degree to which this complicated life for them, one has only to turn to the mileage log that was kept for Fort Walsh in 1881. It shows that out of a total of 14,978 miles travelled by the detachment staff, 8.6 percent were for what was termed 'Indian issues' and 85.9 percent were for the sheer physical survival of the post. A mere 5.5 percent were for what the police themselves termed law enforcement.[13] Construction, laying in a food supply, firewood cutting and hauling, care and feeding of the horses, medical services to the men and the community, and administrative duties such as collecting weather data and conveying mail, occupied the majority of their time.[14] Often, the police also had to devote a considerable portion of their energies to dealing with extraordinary or emergency measures. These included prairie fires, floods or blizzards and hungry American cattle herds that pushed their way across the border.[15]

Also, the attitude of much of the citizenry seems to have worked against

efficient law enforcement. This, to a degree, was undoubtedly a product of the Mounties' difficulties. When witness to the fact that, under frontier conditions, the latter were not firmly in control, even people who came from Great Britain, imbued with Old World ideals, were liable to lose some of their former confidence in the legal system.[16] To a considerable extent, it was also a reflection of gender imbalance. As James Gray and Paul Voisey have illustrated, initially, single young men ventured west in far greater numbers than either married couples or women (Figure 2).[17] This unquestionably helped to diminish respect for the law in a general way. Men who live outside families tend not to be as concerned as their married counterparts about building a stable society where wives and children can be insulated from crime and other forms of violence.

Both the inadequacies of the police force and public irreverence toward the law are indicated by a number of features of the ranching frontier. One that comes instantly to mind is livestock theft. Between the early 80s and the end of the first decade of the 20th century outlaws constantly preyed on both horse and cattle herds. Indeed, so much rustling took place that it can be classified by its various forms.

Much of it was a sort of quick grab approach where a few men got together, made off with herds and disposed of them as fast as possible in a new and far removed locale. This system was particularly well suited to horse theft because of the mobility of that particular animal species. Often rustlers nabbed livestock in the northern States and ran it into the Canadian West. The most famous of the American thieves was probably the Dutch Henry gang. At one stage, in partnership with the celebrated Sundance Kid, that gang ran American horses into southern Assiniboia—there to be sold to local dealers who hawked them to homesteaders needing beasts of burden to start up their new farms.[18] On the Canadian side, Henry and his cohorts joined forces just after the turn of the 20th century with the Nelson–Jones gang.[19] They set up headquarters in the Wood Mountain area south of Swift Current. This region was ideal for rangeland criminals. It "was a heavily wooded terrain, with hills and minor mountains whose canyons and gulches offered ample concealment" for "horse thieves, cattle rustlers and wanted outlaws." The rustlers instigated a reign of terror to prevent local ranchers from helping the police against them. Apparently, at times there were so many criminals in the area that it was "difficult to tell the 'good guys' from the 'bad guys'."[20]

While the Dutch Henry and Nelson–Jones gangs were in Canada they were regularly pursued by the North-West Mounted Police. Ultimately, however, only a handful paid for their misdeeds on this side of the border. Three of them were arrested, tried and imprisoned for theft. Two others were handed over to the authorities in Montana. The rest scattered and headed south where most of them seem to have come to violent ends at the hands of law enforcement agencies of one form or another.

Although trafficking in stolen goods often ran south to north there were

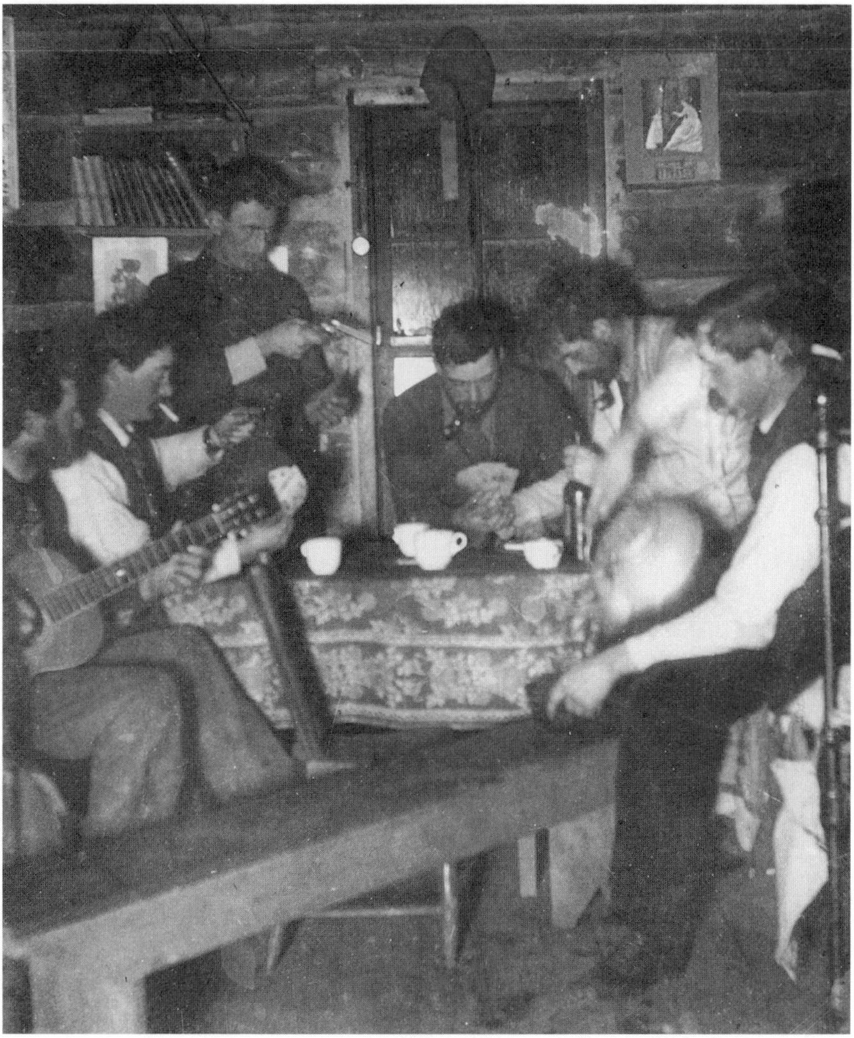

Figure 2. Young cowboys holed up in bunkhouses and line camps during the winter could celebrate a Saturday night with whiskey, cards, and music. Guns were omnipresent, although used in a joking manner here. This group was photographed in a cabin at Box Elder, near Walsh, ca. 1903.

(Glenbow Archives, Calgary, Canada, NA-4061-1)

also lots of cases of it going the other way. In 1885, for instance, two southern Albertans—one a North-West Mounted Police constable—were arrested in Montana with stolen Canadian horses. They quickly learned that American justice could be a lot more efficient than Canadian. In the process of being transported to Fort Benton for trial they were intercepted by a party of cowboys and after "very few preliminaries," were "taken to the

nearest tree" and directed to "the hempline route to the great hereafter."[21] In 1902, Sheriff C. Wallace Taylor, of Choteau, Montana, arrested James Fisher who was wanted for helping to steal 31 cattle at Okotoks. Fisher, not being a complete idiot, waived extradition, and came voluntarily to Alberta for trial. He was found guilty and sentenced to five years in jail.[22]

The kind of rustling that these criminals got involved in was obviously organized but, in some respects, it was not incredibly refined. Basically, it involved a sudden seizure of the livestock and then a very rapid retreat to the supposed sanctuary of the border. Other forms were more sophisticated. Ironically, the Canadian ranchers themselves practiced some of them. In the first place, many of the big operators had the habit of taking possession of every unmarked animal they could find on the range at roundup time. The Cochrane outfit first adopted this practice in 1882.[23] Then it spread. "It is the general custom of the large ranchers and ranch associations at the spring and fall round ups," the commanding officer at Calgary reported in 1896 "to either brand or sell all stray and unbranded cattle, including calves which are known as 'Mavericks' for their own benefit. . . . Thus we find in numerous cases that ranchers have cattle in their possession that legally they do not have the right to."[24]

In an open range system, where all the herds were mixed together and when so many newborn and therefore unbranded calves were gathered, it was much easier for the cowboys to brand everything in their path than to attempt to determine which animals did not belong to them. It was also, of course, next to impossible for the police to step in and attempt to dictate which calves belonged to whom. The large ranchers knew that at least some of the cattle they were gathering were not their own. They usually either slaughtered the mavericks to feed the cowboys during the roundup or sold them later and used the proceeds to help cover roundup expenses.[25]

In both cases the big ranchers could feel that they were working to the good of their kind. There is evidence, however, that some of them needed no such rationalization. In a 1909 legal case, *Rex vs. Dubois*, "a stockman of long and varied experience in all the range country on this continent," and his brother John F. Dubois were tried for stealing a steer from the Hatley Ranch Company. C. J. Sifton, the presiding judge, summarized the evidence as follows:

> *According to the evidence, it would appear that alleged respectable ranchers and stockbuyers do sell, do ship, do kill and do brand cattle which do not belong to them, and, when they are found out, pay for them, which raises a strong presumption that there may be numerous cases which not being found out, soon enough result in financial benefit to the so-called respectable people, and undoubtedly place them in the position of being cattle thieves under sec. 989 of the Criminal Code.*[26]

This suggests that at times some big operations even stole from their own kind. It seems unlikely that it happened very often, however, as it would have made little sense to most of them to risk the wrath of their peers, particularly considering the fact that they were jointly engaged in a fight to defend their herds against the small ranchers. This was no easy fight. What seems to have happened is that, in view of the indiscretions of the big outfits, many of the ordinary cattlemen assumed the right to pick away at any and all big herds year after year, mainly by taking the newborn calves before they had been branded. From there the conflict escalated. Great ranches took every unbranded animal they could find at every roundup and smaller men actively claimed any calves they could get their hands on whenever they came across them. Mavericks thus came to be "considered the property of the first man to run his brand on their virgin hides."[27]

Many of the small ranchers seem to have got their start this way. As David Breen has recognized, they came out to the ranching frontier with little or no capital and no cattle whatsoever and got into the business principally "by stealing the beginnings of a herd of their own from among the strays from the great herds on the open range."[28] In 1893, the *Macleod Gazette* noted the "extraordinary manner in which some men's herds" tend to "increase out of all proportion to their original size." It is about time, the paper declared, that we find a way to "stop the depredations of certain unscrupulous white men who never legally owned a head of stock in their lives but who are waxing fat on what they can steal from their neighbours."[29]

Some reasonably sophisticated schemes were developed to facilitate these thefts. In one area in the foothills, there were three young men on two small ranches who got very adept at it. On one ranch they had a log cabin, a stable, a corral with a spring in it and a closed in shed. A coulee ran "a couple of miles" from the corral to a creek bottom. The men would head out with "lunches in their pockets," and their six-guns strapped to their hips. They would find a herd in the valley and then chase the calves up the coulee using the noise of their guns to scare off the mothers. Within a short time the calves would be herded into the corral and then deposited safely into the shed out of sight of any passers-by. In a few days, when the calves were properly weaned and there was no fear that they would recognize their mothers, or vice versa, they were ready for the young cattlemen to put their own brand on them. Then they could be turned out to pasture once again.[30]

The chief means of facilitating the theft of newborn calves, however, was to pick them up one at a time and then subject them to the so-called 'running iron.' A rustler would travel the range with a small branding iron with a short straight edge on it that could be used to fashion, or even to alter, any brand desired. In 1906, the police officer in charge at Lethbridge reported that the "cattle rustler rides the ranges with a running iron strapped to his saddle generally in stormy weather and picks up calves which have arrived at the age to be easily weaned from their mothers." In no more than a "few minutes," he estimated, these men are able "to rope the calf

and drive it to some place where it is held till it would not be claimed by the mother, or recognized by the owner."[31] As time went on virtually any unmarked cattle—not just those from the big herds but from all the ranches, large and small—became fair game. The same Mountie added that 'fortunately' for the running-iron kind of rustlers, and "unfortunately for the settlers, a number have settled in the district with small bunches of unbranded cattle."[32] These cattle, he was insinuating, were being pilfered.

Another rampant form of rustling on the Canadian range involved networks of thieves trading cattle or horses or both. The participants were for the most part squatters, homesteaders, ranch hands and/or professional rustlers. The usual practice was to go into a certain area, pick up a small herd of either horses or cattle, drive them out of the area as quickly as possible and trade them for other commodities such as cash or grain. Often the other commodity was a second set of stolen horses or cattle. The original livestock thief would contact a thief in a new area, swap animals and move on again to negotiate another trade in a third area. "At present we have under arrest, committed for trial, one Brewster, who is accused of stealing over 30 head of cattle near Red Deer," Commissioner Herchmer reported in 1896. "This Brewster was found at Green Lake after a long search, some 800 miles from the scene of his alleged theft, in possession of a large band of horses, which we held for some time."[33] These horses may also have been well out of their original territory, as the police could find no local ranchers willing to claim them. The advantages of this type of arrangement for the travelling and the local thieves was that both found themselves in possession of livestock that they had not stolen. The local thief held animals that could not be traced or identified easily and the thief from afar could argue if caught, that he had bought his herd.

Ranchers, often of considerable wealth and importance, from the northern United States conducted another form of livestock theft. The best known of these ranchers were the Spencer Brothers, respected cattlemen from Montana. In 1901, the Spencers leased land on the Milk River Ridge, on the Canadian side of the border, in order to gain access to the open range there.[34] Then they developed and perfected two fraudulent methods of exploiting the opportunities it offered. In the first place they would bring in far greater numbers than their lease could support. For a high percentage of the cattle, the open range thus became free grazing land.

To make this even more profitable, when the Spencers rounded up their animals to take them back to Montana in the fall, they had a tendency to incorporate any Canadian mavericks that were found grazing with them (or, one presumes, that the Spencers could encourage to graze with them). The Mounties figured this out by doing some rather simple mathematical calculations. Under the open range system, one of them estimated "the ordinary . . . expectation in the matter of calf crop," was "one calf to three cows or thereabouts." Therefore, John Spencer's "claim, that every one of their cows had a calf, was a sheer absurdity."[35] To confirm that the Spencers were taking cattle that did not belong to them the police visited one of the herds that was in the process of being shipped home. They found "a goodly number of dry cows" that clearly had either lost their original calves or had failed to give birth.

The Spencers were far from the only Americans conducting business in this way.[36] Numerous outfits grazed cattle close to the border and leased land on the Canadian side. One of these was the Circle Ranch on the confluence of the Little Bow and Old Man Rivers.[37] It too took a large lease on the Canadian side. Other American ranchers simply drove their herds north allowing them to spill over onto the Canadian side as if by accident.[38] In this way they accessed the plentiful and inexpensive crown lands and, it would seem, often picked up stray cattle when it came time to take them home.[39]

To complete the overall picture of rangeland crime it is necessary to add that there may well have been a great deal more of it than we are able to document. The observations of men in charge of enforcing the law provide compelling evidence that a substantial portion of the rustling went undetected and therefore unrecorded. "This is an enormous territory to watch," Herchmer complained in 1896 while lamenting the amount of rustling going on.[40] One year later he noted: "we have endeavoured . . . to patrol the country as usual, and while we have been successful in arresting many cattle thieves and other delinquents, advantage has been taken of our small numbers."[41] By 1903 the commanding officer for Calgary sounded frustrated in the extreme and he spelled out precisely the difficulty of crime prevention on the range. "The convictions for cattle and horse-stealing are . . . one more than last year—I can only repeat" that this kind of crime is "the most prevalent and . . . most difficult to detect. The way the cattle and horse business is carried on in a stock country such as this, lends itself to this class of crime. So many have been tempted, that it is very hard to get reliable information."[42]

A huge span of territory, relatively few officers in comparison, and the sheer amount of lawlessness were obviously crucial in the police officers' eyes. These same factors made convictions extremely difficult to achieve when rustling was uncovered. The police simply could not give individual incidents the kind of attention they required. "At present, no matter how carefully our cases are worked up, some technicality almost invariably causes the release of the prisoners," Commissioner Herchmer told his superiors. "Every day the immunity from punishment, so clearly shown, is encouraging rogues to increase their cattle stealing business, and under present conditions, no matter how many are arrested, we cannot stop this nefarious practice."[43] There were "88 cases of horse-stealing entered," the next year, and "several bands of horses" were "brought in from the United States," which the Mounties "had every reason to believe, were stolen." However, "the brands were so well 'worked' that the owners could not be discovered, and, therefore, nothing could be done."[44]

Adding to the problem was the fact that ranchers often refused to help the police. Frequent complaints from the force noted that "the majority of stockmen, especially those doing a small business, will not try to help themselves, and give . . . [us] little or no assistance . . . although they frequently complain of the failure of the police to trace . . . criminals."[45] Numerous ranchers seem to have followed the ancient Biblical adage "let him who has not sinned cast the first stone." A clamp-down on range crime was threatening because it would have implicated too many people. For those who were not, themselves, involved, a major obstacle to helping the police was the possibility of retaliation. "I am bound to say, that more could be done by us if some ranchers were not so reticent in giving information, through fear of reprisals," the commanding officer at Maple Creek estimated in 1903.[46] Recognizing that there were great numbers of his neighbors implicated, the honest man suffered from the distinct sensation that he stood alone and therefore was particularly vulnerable to depredations and even to vengeance should he help the authorities. In the Wood Mountain area, the members of the Dutch Henry and the Nelson–Jones gangs seem to have taken turns terrorizing the smaller ranchers and at times were able to force them into actually aiding and sheltering them. Those gangs are known to have 'punished' informants.[47] L. A. Knafla believes that intimidation was one of the most persuasive tools the Dubois brothers used to keep their neighbors in line in order to maintain their criminal activities.[48]

The picture we get then is not one of ranchers and Mounties working hand in hand to enforce the law. The purpose here is not to suggest that everyone was a criminal or that the police worked entirely alone. While many cattlemen were involved in theft, others tried to help bring a semblance of security to the open range. Under everyday circumstances cowboys patrolled the herds in an effort to discourage rustlers and when district roundups were organized, representatives or 'reps' from ranches in neighboring districts were invited to participate in order to pick up properly branded animals and return them to their original pastures.[49] There are instances, moreover, of ranchers taking it upon themselves to reimburse the owners of strays found grazing far from home.[50] However, both published and manuscript reports indicate that, from a legal point of view, the frontier was anything but orderly.[51] Theft mushroomed, at times out of control, as both ranchers and police grappled with the immensity of open range.

If this helps to give us a different perception of early society in the Canadian West than we are accustomed to, other aspects of frontier life strengthen that perception. One of these was a propensity among the cattlemen to carry and use guns, particularly six-shooters. It is possibly true that Canadians were less likely to resort to firearms in disputes than the Americans. The Mounties expended considerable effort to control guns and they attempted to prevent people from openly using them or threatening to use them against each other.[52] Thus, as one cattleman who moved north in the late 1870s or early 1880s put it, "the American cowboys, coming to work on Alberta cattle ranches, shed their six-shooters at the boundary as trees shed their leaves in the fall, and were glad to do so."[53] However, gunplay was certainly not uncommon here.

Cowboys who did take off their six-shooters when they crossed the border were not at all reluctant to put them back on again when the situation demanded. One of the men who initially came north on the great cattle drives of the early 1880s, George Lane, often carried a six-shooter.[54] Lane had spent a considerable portion of his life ranching in Montana and no doubt picked up the habit of carrying a side arm there. One of his fellow countrymen, Jim Patterson, who became foreman of the Walrond and later the Oxley ranch was renowned for his prowess with the gun.[55] The six-gun culture was passed on to non-Americans as well. Billie Cochrane who became manager of the ranch at Waterton had a revolver, which he thought important enough to replace when it was stolen at a hotel in Macleod in 1885.[56] A lot of the less-well-known cattlemen also kept guns near them if not always dangling from their hips. The ranch hands often did not wear their pieces when working the herds because they were heavy and a bit of an impediment to roping, branding and otherwise handling the cattle.[57] However, many of these men were willing and able to strap on their guns at a moment's notice. This was discovered in 1884 by one very distraught young Englishman who found his fellow herders using his bowler hat for target practice.[58] In the late eighties, a cowboy working for the Cresswell Ranch was looking for stray horses in the Wood Mountain area. He came across two Canadian ranchers and as he approached them he found himself suddenly looking "into the bad end of a rifle and six-gun." The two had heard about some Montana outlaws holding up some of the "boys from the Seventy-six" outfit, and they were not taking any chances.[59] A Mountie who had been stationed in the Wood Mountain area between 1884 and 1888 estimated that Canadian cowboys were "invariably armed, owing to the exigencies of a nomad life in a wild country."[60]

By any standards, furthermore, there was considerable gun fighting and it, rather than recourse to traditional legal authority, was frequently the main means of dispute resolution. The following incidents were gleaned from the newspapers and the annual reports of the North-West Mounted Police. They can be considered only a small fraction of the total incidents in which guns were involved.

Sometimes gun violence was merely threatened by men who had consumed too much alcohol. In 1885, a cowboy with a revolver was found menacing citizens at a tavern in Fort Macleod. Mounties were notified and compelled the man to give up the gun. He was placed in the North-West Mounted Police guardroom for the night and fined 25 dollars for disturbing the peace.[61] At other times serious repercussions were not so successfully avoided. In March 1904 a cowboy in Calgary got into a dispute

with some other patrons in a particular bar and, when the police intervened, he turned his wrath on them. The Mounties had no alternative but to shoot him dead.[62] In 1886 several armed men held up the Calgary–Edmonton coach.[63] The robbers got away with $400.00. A short while later "the cowardly murder" of a young man named Clinker Scott occurred, apparently in relation to this crime. He was shot through the window of his shack, west of Calgary, while he was making bread. "Dead men," it was noted "tell no tales."[64]

There were gunfights too, of the type we have all witnessed time and again in American movies. In July 1885 Ben Hale, a well-known cowboy, shot a man named Bob Casey three times at Medicine Hat. The two had been drinking heavily and they got arguing about something as insignificant as whose horse was the faster.[65] In early 1891 a well known cattle thief named Edward 'Tex' Fletcher shot and killed a man named Peter Dacotah, in a rancher's home near Battleford, after a night of revelry and illegal whisky. He later received a 20-year prison sentence for murder.[66] In November 1895 John Lamar, foreman of the Walrond Ranch, and Gilbert McKay, a former employee of the ranch, got into a heated dispute over a letter addressed to McKay. Some days later, McKay rode out to the Walrond and challenged Lamar to a gunfight. Lamar had his revolver on at the time, but in the hope the other man would go away, he retreated into the house and remained there for some time. When he came out, however, McKay was still waiting for him, and immediately drew his gun. Lamar, was a faster draw and got off the first shot, wounding McKay in the arm. He then fired two more shots in an effort, as he himself explained, "to disable his opponent." Unfortunately McKay "changed his position in the saddle," and "one shot took effect in his chest and the other in the abdomen."[67] Miraculously he seems to have survived after a stint in a police hospital. On 12 June 1896, two longstanding enemies named Godin and Ducharme met on the Bow Marsh Bridge in Calgary. One grabbed the pistol from the other's holster and shot him in the abdomen. The aggressor then attempted to flee but as he turned, the wounded man, having wrenched his gun back again, shot him in the back. Both men died of their wounds.[68]

A few years later a ranchers' feud in the Pot Hole district brought a similarly tragic end. Two men named Lee Purcel and Dave Akers disagreed heatedly over the question of the ownership of some cattle. Purcel took the dispute to heart and decided to seek revenge. One day he grabbed his rifle and hid near his old friend's corral. When Akers came out, Purcel put a bullet through his head. Purcel was later arrested and tried for the crime. He was eventually convicted of manslaughter and given a paltry three years in the penitentiary by a very generous judge and jury.[69]

It is usual to think of Canada as the peaceable, law-abiding kingdom north of the 49th parallel and resisting the violence and chaos that was so integral a part of American society. We are told that on numerous occasions, the Macleod district was infested with horse and cattle thieves from the south. Further, we are reminded that the Mounties often took the liberty of escorting men with bad reputations back to the boundary line and telling them to stay at home, else prison would result.[70] These assertions are not in dispute. It should be recognized, however, that this worked both ways. On frequent occasions Canadian disorder, like stolen Canadian livestock, spilled over into American society and had to be solved by peace officers there. In 1895 a Constable Richardson followed stray horses across the border to Middle Butte, Montana. While there he was shot in a fight with a man named Long whose acquaintance he had first made on the north side of the line. Long then quarrelled with American authorities and was shot and killed.[71] On a number of occasions riders toting six-shooters successfully held up the Canadian Pacific Railway train. On at least one of those occasions Mounties formed a posse and attempted to track them down but the thieves made their way across the U.S. border and were never found.[72]

On the frontier, single young men were drawn to the gun in part because of a culture that was anything but tame. At night their instincts drove them to the urban centres, large and small, where they sought liquor and excitement in numerous forms from brawling to shoot outs. In 1912, L. V. Kelly illuminated this fact with some elegant prose when attempting to extol the virtues of Canadian ranch hands. Cowboys, he estimated, might go on hilarious 'busts' when in town, they might 'shoot-up' a bar-room and smash every light in the place, they might ride into stores on the backs of frantic horses, but they were good men, the kind who worked for their employers. If a flooded river must be crossed to save some of the cattle carrying the brand of the outfit they worked for, they plunged in and braved the torrents with their driftwood and their deadly 'drag.' If a 50-mile ride was necessary in order to save a horse, they took it. If an all-night vigil beside a herd of freezing stock was necessary to save those animals, the vigil was cheerfully undertaken. Many and many a night the cowboys sat on their horses, bundled to the ears, while the bitter winds of ten and twenty below zero swept across the prairies; and there are known instances where cowboys whose feet and legs were frozen remained by the herd and pulled it through until relief came. The employer's stock was their own; a theft was a personal loss. They were 'good,' men—rough, ready and true.[73]

Kelly was a contemporary of the men he was describing. He was merely giving vent to values that prevailed among them. These were basically good young men, he was saying, who often frequented the bars and even on occasion shot them up. But they should be forgiven because, as the old saying goes, 'boys will be boys' and because they helped to forge the ranching frontier with their manly flesh and blood.

The propensity toward bar-room gunfights was really quite general. This is illustrated by an episode that occurred in Macleod. Previously two men named Murray and Leeper had met on the banks of the Kootenay River.

They got arguing and pulled their guns. Leeper beat Murray to the draw, "thrust the muzzle of his six-shooter" into the latter's ribs and then humiliated him by forcing him to take a swim in the river.

Some days later the two happened to be drinking in separate saloons in Macleod. The town was "full of round-up cowboys who were certainly not worrying a bit about the serious side of life." The ranch hands knew about the enmity between the two men and they decided to have some fun with it. One crowd of them formed around Murray and the other around Leeper. Billy Stewart did everything he knew to spark a conflict. He spent time separately with both, telling them the dreadful things the other had said about them. As the liquor flowed "white-hot rage soon took possession of the two, and they talked darkly of dire happenings if only the other could be met with, Stewart and the two parties of cowboys sympathizing with each wronged individual and telling just how to kill most painfully and disgracefully." The cowboys also got both men's firearms out of their holsters, secretly removed the bullets and replaced the guns. Then they brought the men face to face in the Queen's Hotel. In an instant "the big guns leaped like magic to the ready hands." The men "stepped into the clear, and advanced slowly, the 'clickety-click' of the futile hammers on their weapons indicating just how earnest they were." When they realized that their guns were empty the men both tried to "bend the steel frames against each other's head." At that point "the hilarious spectators intervened and patched up a truce that remained unbroken, if strained."[74]

We often think of American cowboys coming north and causing trouble in our bars. And they did. Among numerous others, the occasion when the Sundance Kid pulled his gun to settle a dispute with his partner in a tavern in Calgary, bears this out.[75] However, sometimes our cowboys went down there and returned the favor. One night Tom Lynch, Bob Newbolt and a group of British, Canadian and American riders on a cattle drive went drinking in a bar on the Montana side of the border. After they "had several drinks they proceeded to shoot up the saloon."[76] Admittedly the tendency toward this kind of behavior was tempered somewhat in Canada by the police. In Maple Creek, for instance, the Mounties were known to confiscate six-guns from men they did not like or trust.[77] Even so, it clearly cannot be argued that bar-room shoot-ups were anything like rare. "Blazing away with a pistol, whenever a man gets drunk, whether it be in the hands of a policeman or a citizen is getting monotonous"[78] a reporter complained in 1886.

Evidence suggests, in fact, that gunplay was so much a way of life in the Canadian West, both within and outside the saloon, that it became a part of the popular culture. "Shooting seems well on the highway to becoming a common pass-time in the vicinity of Macleod" wrote the editor of the local newspaper in 1885.[79] In the 1930s an elderly pioneer who had witnessed the ranching frontier first hand remembered that "most cowboys had only one aim, that was to buy as much ammunition as they could, become as

'quick on the draw' as possible, and become deadly accurate shots."[80] If this brings us closer to a Hollywood depiction of the Canadian West than we might expect, so does the cowboy versus Indian violence that erupted from time to time both before and after the celebrated Riel Rebellion of 1885. Indians were regularly accused of killing the ranchers' cattle.[81] Undoubtedly they were sometimes wrongly blamed for crimes committed by others but, particularly when the winters were long and the buffalo scarce, they do seem to have been willing to take livestock to survive.[82] Therefore they were involved in a portion, at least, of the rustling in which so many of the white cattlemen were engaged. This seems to have caused far more racial strife than some scholars believe.[83] In August 1887 a rancher near High River was reported to have caught two Blackfoot Indians killing his cattle. A gunfight ensued in which the rancher shot one of the Indians dead on the scene and "fatally wounded the other."[84] The fact that there was little shock or dismay expressed in the media about the deaths suggests that there was a general and widespread value system which inclined cattlemen to use the gun to protect their stock from Natives whenever necessary. [85]

There were no large scale Native–white massacres on the ranching frontier of the type once glorified by American film, but there was a great deal of bitterness and racial animosity that often manifested in violence and death.[86] In 1888, for instance, white settlers near Canmore, enraged by the shooting fatality of one of their neighbors, were reported to have formed a posse, and hunted down and lynched two local Indians from the Kootenay Tribe.[87] On 10 February 1897, Charcoal, a member of the Blood Tribe, was hanged for shooting Sergeant A. B. Wilde of the North-West Mounted Police. Charcoal had previously also murdered a fellow tribesman and shot and severely wounded a white farm agent.[88] In the same year Sergeant Colebrooke of the Mounties was shot by a Cree Indian named Almighty Voice.[89] The latter was finally killed after an extensive and much publicized manhunt. Some years later the newspapers reported a particularly gruesome discovery on the Blood Reserve. A prospector's dead body was found with the legs severed and clothing burned.[90]

In many of the cases where Native–white violence occurred, the consumption of whisky also undoubtedly played a part just as it did in white–white violence. To those of us investigating the propensity towards lawlessness in the Canadian West, one of the interesting things about the fact that so much of it was associated with the consumption of spirits, is that until 1892 the liquor trade itself was illegal. It is testimony to a common willingness to break the law that the trade infected frontier society at all levels, traversed all ethnic lines and fostered extensive commercial activity both across Canada and across the international border.

By the North West Territories Act of 1875 intoxicating liquor was strictly prohibited in the territories except by permits issued to individuals by the Lieutenant Governor. These were for the importation of a small

Figure 3. Most roundups were 'dry,' hence the sometimes riotous celebrations when the work was over. However, these three cowboys relaxing beside the chuckwagon were obviously enjoying a drink. (Glenbow Archives, Calgary, Canada, NC-39-207)

quantity on a yearly basis for personal use only. The permits were apparently intended only for the wealthy and influential and they were granted in the beginning to the select few.[91] However, the ranching frontier was anything but dry (Figure 3) as a result of a thriving smuggling trade. The first smugglers were Americans who concentrated on specific locations such as Fort Whoop-Up and who supplied the Natives before there was a considerable white population. In time much larger numbers of Canadians replaced the Americans. Most of the liquor seems to have come from Montana but a considerable amount was also transported from Ontario via the Canadian Pacific Railway after 1883.[92] The Canadians had no racial biases in their commercial dealings and proceeded to supply anyone who could afford it.

In 1884, the trade was greatly facilitated when the government, in recognition of the fact that settlement was increasing rapidly, decided to issue the permits to practically any European who applied. Then the system was misused in almost every possible way. First, a great many people took out the permits, imported the whisky and, since the permits were never collected and cancelled, kept them to justify all the illegal liquor they were able to get their hands on in future from smugglers. Before long public carriers were approved to bring whisky in from Fort Benton. The carriers were careful to use the permits to cover every bottle they transported. The problem was that they managed to acquire a great many permits from people who did not intend to use them. This left them a sizable volume of illicit liquor to put on the open market.

Abuse of the permits was also crucial to a burgeoning saloon business in every ranching community from Fort Macleod to Calgary, Lethbridge and Maple Creek. In 1888, one of the highest-ranking North-West Mounted Police officers in the territories reported with obvious frustration that there was great temptation

> *to a certain class to smuggle illicit whisky of the worst description . . . . A few individuals . . . for the sake of a dollar or two will supply Indians . . . or a flowing population off the ranches who frequently make up for their solitary life on the range by making the most of every opportunity for conviviality when they come to town . . . . A saloon keeper of any experience keeps about enough liquor on his premises to fill his permits and whenever "pulled" by the Police he produces his permits, or those of his friends, and keeps his reserve stock of contraband liquor in hay stacks and manure heaps, [and] closets.*[93]

The whisky trade was, like gun fighting, rustling and other forms of violence, a product of the weakness on the frontier of both law enforcement agencies and of the family. Single young men, as most of us who at any stage of our lives have suited that description would agree, are disproportionately disposed to alcohol consumption. If in the following depiction, the writer is guilty of some embellishment he cannot be charged with representing the ranching frontier in anything but its true colors (Figure 4).

> *Whisky rolled into the land in every conceivable way. It came branded as red ink, it came in bales of hay, in loads of oats, even in kerosene cans, boots, boxes and kegs. A shipment of Bibles arrived at one town, and the settlers purchased them so avidly and hastened away so rapidly to commune with themselves and the book's contents that the Mounted Police smelled a rat, the study of the Bible not being a pronounced habit of the majority of Westerners in those days. Upon purchasing one of these coveted volumes the Police smelled more than a rat, for the 'Bible' was a little metal cask, formed like a book, branded like a book and entitled 'Holy Bible' in gilt letters, but filled with whisky!*[94]

Arrests were difficult to make because the permits were preserved religiously by a very thirsty society. Even when there were arrests,

Figure 4. Whisky rolled into the land in every conceivable way. Bottles had been concealed in the carcasses of these dressed hogs seized at Tete Jaune Cache railway Construction camp in 1910. (Glenbow Archives, Calgary, Canada, NA-2651-1)

convictions were often virtually impossible to achieve because of collusion by all the men who supported the trade, either because it supported them or because it brought them one of their principal items of entertainment, or both.[95] "Conviction after conviction was quashed" by the inability to get reliable witnesses or by understanding male judges.[96] Many of the single male police officers themselves participated in the trade and alcohol consumption within the ranks became a real problem.[97] Colonel James F. Macleod himself believed that "for every successful (whisky) patrol there were many unsuccessful ones."[98]

One should not be surprised to discover that both assault and prostitution were also rife in this predominantly male, alcohol-consuming society. The researcher finds these as well as a regular smattering of other indiscretions including arson, break and enter and trespass recorded in the annual reports of the North-West Mounted Police and in the frontier newspapers.[99] Ostensibly, these types of crimes were not specific to the ranching era. They were to be about as common after this period had ended as before. Even so, in combination with the crimes that we have investigated in some detail, they help to illustrate irreverence towards legal authority.[100]

Recently, a well-known expert in British and Canadian legal history lamented that "proper quantification of crime on the frontier is impossible."[101] The principal reason is that so much of it, as we have seen, was never recorded. This makes it impractical for the historian to attempt to compare Western Canada with other societies in order to assess relative degrees of lawlessness. One cannot do much more than point out that men here regularly stole cattle, drank excessively, dealt in illicit goods, carried and used guns and took part in the usual range of nefarious activities. One can also examine some of the important underlying factors. It was the frontier environment that made proper policing extremely difficult and encouraged the citizenry to be relatively uncooperative. If nothing else, this furnishes concrete evidence that the ranching frontier's law-abiding image has been grossly overplayed. In the final analysis, the 'Tame West' appears to be a Canadian myth about a civilized society that never really existed.

A Century of Ranching at the Rocking P and Bar S

Henry C. Klassen
University of Calgary

In 1990, the Rocking P Ranch's 108th anniversary and the Bar S Ranch's 103rd anniversary marked important points in their development. The Rocking P ran 2,600 cattle, enjoyed $700,000 in annual sales, controlled 33,000 acres of land, and occupied a significant position in three industries: cattle, horses and buffalo. The Bar S had 2,000 cattle, recorded $500,000 in annual sales, controlled 25,000 acres of land, and commanded a major position in one industry, cattle. Both were medium-sized businesses—economic ventures that possessed facilities at sites in southwestern Alberta and sold their products to buyers in Canada and the United States.[1]

The two ranches celebrating their anniversaries were remarkable human organizations. Both the Rocking P and the Bar S people used complex machinery and advanced technology to carry out their work. The owner-managers employed the most up-to-date accounting and financial methods to monitor their enterprises. At both the Bar S and Rocking P, the owners, who were also the managers, ran their business in an informal way. Responsible for the ranches' day-to-day management, they personally worked with animals and handled finished products.

The Rocking P and the Bar S of 1990 were a far cry from the new ventures formed in southwestern Alberta in 1882 and 1887 respectively. The founders, George Emerson at the Rocking P and Walter Skrine at the Bar S, could not have foreseen how the businesses they started would evolve over the next century. Perhaps the only similarity between the fledgling ranches of the late 19th century and the sophisticated modern firms of 1990 was that both institutions were livestock raising businesses whose owners invested capital in land, animals, buildings, and equipment; who recruited and rewarded ranch hands; and who arranged the marketing of finished products in order to make profits. Apart from the basic fact that the institutions were livestock raising businesses, the differences between them were amazing. The most obvious difference was that by 1990 the Bar S and the Rocking P were no longer small ranching firms.

George Emerson and the Founding of the Rocking P Ranch

Born in the United States in 1846, George Emerson grew up in Danville, Quebec. After working in Iowa and Montana, he came to Alberta seeking his fortune in 1869.[2] He first participated in the Hudson's Bay Company trade in the Canadian prairies, and then became involved in the cattle-drover business in Alberta and Montana. Emerson stumbled into the ranching business, and struggled in it, as did other ambitious entrepreneurs in many other industries. Emerson spent part of 1882 seeking a location for ranching, eventually choosing a homestead southwest of High River, along Pekisko Creek several miles upstream from the Bar U Ranch, in township 17, range 3, west of the fifth. Here he established his ranch.[3] He had for some time admired the Rocking P Ranch in Montana; and when he set up his ranch on Pekisko Creek, he gave the business the Montana ranch's name. Emerson's was a small cattle business, founded in an area of Alberta that was in the early stages of the ranching industry. The Rocking P employed a handful of people, operated mostly with local capital, and sold its beef in a limited region. Directly involved in the ranch's daily management, Emerson personally looked after the cattle and handled the marketing of beef. Because of his unsurpassed knowledge of the country, he emerged in one of the High River roundup outfits as the trusted guide, riding ahead of the wagons on a handsome horse to locate water and a campsite. Even after losing at least 40 percent of his cattle during the harsh winter of 1886–87, Emerson continued to serve as the guide for the roundup.[4] By 1890, he had begun to recover from the blow and possessed a herd of 700 cattle.[5]

Emerson was the initial driving force at the Rocking P. But the physical environment, as well as planning, determined some of the early developments at the ranch. As was the case with many other cattlemen in southwestern Alberta, Emerson kept down production costs by running his cattle on the open, unfenced range, where they enjoyed free grass. To control valuable waterfronts and pasturelands, he had spent $500 on building eight miles of barbed-wire fence on his holdings by 1900. By this time, he had expanded his herd to 1,000 cattle.[6] Looking for new opportunities, Emerson sold his ranch on Pekisko Creek to the Bar U in 1905 and moved east to the short grass country south of Brooks where he ran cattle free on Canadian Pacific Railway land in partnership with George Lane. Together, Emerson and Lane invested heavily in cattle from Mexico and Manitoba. Still, there were problems: the partners lost 90 percent of their cattle in the severe winter of 1906–07. In an effort to cope with the difficulties growing out of his losses, Emerson went into partnership with Rod Macleay, a rancher in the foothills country where the losses were quite moderate. To protect their investments, Emerson and Macleay used the foothills country to provide winter pasture for their cattle.[7]

Figure 1. Rod Macleay, a hale and hearty young man, who started ranching in the foothills early in the 20th century. Before Macleay came to Alberta to ranch, the family doctor in Quebec gave him only six months to live. Macleay was active on his ranch until his death at the age of 75. (Courtesy of Ernest Blades)

Born in Castlegar, Quebec in 1878, Rod Macleay eventually moved to Danville.[8] Medicine attracted Macleay, and he graduated from McGill University. But he never opened a medical practice, because he was suffering from rheumatic fever. The family doctor gave him only six months to live, but when he first came to Alberta in 1899 his health improved (Figure 1).

In 1901 he started on his 160-acre homestead with a few head of cattle in the Pekisko area, in township 16, range 1, west of the fifth, south and east of Stimson Creek in the rolling foothills of the Canadian Rockies.[9] At the same time, Rod Macleay was joined in partnership by his brother Alexander and his cousin Douglas Riddle, each of whom had his own homestead. By the spring of 1906, the Riddle & Macleay Bros. Ranch Co. was running 800 cattle on the northern flanks of the Porcupine Hills close to the headwaters of Mosquito Creek.[10] Over the years, the company's main source of water consisted of a number of natural springs, but it also relied on a tributary of Mosquito Creek which ran through the new ranch.[11] Sheltered by hills and willow brush, the cattle depended especially on the free grass that grew everywhere on the open range. A few miles of barbed-

wire fence on the homesteads allowed the company to control its pasturelands and waterfronts.[12]

Rod Macleay and his partners entered the ranching business just a few decades after its beginning in the Canadian prairies. By the late 1890s, livestock raisers in southwestern Alberta were offering cattle for sale in Canada, Great Britain, and the United States. Alberta proved to be a hospitable environment for the conduct of the livestock raising business. Geography and bountiful natural resources played important roles in this period, as they would in later years. Albertans were the beneficiaries of land capable of supporting diversified agriculture, virgin forests providing lumber for buildings, and rivers, creeks, and natural springs supplying water for livestock and people. Albertans were also aided by being part of a world economy that was growing and thereby adding to business opportunities.

Rod Macleay and his associates derived much of the support for the founding of their ranch from friends and family. At its beginning, the ranch resembled most new Alberta businesses, then and now; enduring personal trust was necessary for securing the start-up capital. Rod's father, Sandy Macleay, who was a prominent businessman in Quebec, accounted for much of the financing. In 1901, Sandy provided Rod and Alexander each with a money gift of $6,000 as well as with a gift of machinery and lumber.[13] A very persuasive businessman, Rod reached beyond his father to tap an additional source of capital in Calgary. The key lay in his relations with the manager of the Calgary branch of the Bank of Montreal, who gave the ranch a large line of credit.[14] Most of the capital was used to purchase cattle, but part of it was employed to acquire some land. The backing of Sandy Macleay and the connection with the bank were important to the success of the business. However, even with all this support, the ranch started operations short of capital, a problem that contributed to its bankruptcy and to Alexander Macleay and Douglas Riddle's withdrawal from the enterprise around 1903.[15]

But Rod Macleay was a persistent businessman. He never lost heart, even during the worst of his troubles. His own commitment and enthusiasm—his willingness to try again—helped his case tremendously. With the ongoing backing of the Bank of Montreal and his father, he was able to continue in the ranching business at the Rocking P. In the foothills around his original homestead, Macleay steadily increased his deeded and leased acres of land. In 1904, he expanded his livestock-raising operations by acquiring the John Ware Ranch and 100,000 acres of leased land complete with fence at Brooks.[16] Thus, the Rocking P comprised two major land holdings, and two herds of cattle, one in the foothills which offered natural shelter for a cow-calf operation and the other in the open plains for grazing and fattening steers. They were effectively run as an integrated enterprise to make the best use of the advantages of the two rather different areas. In 1905, Macleay was optimistic enough about his future to marry Laura

Sturtevant of Newport, Vermont, who was educated at the Newport Academy.[17] Before long, the couple had children: Dorothy, born in 1909; and Maxine, who arrived in 1911.

Macleay spent much of 1906 developing his Brooks Ranch. Yet, this was a risky time for Alberta ranching businesses, a period full of dramatic ups and downs in the Canadian business cycle. In addition to the terrible winter of 1906–07 which destroyed most of Macleay's Brooks cattle herd, the depression of 1907 also hurt his business.[18] But with Macleay's persistent entrepreneurship, his enterprise survived these hard times and expanded during the next decade to become a regional ranching concern of some repute. An important step in this direction came in 1909, when he went into partnership with George Emerson; the two partners adopted the Emerson brand, Rocking P.[19] Five years later, in 1914, Macleay became sole owner of the Rocking P Ranch by buying out Emerson, who then moved his cattle to the Sand Hills north of the Red Deer River and ran them on a Canadian Pacific Railway lease until his death in 1920. By World War I, the Rocking P had emerged as one of the most successful ranching concerns in Alberta.

Rod Macleay and the Development of the Rocking P Ranch

Rod Macleay became sole owner the Rocking P Ranch at an auspicious time. The World War I years, 1914–18, proved to be a period of enormous expansion for Alberta ranching business, as Canada became a more industrial and urban nation. From a country based on small towns and farms in the mid-19th century, Canada became a nation of growing factories and rising cities by the end of World War I. Between 1911 and 1921, Canada's population rose from a little over seven million to nearly nine million. Along with the demographic force contributing to the unsettling of the older order in the nation came increasing affluence which meant more per capita beef consumption. The Rocking P's leading product for this period, cattle for beef, benefited enormously from this growth.

In 1916, Macleay greatly increased the size of his holdings in the foothills by purchasing the TL Ranch on the south fork of Willow Creek from Edmund Thomson and Dan Riley. This purchase added 29 sections of deeded and leased land to Macleay's acres and provided him with a very important additional source of water as well—Willow Creek.[20] Macleay's most pressing problem now was the debt of $14,000 he owed Thomson and Riley, but by 1919 he had paid it off.[21]

As it grew, the Rocking P continued to produce beef cattle in the foothills as well as in the plains. Under Macleay's leadership, the ranch became well known for experimentation. Experimentation has always been essential to the development of the cattle industry. Macleay was one of the

Alberta ranchers who pioneered in the production of a Hereford–Galloway–Angus cross.[22] These high-quality animals insured that the Rocking P not only maintained, but also increased its market share in the beef industry.

To diversify his operation and to take advantage of the opportunity to make profits in expanding markets in Alberta farming communities during the World War I years, Macleay started raising horses on a moderate scale. As early as 1910, Macleay had purchased 101 mares at $90.25 each in Oregon.[23] The following year, he expanded his herd by buying additional 87 Oregon mares. Assisted by a few competent cowboys, including Joe Case, who was born in England, as well as by a good cook, Scotty Porteous, a native of Scotland, Macleay was able to get ahead.[24] Between 1914 and 1918, the Oregon mares produced many fine saddle and work horses, most of which the Canadian Army purchased for use in the cavalry and artillery.

Prosperity allowed Macleay to expand in 1919 by acquiring the Bar S Ranch, just south of the Rocking P Ranch. This involved not only the purchase of 11,200 acres of Bar S land, but also the acquisition of many Bar S cattle.[25] The Bar S was certainly an important addition to Macleay's ranching business.

The Establishment of the Bar S Ranch

By the time Rod Macleay acquired the Bar S Ranch in 1919, it had been in existence for thirty-two years. The Bar S was founded by Walter Skrine, son of the wealthy Henry Duncan Skrine.[26] Born in 1860 in Somerset, England, Walter Skrine was a graduate of Oxford University. In 1884, following his experiment with a career in the coffee plantation business in Ceylon, he came to Alberta.[27] In July 1887, after ranching for three years along the Highwood River and after seeing seventy percent of his cattle frozen to death during the hard winter of 1886–87, Skrine established the Bar S Ranch.[28] He did so on land at the headwaters of Mosquito Creek in township 16, range 1, west of the fifth, first entering it as a squatter and then acquiring it as a 160-acre homestead.[29] Certainly one reason for the move was the need for shelter for his herd of 200 cattle. The Bar S Ranch, with its hills and willow brush, offered the means to secure the desired shelter. Also important in explaining the move was the presence of Mosquito Creek and natural springs which provided Skrine with all the water he needed. Then, too, relocation allowed him to get away from homestead farm settlement around High River.

Skrine, however, was cash-poor, because of the financial reverses he suffered in the severe winter. It is likely his father helped rescue the business, providing assistance to improve the Bar S's finances. By 1890, Skrine was running 600 cattle on his homestead and on 15,807 acres of leased land.[30] In an attempt to control the waterfronts and pasturelands on his homestead, he had spent $700 constructing five miles of barbed-wire fence by 1893. As well, by this time he was raising grain crops on 14 acres of homestead land to feed his saddle horses, bulls, and some calves and weak cows during the winter.[31]

Optimistic about his future, Skrine married Agnes Higginson of Rockport, County Antrim, Ireland in 1895, a gifted writer who used the penname Moira O'Neill.[32] In July of that year, he brought his wife to the Bar S.[33] As he built a new, two-storey, frame and log house, steadily added land, and irrigated some of it, Walter Skrine was trying to make his environment take the shape he needed.[34] Like some other Albertans, Agnes Skrine saw the owners of small ranches as symbolizing all that was best about the Alberta way of life. She also understood the critical importance of water in the development of the ranch. "I like the herds of cattle feeding among the foothills, moving slowly from water to water. I like the clear rivers that come pouring out of the mountains," she observed.[35] Together, the Skrines built up the Bar S. By 1898, they were running 700 cattle on the ranch.[36]

At the same time, Walter Skrine was affected by the larger business environment over which he had limited control. He had joined the Mosquito Creek roundup as early as 1887, and he was soon co-operating with A. E. Cross of the A7 Ranch in purchasing cattle, herding them, and marketing them.[37] But as the years passed, some of Skrine's correspondence with Cross concerned the growing number of settlers who were taking up land near the Bar S.[38] Even a few settlers along a creek often took up the bottomland and made wild hay and winter pasture unavailable. The arrival of the settlers helped to put the local ranching economy into a downward spiral and this, in turn, led Skrine to sell the Bar S to his neighbor, Peter Muirhead, in June 1902, and together with his wife return to Ireland.[39]

Born in 1856 on a farm in Oakland County, Michigan, Peter Muirhead was the son of parents who had grown up in Sterlingshire, Scotland.[40] As a boy he performed chores on the family farm and attended the local school. He then went to work for his friend David Ward in a lumber camp, where he rose to become foreman. Intrigued by what he saw in the lumber industry, Muirhead started his own business, the Blue Lake Lumber Company, at Mancelona, Michigan. He played an active role not only in Ward's venture but also in his own enterprise, remaining at Mancelona until 1898, when he sold his company and moved to his 160-acre homestead in the foothills country west of Nanton, close to the Bar S Ranch.[41]

Muirhead's career change and move to the foothills country set the stage for his entrance into the ranching industry. He obtained much of the support for the development of his ranch from his old friend David Ward, who at the time of his death in 1900 left him a substantial part of his estate.[42] This enabled Muirhead to pay cash for Walter Skrine's Bar S Ranch and make it the center of his growing operations in 1902.[43] Between 1904

and 1907, Muirhead ran from 1,700 to 2,200 cattle and from 150 to 240 horses on the Bar S.[44] He achieved greater control over his pasturelands and waterfronts by building a barbed-wire fence all around his ranch.[45]

Yet, these years were also a risky time for the Alberta ranching business. During the severe winter of 1906–07, there were many losers, and Muirhead was one of them. "Loss larger than expected," he wrote his sister Elizabeth Harger in the spring of 1907. "Will sell all cows next summer and not raise any calves. Will buy them." He added: "I still have lease on the Red Deer River. Is a good place to raise horses. There is double the money in them than cattle. Little work and no expense."[46]

Nevertheless, Muirhead continued to raise cattle on the Bar S. He survived the winter of 1906–07 and started to expand during the next few years. To provide his cattle with feed during the winter, he began to put parts of his ranch into grain in 1908.[47] But the arrival of more and more settlers led to the opening up of his leased land at the Bar S to homesteading and shattered hopes for further growth.[48] The extensive methods of the previous era were rapidly coming to an end, a situation that brought further changes. Recognizing that his plans for expansion were not working out well, Muirhead sold the Bar S, in 1909 to a Vancouver meat packing company controlled by Pat Burns and established a new horse ranch at Seven Persons.[49] Later, in 1919, Rod Macleay purchased the Bar S Ranch from Pat Burns.

The Growth of the Macleay Ranching Business

The acquisition of the Bar S reinforced Macleay's decision to enlarge his holdings in the foothills area. The purchase, combined with the expansion of his cattle operations, meant that he needed much bank credit. In 1921, Macleay borrowed $320,000 from the Bank of Montreal. This loan carried an annual interest rate of seven percent, a charge similar to many commercial loans of the day, and a reflection of the Bank of Montreal's confidence in the soundness of Macleay's business.[50] But a nationwide depression between 1919 and 1923 temporarily demolished hopes for growth. The slump slowed the development of Alberta's ranching industry. For Rod Macleay, who was still trying to expand his cattle raising operations, the results of this depression were extremely difficult to bear.[51]

Far from discouraged, however, Macleay continued to seek opportunities to develop his ranching enterprise. As always, during the 1920s the availability of grass was essential to the development of the business. From time to time, some of the cattle were trailed from the foothills area to Macleay's Brooks Ranch, where grass was plentiful.[52] Access to water in the Red Deer River and its tributaries aided the venture as well. Macleay also purchased hay from the farmers in the vicinity of Brooks to feed the cattle during the winter. Fortunately for him, the federal government opened the forestry reserve west of the foothills to ranchers during the summer season around 1919. Beginning at that time, Macleay followed a strategy of allowing a considerable part of the winter pasture on his foothills ranch to rest in the summer months, thereby giving the grass an opportunity to grow. Every year he moved a portion of his Rocking P and Bar S herds, and a portion of his TL Ranch herd on the south fork of Willow Creek, to the forestry reserve, where the cattle grazed from mid-May to the end of October.[53] At a cost of five dollars per head for the summer, Macleay was able to use the forestry reserve to fatten about 1,800 cattle, mostly yearlings and two-year-olds.

Alberta had other things, such as railway connections to regional, national, and international markets, to offer enterprising ranchers like Macleay. The Canadian Pacific provided direct links to Calgary, Vancouver, Winnipeg and Montreal, as well as ties to American railways that could take cattle to Chicago. Macleay sold most of the cattle on his ranches to meat packing companies such as Canada Packers, but he also made some shipments to the United States, for example sending about 2,300 head of cattle to the Chicago stockyards around 1919.[54] Generally speaking, Macleay's strategy—great emphasis on high-quality cattle—resulted in an expanding enterprise. Nevertheless, his heavy debt load presented a basic business problem. Only when Macleay purchased Gordon, Ironsides and Fares' Mule Creek Ranch in southern Saskatchewan in 1924 and then sold it to Pat Burns at a profit four years later was he able to get rid of the debt on his Bar S Ranch.[55]

In early 1930 Rod Macleay thought that the time had come to incorporate his cattle raising business, and in February he transformed the venture into an Alberta corporation, Macleay Ranches Ltd.[56] In doing so, he consolidated his existing ranches—the Rocking P Ranch, the Brooks Ranch, the Bar S Ranch, and the TL Ranch—into a single business organization. Capitalized at $500,000 (5,000 shares of stock valued at $100 apiece), the new firm had three family stockholders: Rod Macleay, his wife Laura and their oldest daughter Dorothy. In addition, Stewart Riddle, who had served as ranch foreman since 1915 and who was outside the family, had a small interest in the enterprise. Still, it was a closely held family firm.

One reason for incorporation was the growing firm's need for capital. With its promise of limited liability to investors, the corporate form of organization offered a potential way to secure the required additional capital. As time passed, the existing capital was insufficient to meet the Macleay's needs. The capitalization of the new firm was increased to $1 million, 20 years after its founding, in 1950.[57] However, apart from Stewart Riddle's small interest in the firm until 1942, incorporation brought in no outside investment. Unwilling to yield control of their firm to outsiders, the

owners did not diminish family ownership in the corporation. Rather, the firm remained a closely held family enterprise throughout its existence. In 1942, Maxine Macleay, Rod and Laura's second daughter, became a stockholder.[58] When the capitalization of the firm was raised in 1950, only the family stockholders were permitted to purchase additional shares.

Organization of the management structure at the Macleay Ranches followed a standard pattern. Each year stockholders elected a board of directors who, in turn, chose the officers of the firm: the president, and a secretary. Authority on a daily basis rested with the president, who was assigned the general supervision of all the firm's affairs, and the ranch foreman, who served as manager. At the Macleay Ranches, the owners personally managed their corporation. Rod Macleay was the firm's president, while his daughter Dorothy became the first secretary. She was succeeded by her sister Maxine by 1950.[59] Throughout this period the board of directors—originally composed of Rod, Laura, Dorothy, and Riddle—changed very little. Only in 1943 did Riddle drop out of the board, while Maxine Macleay had entered it one year before.[60]

Stewart Riddle was an important member of the Macleay Ranches' management. Born in Danville, Quebec, Riddle was the son of a prominent lumber entrepreneur. Educated in the local school, he began working in 1910 for his cousin, Douglas Riddle, owner of the Wheat and Cattle Company west of Nanton, where he served for five years as a cowboy. In 1915, Stewart Riddle entered the employ of the Macleay ranching business as the ranch foreman, a position he held until he retired to Calgary in 1954.[61] He proved to be an outstanding foreman. A person of enormous energy, Riddle got along well with Macleay. Given a free hand by Macleay, Riddle supervised the work on all four ranches and spent considerable time on the Brooks Ranch developing its operations. The supervision of the Macleay Ranches required Riddle to take responsibility for all the cowboys, assign them to the tasks he expected them to perform, and report regularly to Rod Macleay. This was a time when basic ranching knowledge and skills were still spreading throughout the Alberta livestock raising community. Under the leadership of Riddle, who never forgot his cowboy beginnings and skills, the men worked effectively and gained a reputation for reliability. He labored alongside the cowboys and was well liked by them.[62]

In establishing the Macleay Ranches as a corporation, the appointment of Dorothy Macleay as secretary in 1930, and of her sister Maxine to this position twenty years later, was of great significance. With their assistance, Rod Macleay kept the books and wrote the business letters.[63] In this way, the books, accounts, and documents of the Macleay Ranches were kept in order. Both Dorothy and Maxine graduated from the University of Alberta with degrees in agriculture. Both were excellent riders, and when they were home in summer, during their university years, they helped their father with the ranching work.[64] As the seasons passed, they assisted in the various

cattle operations—weaning and branding all calves, castrating bull calves, culling old cows, and herding cattle. In addition, Maxine had a natural veterinarian talent, for example in spaying heifers.[65] As a gifted artist, she also portrayed the life of a cowboy of the 1930s on the Rocking P Ranch in her sketches.[66]

Yet, as the Great Depression blanketed the Alberta cattle industry, the Macleay Ranches and its owners were besieged. The firm was hurt by slumping cattle sales and falling cattle prices, and it sustained heavy losses. Unprecedented in its severity, the depression hit most Canadian businesses hard and very much restricted available choices for ranchers. Nevertheless, Rod Macleay worked to develop overseas sales. There was an important reason for his eagerness to sell his cattle in Great Britain; he hoped to avoid the new tariff barriers erected by the United States. The Fordney–McCumber tariff took effect in 1922, and its impact was intensified by the passage of the Hawley–Smoot tariff in 1930. There was no prospect of profitable sales south of the border. As chairman of the newly formed Council of Western Beef Producers, and with the assistance of the federal government, Macleay secured lower steamship freight rates from Montreal shipping companies.[67] In November 1930, he cooperated with local ranchers like A. E. Cross in making a shipment of his cattle to Great Britain.[68] With the success of this shipment, Macleay's British sales grew the next year. In 1931, he also sold 80 high-quality Rocking P cattle for distribution to the Dominion Stores.[69] However, these sales proved only partly successful in protecting the Macleay Ranches from the hardships of the depression—the 1930s were poor years for the firm and its owners.

Especially bleak was the middle of that decade, when dry summers combined with cold winters to kill the firm's aspirations of developing a profitable position in cattle.[70] Providing the cattle with grass also proved difficult. Robbed of rain, the pastures needed time to adjust to the drought, especially enough time for the roots of the grass to go down to the water, so Rod Macleay allowed the grass to grow for two years before permitting his cattle to graze it.[71] Yet, finding the right balance between the cattle business that drove the Macleay Ranches and the development of the pastures was not easy. Still, Rod Macleay made every effort to restore the grass.

Like other Alberta ranchers, Rod Macleay also responded to the Great Depression with retrenchment. Despite calls from government authorities for increased capital spending projects to help Canadians cope with the depression, most firms cut back on spending and employment in the 1930s. Cutbacks in wages also took place on the Macleay Ranches. In the 1920s, most cowboys on Macleay's ranches received $30 per month plus board and room. While they continued to receive board and room, their wages were cut by about 33 percent during the next decade.[72] Despite these cutbacks, able cowboys like Pete Smith and Lou Russell, both of whom hailed from

Texas, continued to work for Macleay.[73] So did Charlie Glass, who was born in Alberta. First employed as a cowboy by Macleay in the early 1920s, Glass performed well and stayed for many years.[74] Serving as foreman of the Brooks Ranch from 1935 to the early 1940s, Glass began as foreman of the Rocking P Ranch in 1945 and held that position until his retirement in 1980. Altogether, there were about 10 cowboys on the various ranches, some of whose wages were cut to $10 a month during the depression. Macleay's retrenchment work was successful, but it did not solve all the problems facing him during the 1930s.

Canada recovered from the Great Depression slowly. In the late 1930s, the nation's economy grew, with full recovery occurring during World War II. The Macleay Ranches participated in Canada's economic recovery and by 1942, Rod Macleay was running 4,300 cattle.[75] In that year, he sold the Brooks Ranch and used the proceeds of the sale to pay off some of his debts.[76] At the same time, through his personal business connections, he borrowed $190,000 from Carl Christensen, an Alberta farmer, using the funds to pay off his loan from the Bank of Montreal.[77] Later, Rod Macleay also obtained loans from the Royal Bank of Canada to finance his cattle operations.[78]

The Macleay Ranches entered the post-World War II period well financed for its size and and still possessing a name that retained importance in the marketplace. Rod Macleay, attracted by the prospect of a growing market, reaffirmed his commitment to the cattle industry. In the late 1940s and early 1950s, the Macleay Ranches flourished. By this time the roads in southwestern Alberta had improved, but Rod Macleay never learned how to drive a car. His wife Laura drove him wherever he wanted to go until her death in 1952.[79] Rod Macleay lived to see his firm benefit from a period of expansion before he died of a heart attack on 27 October 1953 and, as a major stockholder in the firm, he enjoyed the fruits of that growth.[80] Some remembered Rod Macleay "for the high quality of his cattle and on numerous occasions steers from his big spread in the foothills country topped the market at both Calgary and Chicago."[81] But there was more to him. He was also known as "a man of many quiet charities, and was intensely loyal to all ranch employees, following their welfare."[82]

Rod Macleay gave careful attention to his will, liberally providing for his two daughters. He bequeathed the Rocking P Ranch to Dorothy and the Bar S Ranch to Maxine.[83] Like many other Alberta livestock raisers, he viewed his ranching business not simply as a money-making device, but as a family enterprise to be developed and handed down to his heirs. One of Rod Macleay's strengths was that he was careful to groom successors, Dorothy for leadership at the Rocking P, and Maxine to head the Bar S. Clearly, he saw in his two daughters, the potential for leadership. At the same time, Rod Macleay personally led his ranching enterprise as one business organization until his death.

New Management Teams

Management succession proceeded smoothly after Rod Macleay died. A new stage now began, one in which there was continuity and change. Experienced women—Dorothy and Maxine Macleay—guided the Macleay Ranches, as the corporation continued to be led by the owners. The executors faithfully implemented the terms of Rod Macleay's will as he had directed with respect to ownership. Dorothy and Maxine became the owners of the Rocking P and Bar S Ranches respectively and they managed their ranches with the same diligence and prudent care their father had exercised in his business. On 2 April 1954, after the affairs of the Macleay Ranches had been wound up under the laws of Alberta, each of the two sisters incorporated her ranch.[84] By this time Dorothy had married Ernest Blades, while Maxine had married George Chattaway. Family ties and personal friendships remained of considerable importance to the managements of the Bar S and the Rocking P. Dorothy and Ernest Blades served as the directors of the Rocking P; and Ernest acted as secretary and manager. Similarly, Maxine and George Chattaway became the directors of the Bar S; and George served as secretary and manager.

Capitalized at $20,000, each ranch had several stockholders. The stockholders of the Rocking P were Dorothy and the infant children of Dorothy and Ernest Blades: Rod, Mac, Betty, Ethel, and Lynnie.[85]

Maxine and the infant children of Maxine and George Chattaway—Clay and Carol—were the stockholders of the Bar S.[86] Clearly, both the Bar S and the Rocking P remained closely held family enterprises.

The Growth of the Rocking P Ranch

Ernest and Dorothy Blades (Figure 2) led their corporation into a period of significant growth and prosperity. In 1954, the Rocking P Ranch controlled about $1 million in assets and was running 2,000 cattle. Two years after Dorothy's death in 1988, it had about $15 million in assets and was grazing 2,600 cattle in its pastures.[87]

Ernest Blades was an important addition to the Rocking P's management in 1954. Born on a farm in Lincolnshire, England in 1909, Blades was educated in the local school.[88] As the son of a farm laborer, he learned much about horses on the farm. Later, after working as a wagoner in England, he sought opportunities in Canada. Impressed by what he read in Canadian immigration literature, Blades came to Alberta in 1927, where he served for one and a half years as a hired man on a farm at Delburne. In 1929, he got a job taking Rod Macleay's bulls by train from his Brooks Ranch to Cayley for service in his Pekisko herds. As events would show, the trip to Pekisko brought Blades luck, landing him at the right place at the

Figure 2. Ernest and Dorothy Blades, owners of the Rocking P Ranch and long-time ranchers in the rolling foothills of the Canadian Rockies, happily celebrated their 40th wedding anniversary in 1980. (Photo courtesy of Ernest Blades)

right time for the kind of business he wanted to work in. He immediately started as a cowboy with Rod Macleay at the Rocking P Ranch at $50 a month plus board and room.[89] A hard worker and a superb rider, Blades was an assest to the ranch. With the deepening of the Great Depression, however, the job dried up in 1931, resulting in the departure of Blades to follow rodeos in California and other states in the American West. In this way, he made a little money riding and roping horses, albeit barely enough to live on.

In 1933, at a low spot in Blades's life, Rod Macleay intervened to improve his fortunes. Paying him $20 a month in addition to giving him board and room, Macleay again employed Blades as a cowboy at the Rocking P.[90] At the ranch, Blades continued to find a supportive family. In 1940, he married Dorothy Macleay. The two had known each other since 1929, when Blades made his first trip to Pekisko.

Ernest Blades spent part of 1941 seeking a ranch that might be for sale, eventually in that same year deciding to purchase the 3Vs Ranch, just west of the Rocking P. Ernest was sole owner of the 3Vs Ranch, while his wife Dorothy continued to have an interest in the Macleay Ranches. From 1941 to 1954, Ernest and Dorothy lived on the 3Vs Ranch, which consisted of two sections of land. Raising Herefords, Ernest saw his herd grow from 100 to 250 cattle during this period.[91]

In these years, Dorothy was really Ernest's business partner on the 3Vs Ranch in a practical way, keeping the books and sharing the riding responsibilities with him, as well as spending much time with their children.[92] Naturally, Dorothy and Ernest shared the fruits of their cattle operations on the ranch. Like most small, struggling businesses, the 3Vs Ranch had to finance its initial development internally through retained earnings. In fact, retained earnings accounted for most of the ranch's growth from 1941 to 1954[93] and Ernest Blades did not have to borrow money.

Even as the growth of the cattle operations on the 3Vs Ranch was taking place, Ernest and Dorothy diversified into raising pigs.[94] Besides feeding the pigs grain, they ran them on the pastures. Pig sales paid virtually all operating expenses on the ranch. Dorothy and Ernest sold their pigs to Swift Canadian and Burns in Calgary, while they sold their cattle to Canada Packers and Swift's. Each year, they marketed about 25 percent of their cattle herd.

In 1954, a few months after the death of Rod Macleay, Ernest and Dorothy Blades and their children moved to the much larger Rocking P Ranch, and thereafter its operations were combined with those of the 3Vs Ranch. At this point, they discontinued the pig-raising operation and devoted all their energies to the many cattle. Their cattle marketing efforts generally bore satisfactory results, as manager Ernest Blades undertook direct supervision of the daily operations of the two ranches, assisted by his foreman, Charlie Glass, who had served Rod Macleay in the same capacity. A fine worker and a skilled rider, as well as a man who was liked by the other cowboys, Glass was able to assume much of the management burden.[95] Most of the time, Blades did not have tell him what to do and the two men got along well. Indeed, Glass became his friend, and came to be regarded as one of the family. By the time he retired in 1980, Glass was paid $200 a month plus board and room.

As the principal owner of the Rocking P, Dorothy Blades remained of great importance to its management.[96] When the firm needed to sell cattle, she had talks with Ernest, after which he sold them. Dorothy also assisted her husband in keeping the books, as well as helping with much of the outdoors activity, especially in taking on riding responsibilities. Together, they ran the Rocking P.

As the Rocking P cattle operations grew in size, the firm sold from 700 to 1,000 head of cattle each year.[97] Ernest and Dorothy Blades were drawn especially to Herefords, and over the years they crossed them with Angus, Galloway, and Shorthorn cattle. The strategy first adopted by Rod Macleay of producing similar cattle proved to be a viable formula for success. Every year Ernest and Dorothy put up hay and grew oats for their cattle, but for the most part they relied on grass on the ranch and on the forestry reserve to fatten them. As conservationists, they were nonetheless alert to the need

to prevent overgrazing on the Rocking P.[98] Indeed, their policy of running a substantial part of their herd on the forestry reserve several months each summer allowed the grass on the Rocking P to come back. They faced low prices for their high-quality cattle in 1954, but later the prices improved.[99] Retained earnings continued to be a mainstay in the financing of the growth of the cattle operations of Ernest and Dorothy Blades. Only in 1969 did they borrow $100,000 to purchase the LeMan Ranch, but they paid off this debt within six months.[100]

Dorothy Blades lived to see the size of the Rocking P herd grow to nearly 2,600 cattle before her death in 1988, and as the main shareholder in the firm she enjoyed the fruits of that expansion.[101] Under the supervision of Ernest Blades, the Rocking P continued to produce top-quality cattle.

The Development of the Bar S Ranch

Meanwhile, George and Maxine Chattaway guided the Bar S Ranch's expansion and development. In 1954, there were 1,000 cattle grazing on the ranch. A decade and a half after the death of Maxine in 1974, the Bar S was running 2,000 cattle.[102]

George Chattaway was a significant addition to the Bar S's management in 1954. Born in 1912 in Fort William, Ontario, Chattaway graduated from Olds Agricultural College and the faculty of agriculture at the University of Alberta.[103] During the 1930s, he began working for the federal government in the department of agriculture.[104] Having met Maxine Macleay at the University of Alberta, Chattaway married her in 1943. Thereafter the couple lived and worked on the Bar S. A speedy introduction to ranching life came to George Chattaway, and he soon learned to handle saddle horses and cattle well. In 1954, he became the Bar S's secretary and manager as well as one of its directors.

Maxine Chattaway, the other director, was the main owner of the Bar S Ranch. Both Maxine and George Chattaway were flexible in their way of doing business, and were eager to carry the Bar S into the future. They were energetic persons who got things done. When they took the reins at the Bar S, George and Maxine stressed the need to continue producing high-quality cattle. Like Rod Macleay before them, they crossed Hereford, Galloway, and Angus cattle, but over the years the Hereford element became more dominant.[105] They sold their cattle especially to Canada Packers, but also to Swift Canadian, Burns, and Katchen Brothers. In 1954, the Bar S enjoyed about $150,000 in annual sales.[106] The capitalization of the ranch was raised to $320,000 in 1958, just four years after Maxine took over.[107] As was typical of small businesses, the Bar S's management favored a program of internally generated growth. Most of the Bar S's earnings were plowed back into the firm. While retained earnings accounted for much of their ranch's growth, the Chattaways also financed expansion through substantial loans from the Royal Bank of Canada.[108] Under the careful management of George and Maxine Chattaway, the ranch continued to prosper during the 1970s and 1980s. In 1990, annual sales amounted to half a million dollars.[109]

Management succession dominated the thoughts of George Chattaway long before he died in 1994.[110] An important strength of Maxine and George Chattaway was that they groomed their son Clay as their successor.[111] Born in 1946, Clay Chattaway from an early age wanted to become a rancher. After graduating from University School in Victoria, British Columbia, he went on to Olds Agricultural College, the second generation of his family to attend that institution. There he participated in a general agricultural program and graduated in 1967.[112] Shortly afterward he married Pat Jevne, whom he had met at Olds Agricultural College. Business partners in the Bar S from the beginning, both Clay and Pat liked the beautiful countryside and their inspired performance in working with saddle horses and cattle impressed everyone.

Clay Chattaway had, of course, been introduced to the practical side of ranching early in life, getting to know horses and cattle, and working with machinery. He benefited from an upbringing in which his father had taught him how to make the most effective use of his skills. Rod Macleay had given his grandson a financial stake in the Bar S, and this was gradually increased by his mother after Rod's death in 1954. By 1981, Clay had proved his ability and was president of the Bar S.[113]

Cattle ranching experienced a fundamental transformation in the last third of the twentieth century. With the advent of improved breeding practices, the extensive use of power machinery, and the new conservation age, new methods became important for ranchers. The Bar S participated fully in these changes. The alterations Clay and Pat Chattaway made profoundly shaped the ranch for the next two decades. Beyond continuing to cross Hereford, Angus, and Galloway cattle to produce high-quality beef, they relied on new genetic research in government laboratories to raise better cattle. Biological information on reproduction dynamics had improved, and this was reflected in the breeding stock at the ranch. Active as conservationists, Clay and Pat maintained and improved the natural grass on their ranch by rotating the use of pastures.[114] During the dry years of the 1980s, they succeeded in solving the water shortage problem by building new dams in coulees as well as by making new dugouts. Automation eliminated the back-breaking labor previously required to provide hay for the cattle. By this time manufacturers were offering front-end loaders on tractors, which allowed the Chattaways to handle huge, round hay bales and thus participate in new ways of making hay.[115] Also, horse-drawn wagons had given way to modern trucks, which the Chattaways used to move hay bales quickly over long distances. They capitalized on new

opportunities to make their operations more efficient and, as a result, continued to grow.

The decision to invest heavily in new technology saved on labor expenses and heralded a new future for the Bar S. Only those ranches willing to spend liberally to constantly update their production facilities could hope to remain competitive in the livestock raising industry. As the Bar S became increasingly capital-intensive, it was important for Clay and Pat Chattaway to use labor effectively to achieve a smooth flow of beef cattle through their ranch. They and their children—Scott and his wife Lee, Chris, and Morgan—made up the most important part of the small workforce and did most of the riding. In addition to relying on their horses, each of them used a dog to assist in gathering the cattle. Education remained important to the Chattaway family: Scott took a general agricultural program at Olds Agricultural College and Chris studied range science and Morgan animal science at Montana State University, Bozeman. Clay and Pat also recruited a few workers to help them in conducting their business. Central in importance for the ranch's future was the cook. Beginning a new trend after World War II that would become more pronounced in later decades, women began to replace the male cooks. By 1997, Norma Ozeroff had performed splendidly in this position for 25 years. In addition, two or three men served as laborers on the Bar S, carrying out tasks such as running the tractor, feeding cattle, and repairing fences.[116]

Rocking P Ranch Growth and Division

By this time, significant changes had occurred at the Rocking P Ranch. Most important, the ranch was divided among the five children of Ernest and Dorothy Blades in 1996. This change took place against a background of development efforts in the firm.

All the children had, over two decades, helped their parents build up one of Alberta's important ranching businesses, a firm known throughout the foothills country for the quality of its cattle. Among the children was Mac Blades, who as a young boy on the Rocking P was inspired by his father and foreman Charlie Glass. Mac spent many a day riding a saddle horse and looking after cattle, which convinced him that the life of a rancher was for him. In 1965, he finished high school and went to work full time on the Rocking P.[117] By 1973, his father, while remaining active in running the ranch, had come to rely heavily on Mac who was now manager and had a small interest in the enterprise. Over the years, Mac's ownership in the ranch increased. Like his father, who went into semi-retirement in the late 1970s and 1980s, Mac honed his understanding of the realities of the ranching business. By this time, Mac had married Renie Jones of Harrison, Idaho. Born on her parents' cattle ranch, Renie shared a similar background

Figure 3. Mac and Renie Blades (foreground) on their 1996 trip into the Bow-Crow Forestry Reserve, where they ran their yearlings on the Livingstone and Oldman rivers from 15 June to 15 October. (Photo courtesy of Mac and Renie Blades)

with her husband, and the couple became a strong management team for the Rocking P. They led the family ranch into a new period of growth and prosperity. The ranch controlled 37,000 acres of deeded and leased land by 1973. The profitability of the family enterprise during the next two decades allowed its owners to significantly increase the firm's productive facilities. In 1996, the year when the division of the Rocking P occurred, it controlled 42,000 deeded and leased acres.[118]

Like Clay and Pat Chattaway, Mac and Renie Blades participated fully in the changes occurring in the Alberta livestock raising industry in the last third of the 20th century (Figure 3). This period, and with it the rapidly growing importance of conservation, new power machinery, and fresh breeding methods, presented a variety of new challenges that Rocking P owners had not fully experienced earlier: rising capital costs, grass and water management problems, and the complexities of breeding cattle.

At the Rocking P, Mac and Renie Blades proved innovative and flexible in their approach to business. While their traditional technique of crossing Herefords and Galloways to produce top-quality beef remained important, they benefited from investing large sums of money in better purebred bulls. Although cattle continued to be their leading product, they consciously chose to become a diversified ranching enterprise. In addition to Herford–

Galloway cattle, they raised some quarter horses and buffalo.[119] Most of the buffalo sales occurred in Fort Macleod, while quarter horse sales usually took place through word-of-mouth to prospective customers around Nanton and nearby towns such as High River. But the main growth was accomplished in cattle, which buyers purchased right on the Rocking P. In the early 1970s the ranch specialized in sales of two-year-old steers, but changing demands in the market prompted a gradual switch to selling mostly yearling steers. From the outset, Mac and Renie Blades emphasized the need to maintain the high quality of all their products. They sometimes worked together informally with Clay and Pat Chattaway in things such as marketing cattle where a network of family ranches like this helped to reduce the cost of operations.

Mac and Renie Blades devoted considerable time to the protection of precious natural resources and grass management. There was no single, comprehensive path to conservation. But very naturally, Mac and Renie toiled as environmentalists, carefully managing their land to conserve grass and water. The forestry reserve remained important as they grazed some of their cattle there in the summer, but the ranch continued to be their main source of grass. Mac and Renie fully understood how quickly the grass on the ranch might disappear from overgrazing. They played their parts well, rotating the use of pastures to allow the grass to rest and recover. In doing so, they also ensured that the cattle would find enough grass in the pastures during the winter. At the same time, they seized the opportunity to provide their cattle with an ample supply of water. Although Mac and Renie depended heavily on the many natural springs of water on the Rocking P, they also invested much capital in sinking wells, creating dugouts, and building dams in coulees, especially during the dry years of the 1980s.[120] The ranch suffered a blow in February 1987, when a big fire from outside its boundaries swept over it, causing a great deal of destruction. It was a difficult struggle for Mac and Renie Blades during this time, but they gradually recovered from the devastating impact of the fire.

The prosperity of the Alberta economy in the 1970s provided the Rocking P with profit opportunities. When the boom ebbed at the start of the 1980s, however, the ranch found it more difficult to earn profits. Other ills that befell the Rocking P in these years included plummeting cattle prices, a situation it faced again in 1995 and 1996. The ranch nevertheless successfully weathered these unsettling developments. With favorable cattle prices in 1997, the Rocking P's future looked more promising.[121]

In organizing the small workforce at the Rocking P, Mac and Renie Blades developed a basic strategy: a strong emphasis on co-ordinating the efforts of the family with those of a few cowboys. The responsibilities of one of the cowboys included looking after the cattle on the ranch on a daily basis, while the main task of another one was to watch over the cattle when they were on the forestry reserve. Much of the additional seasonal work with the cattle was done by Mac and Renie Blades and their children—Justin, Shauna and her husband Manerd Bird, and Monica and her husband Blake Schlosser. As people knowledgeable about the weaning of calves from their mothers, they decided to slow down the weaning process, thus enjoying the advantage of seeing the calves enter their new environment and become independent with more confidence and less weight loss.[122]

Beyond helping with all the riding work at the Rocking P, family members specialized in certain activities, with Monica and Blake Schlosser giving attention to the quarter horses, Justin devoting his time to the cattle, and Shauna and Manerd Bird doing the family ranch books. They brought appropriate educational experiences to their tasks: Shauna took business administration at SAIT, and both Monica and Justin studied animal science at Montana State University, Bozeman.[123] Led by Mac and Renie Blades, the Rocking P remained competitive in the cattle, quarter horse, and buffalo markets in which it participated.

As the Rocking P grew in size and complexity, ranch division dominated the thoughts of the owners. In 1996, the widespread enterprise was divided among the five children of Ernest and Dorothy Blades—Rod Blades, Betty Wideman, Ethel Schlosser, Mac Blades, and Lynnie Blades. As a result of this division, Mac Blades received the part called the Rocking P Ranch, Rod Blades the TL Ranch, Betty Wideman the Mapiatow Ranch, Ethel Schlosser the Anchor P Ranch, and Lynnie Blades the Big Fire Ranch. In running their individual ranches, each of the children successfully balanced a quest for growth with a desire to enjoy life within the larger family circle. As third generation owner-managers, these ranchers often co-operated with one another in operations such as branding and running their cattle on the forestry reserve, thus creating a network of family ranches that provided an effective way for securing stability, saving on labor costs, and permitting development to take place.

Conclusion

By 1996, the Rocking P and Bar S ranches were much larger and more complex than they had been a century before. Although relying on significant traditions such as producing top-quality beef, the firms' owners also followed new trends in strategic thinking in the Alberta ranching community. Most important were ideas about scientific research, new technology, and conservation. Profitable growth remained important to their development as assets, sales, and earnings rose. The two ranches kept up with their medium-sized counterparts in Alberta in raising cattle. Over the previous one hundred years, the Bar S and the Rocking P seized golden opportunities in cattle, then the most rapidly expanding segment of the livestock industry. Their pioneering efforts in cattle in the 1880s and 1890s gave them advantages over many of their competitors who did not enter the cattle business until the early 1900s.[124] In addition to their edge in water

and pasture control, the Bar S and Rocking P also enjoyed ties to major meat packing houses. During the first six decades of the century, capital investments were made to insure the Rocking P and Bar S's success in the future. As a result, they and the Alberta economy as a whole succeeded in harvesting many of the fruits of the economic developments in the last third of the century.

The sense of family identity instilled in the Bar S and Rocking P by Rod Macleay remained throughout the second half of the 20th century, as the second and third generations took over ownership and management. The traditional personal commitment to the development of the Rocking P and Bar S continued as new owner-managers balanced personal family control with the needs of the firms. The owner-managers worked hard, putting in long hours. Risk-taking business people, they had a direct personal stake in the success of their firms and identified closely with them. They regarded the Bar S and the Rocking P as their firms, in which the personal ways of Rod Macleay and his predecessors had not been forgotten. In the second and third generations, the owner-managers continued to take a long-term approach to business, making long-term investments in development and looking upon the ranches in personal terms, as family ventures to be nurtured and passed on to their heirs. Clearly, young members of each family ranch acquired a good knowledge of their enterprise as they grew up, providing them with valuable expertise by the time they began making decisions. Through orderly succession at the Rocking P and the Bar S, stability of leadership was achieved.

The Impact of the Depression on Grazing Lease Policy in Alberta

Max Foran
Western Heritage Centre, Cochrane

The ranching industry in Western Canada received valuable support from the federal government's generous leasehold system instituted in 1881. Over the ensuing 50 years ranchers fought to preserve the integrity of leaseholds in the face of relentless pressure from cash crop agriculture. These efforts were directed primarily towards security of tenure, and while rental and taxation levies were sources of disquiet, they were never factored into production costs and market prices. Instead, ranchers seemed to accept the same flawed notion that justified the uniformity of the homestead system, and which held that land was a constant, a product unto itself regardless of the fruits of labor it bore. Any debate over rates and taxes before 1937 had devolved on the amount levied rather than its applicability to the land being leased. It took the misery of the Depression to change this time-honored perception of land as total product. Amid the economic travail of the late 1930s, a group of southern Alberta stockmen began advocating a change from rentals based on gross acreage to those linked with production costs and market prices. The adoption of the new system by the Alberta government in 1945 evinced official recognition of this radical shift in philosophy, and essentially recognized the primacy of grass rather than the land upon which it grew.

Security of leasehold tenure was easily the most pressing problem confronting Alberta cattlemen in managing their operations.[1] It was a source of concern almost from the beginnings of the open range era. Though the expansive regulations of 1881 allowed 25-year leases of up to 100,000 acres for one cent per acre per year, a two-year cancellation clause was a threat to any sense of permanency. Within three years even this time frame had been abolished. Further restrictions provided for immediate withdrawal of even-numbered sections for homestead purposes, and prohibited grazing on the public domain without permission. Then in 1896 the old lease system was terminated and lessees allowed to purchase 10 percent of their leaseholds for $1.25 per acre. The results were immediate. In 1887, a total of 4.66 million acres were held by 132 leaseholders including 16 with holdings

over 100,000 acres and 20 with over 50,000. By 1897 the leasehold acreage had dropped by almost half. The largest holding was 7,500 acres.[2]

This constriction of the large leaseholdings between 1885 and 1896 was intensified in the first decade of the 20th century under the pressure of agricultural settlement. Except for a few closed leases issued by Clifford Sifton during the final days of his tenure as Minister of the Interior, the demands of the homestead system preempted those of the ranching industry. Though approved leaseholds were ostensibly protected from homestead entry by being unsuitable for agriculture, an extreme definition of the latter kept ranchers in a state of constant unease.[3] For example, government inspectors were instructed not to recognize climate in determining a piece of land's fitness for agriculture.[4] By 1909, the boundless optimism over the future of cash crop agriculture and dryland farming techniques, and the beginnings of viable mixed farming enterprises had obviated any urgency to retain long-term leases for purely grazing purposes.[5] In 1911 P. C. H. Primrose, the North-West Mounted Police Superintendent at Fort Macleod succinctly summed up the situation when he wrote "there is no doubt that the rancher's day is a thing of the past."[6]

Primrose was right. In the face of record homestead entries[7] and the insecurity of their own leasehold tenures, the ranchers were taking flight. Hundreds of ranchers throughout Alberta simply gave up their leases. Some moved to the open unsettled areas of cheap grass in south-east Alberta.[8] Others went into farming.[9] Canada's Veterinary Director General echoed the passing of an era when he commented in 1912 that the "ranching industry in Canada is rapidly passing. Dry farming and irrigation will bring lands unfit for general agriculture under cultivation."[10]

Faced with the loss of their livelihood, the ranchers, fought back. After 1911, the Western Stock Growers' Association (W.S.G.A.) desperately lobbied its old allies in the newly-returned federal Conservative government. Following a tour of the West by the federal Livestock Commissioner, the chaotic state of the cattle industry evinced an official response in the form of an Investigative Commission. After taking evidence from hundreds of cattle operators across the West, the Commission concluded that the ranching industry had declined 75 percent over the previous five years, and in part equated the problem with a lack of leasehold security. Regulations enacted in 1914 approved the issuance of closed leases of up to 12,000 acres for a period of 10 years.[11] Since these leases were for land deemed unsuitable for agriculture, the chief leasehold areas were confined to the short grass country of southern Alberta (Figure 1). The system worked well, especially in the years following the bumper crop of 1915 when the miseries of drought and unproductiveness in marginal farmlands in southern Alberta underscored an agricultural vulnerability undreamed of fifteen years earlier.[12] Revised grazing regulations promulgated in April 1922 provided for 10-year leases on land irrespective

Figure 1. Cattle drive across the short grass country, 1921. There is a widespread perception that ranching on a large scale ended soon after the killing winter of 1906–07. This was not the case. Huge areas remained available for grazing. This paper describes the battle by ranchers to obtain satisfactory tenure to their range, which continued through the 1930s. (Glenbow Archives, Calgary, Canada, NB(H)-16-495)

of soil quality if it was located more than 40 miles from a railroad.[13] Then in 1925 these regulations were amended, increasing the maximum holding to 25,000 acres and providing for 21-year closed leases. In the same year, the W.S.G.A. moved to consolidate its success in lobbying for the lease revisions by passing a resolution opposing any transfer of natural resources from the federal to the provincial domain.[14] Clearly the stockmen's organization, wanted to maintain an optimum situation, a sure indication that it believed it had done all it could with respect to security of leasehold tenure.[15]

The W.S.G.A.'s fear was partly realized in the new grazing regulations issued by the Provincial government following the transfer of natural resources in October 1930. These regulations covered 3,778 leaseholds on 3.22 million acres,[16] and though mirroring the old federal regulations in many respects right down to the actual wording, they contained two major deviations. First, the 21-year lease was abolished in favor of a 10-year tenure. Secondly, and far more threatening to ranchers, was the insertion of a three-year cancellation clause.[17] Understandably, the ranchers saw the new regulations as a major setback. Writing to his board of directors in 1932, the chairman of the W.S.G.A. Grazing and Taxation Committee commented that "if grazing is to continue in the short grass country (the location of most leases), and those in it not go into liquidation, some drastic adjustment must be made by the Province."[18] An old debate was to start up again, this time at a new government level.[19] From 1932, the

W.S.G.A. kept security of tenure at the top of its priorities, and by opening an immediate dialogue with the government over the matter, the Association gained early recognition as the official voice of ranching in Alberta.

The costs of leasing land, though of less serious consequence than security of tenure, became increasingly contentious in the 1920s. As long as beef prices ensured a reasonable profit margin, lease rental costs and taxes were generally accepted as necessary evils. With profits assured during the open range era to 1907, and beef prices rising steadily between 1910–1919, the rent and tax issue was never really a major factor before the 1920s.[20] Throughout the period under discussion, annual rental rates on crown land were stabilized at 2 cents an acre, a figure based on an arbitrary assessment of all western grazing land at 25 cents an acre with 8 percent interest.[21] Other rental rates were higher. Leases on school lands were assessed at 6 cents per acre, and after the federal government allowed grazing on forest reserves, ranchers had to pay 8 cents per animal per month for a six month permit. Land taxes varied according to municipal district but for the most part averaged from 2 to 4 cents per acre per year. Yet, it was not so much the rentals and taxes on leased lands that became excessively burdensome by 1930, but rather the taxes on deeded land. The differentials between taxes on leased and deeded land were considerable. In 1922, Rancher Alfred Ernest Cross paid $5.20 tax on a quarter of leased land. Another deeded quarter in the same township cost him $26.34 in taxes.[22] One stockgrower who ranched only on deeded land told the Southern Alberta Survey Board in 1921 said that he paid roughly 15 cents per acre in all taxes on deeded land whereas leaseholders in the same area were only remitting 5.75 cents per acre.[23] In terms of the leaseholders however, the increasing financial hardships impacted heavily on them as well since their operations included both deeded and leased land. Indeed, the building restrictions on leased lands virtually precluded leasehold operations only.

The burden of these taxes and rentals was felt in the early 1920s when arrears of taxes began to build, and up to 1929, uncollected taxes exceeded the actual levy in Alberta's municipal districts.[24] The situation was so bad by 1924 that the W.S.G.A. successfully negotiated tax reductions on leased lands, a measure which led A. E. Cross to write to provincial Agriculture Minister, George Hoadley, expressing his thanks on behalf of the short grass stockgrowers who had had "a difficult time these last few years making ends meet."[25] In 1928, the Dry Belt Ranchers' Association unsuccessfully petitioned the federal government for a 50 percent reduction in rental rates.[26] Then, when beef prices began collapsing further following the prohibitive U.S. Hawley–Smoot tariff in 1930,[27] the pressure of rentals and taxes escalated to unbearable levels. In 1930, taxation arrears exceeded the levy in municipal districts by $1.6 million.[28] Even before the full impact of the Depression, Alberta ranchers were already in dire straits. One source

Figure 2. Loading chutes at Maple Creek. From 1913 until 1921, Canadian ranchers enjoyed 'open' access to the Chicago market (they paid no duty). This profitable situation was interrupted when the U.S. government placed a tariff on Canadian cattle in 1922. The higher Hawley–Smoot tariff initiated in 1930, virtually closed the United States to Canadian cattle. (Glenbow Archives, Calgary, Canada,1368-13)

quoted a rate of return of 0.83% on the typical ranch balance sheet between 1926–31.[29] A survey by Manyberries Research Station of 27 ranches concluded that stockmen barely met their operating costs in 1931 and that 10 of the 27 had to use reserve capital or borrowed money to keep afloat.[30] By late 1933, the *Calgary Albertan* was claiming that ranchers' operating costs exceeded revenues by 240%.[31] And as the Depression deepened, the problem worsened (Figure 2).

The concept of the range itself as a dependent and fragile variable was much slower to emerge in leasehold considerations before 1925. Ranching stewardship over leasehold land manifested itself in attacks on cash crop farming as the best land-use policy. The negative effects of unrestrained breaking of land to the plough had been noted as early as 1915 by the federal Inspector of Ranches when he wrote in his report of a patch of 20 acres broken in 1885 which "had never grown back to its natural state."[32] His warning that ploughed land was forever rendered useless for grazing went unheeded, as witnessed by the findings of the Southern Alberta Survey Board appointed in 1921 to inquire into the agricultural future of Southern Alberta. Clearly, the board members were convinced that cash crop farming was still the best way to ensure both population growth and optimum land use in southern Alberta:

> *It is doubtful if there are any great stretches of land in the world of a character so uniformly rich as to the soil itself and as to potentialities if carefully used for quick convertibility at the hand of man to immediate wealth by the production of grain.*[33]

Stung by the board's recommendation that leaseholds be discontinued and a system of community pastures instituted to support farmers, A. E. Cross laid the ranchers' case before the board:

> *If the old cattlemen were allowed to utilize the country and settlers prevented from settling on dry and arid lands, there would be no need of a survey board today for southern Alberta . . . a lot of the country more or less destroyed by being ploughed up, the surface earth blown away and bountifully sowed with injurious weeds where the country was originally covered with the finest quality of grasses which cannot be replaced.*[34]

Time was to prove Cross correct. By the end of 1926, almost 2,000 southern Alberta farming families had gone from the land thus ensuring, in part, a tragic recognition that leasehold grazing was the best land-use for most of the short grass country.[35]

Range management was the last factor to emerge as a major issue regarding leaseholds. Through the first quarter of the 20th century, government officials were abysmally ignorant of the principles of effective range management.[36] The federal research stations during this period were replete with reports of experiments designed to improve cash crop farming. Livestock experiments concerned themselves with nutritional studies mostly involving grain finishing and legume forages.[37] Factors affecting range degradation and carrying capacities were scarcely recognized, let alone explored (Figure 3).

The stipulations on stocking rates in the various grazing regulations show that official interest lay in securing maximum use of the land. In the 1914 regulations, the Minister of the Interior could compel a rancher to stock more cattle if he felt it necessary. In 1925, the new provisions for 21-year leases contained a clause which prevented renewal if the leasehold was not being used to its fullest extent. All regulations, including the provincial regulations of 1931 referred to 30 as representing the maximum number of acres per animal. When the federal government rejected a request by the Dry Belt Ranchers Association in 1928 to set the stocking rate at 60 acres per animal in the short grass country it was a clear indication that land differentiation was still not part of official policy.

The ranchers, too, accepted this concept. Accustomed to an extended period of favorable grazing conditions, they seemed to accept the notion of unlimited grass.[38] All they wanted was equitable access to it. Indeed, when A. E. Cross was asked by the Minister of the Interior to comment on the 1914 Regulations prior to their issuance, he argued that the stocking rate of 30 acres to one animal was too stringent in foothills country but that it was quite sufficient in the dry areas.[39]

Yet, it was the stockmen and not the government research stations who first recognized the implications of range degradation. Ten years after

Figure 3. A roundup in the short grass country in the 1920s. Techniques remained largely unchanged from those developed during the 1880s. Here, cowboys select their horses from the remuda in the early morning. Note the rope corral erected by the horse wrangler and anchored to the chuckwagon, and the piles of horse tack in the foreground. (Glenbow Archives, Calgary, Canada, NB(H)-16-503)

Cross' optimistic recommendation, the visible evidence presented by deteriorating range conditions caused by overgrazing, and the vegetative degradation associated with the reversion of abandoned cropland to its natural state brought stockmen face to face with the fragility of the land. The ensuing ten years marked the beginnings of an understanding of the principles and merits of range management. The question of equitability of leasehold rentals emerged as a corollary of this new awareness.

In 1924, the W.S.G.A. appealed to the federal government for assistance in arresting the erosion of grazing lands.[40] The subsequent establishment in 1927 of a research station at Manyberries,[41] in the heart of the short grass country led to the first studies of range management principles. This initial program focused on attempts to assess the carrying capacities of range lands, and methods of management thought likely to secure the best utilization of grazing resources.[42] Experiments on rotational and deferred grazing, forage crops, regrassing,[43] and water conservation methods were well underway by the time of the natural resources transfer in 1930.

The Alberta cattle industry moved into the early 1930s already in a state of extreme volatility. Ranchers were wrestling once more with the familiar issue of security of tenure. Their debts were rising rapidly, and science was questioning, rightly it seemed, traditional grazing practices. As the depression-filled decade deepened, the cumulative impact of these three factors was to force its own solution on leasehold management in Alberta.

The collapse of cattle prices really commenced in 1931, and continued throughout the decade. Between 1931–38 the highest average yearly price paid for good butcher steers in Toronto was 23 cents less than in 1924 when a dismal $6.75 per hundredweight marked the low point of the 1920s.[44] Livestock Commissioner, S. G. Carlyle, referred to 1931 as recording the lowest prices for livestock in the past 30 years,[45] a situation exceeded in the following year when cattle brought $2.90 at the Calgary Stockyards.[46] Again, in 1933, the Livestock Commissioner spoke about the lowest prices on record when steers off the range brought a meagre $1.75–2.25 per hundredweight.[47] Some cattle shipments actually brought less than the cost of transporting them, while Grant MacEwan, then Professor of Animal Husbandry at the University of Saskatchewan, tells of 'canner cows' being worth as much for their hide as for their meat.[48] This sustained period of low cattle prices had two main ramifications. The first was the increasing burden of debt carried by ranchers. The second concerned the accelerated rate of range degradation.

Although statistics varied with year and area, it was a proven fact that, during this period, a rancher's land costs were an unacceptable 15–25 percent of the costs of total production, and that the value of his cattle represented only 20 percent of his equity.[49] One expert told the 1935 W.S.G.A. Convention that the land charges on beef production were double that of grain.[50] Figures released by the federal government during this period showed that ranchers needed a floor price of $6.00 per hundredweight to break even, and to justify the leasehold rentals and taxes which had been set at a maximum of 4 cents per acre.[51] With this floor price unattainable for most of the decade, many ranchers simply could not cope. Arrears in rentals and taxes piled up and lease cancellations increased dramatically.[52] In 1929, the annual provincial tax levy for municipal districts at $3.6 million was equal to arrears and indicated a slowly improving position since 1924. Between 1933–37, taxation arrears for municipal districts averaged $6.2 million, more than double the tax levy. The trend continued well into the 1940s, the period 1938–42 continuing to average about $6.0 million annually in tax arrears. The situation in the major leasehold municipal districts was proportionally worse. In 1935 the five municipal districts with the largest leasehold acreage were in taxation arrears of more than half a million dollars, roughly five times their annual tax levy.[53] The leasehold arrears themselves showed a significant increase in the period. At the time of transfer of natural resources to the province in 1930, leasehold arrears totalled $39,771.46. Eight years later the corresponding figure was $279,873.44.[54]

Faced with these appalling economic circumstances, the stockmen appealed to the provincial government for help.[55] In 1935, the W.S.G.A. successfully negotiated for a reduction in rentals and taxes.[56] Then in January 1937, leasehold arrears in rentals and taxation were amalgamated, and arrangements made to forego accumulated interest charges while consolidating all debts over a seven year period at 4 percent.[57] This consolidation of arrears and rentals meant that all future lease payments would be under a single levy instead of one for rent and another for taxation. Under this new arrangement, the costs of maintaining rented land could be more easily measured against the actual productivity of the land itself.[58] Another change which helped the struggling ranchers occured in 1936 when the Department of Lands and Mines replaced the Department of Municipal Affairs as the body responsible for collecting the new single levy.[59] With leases now consolidated into a single payment under the auspices of a government department more in tune with the problems of the land itself and less interested in fiscal accountability, the ranchers suddenly found themselves with a much more sympathetic ear in Edmonton,[60] especially when the new Social Credit government, elected in 1935, seemed to indicate more sensitivity to ranching problems than the previous U.F.A. government.

Accompanying this build-up of indebtedness was the accelerating degradation of the range. The prevailing low prices compelled many stockmen to retain large cattle numbers that ordinarily would have been marketed.[61] The result was chronic overgrazing. In 1936 the provincial Supervisor of Grazing warned of the "probability of Alberta grasslands being completely overgrazed and developing into a desert." He argued that the existing system of requiring one head per 30 acres would have to be amended.[62] In the same year, the District Agriculturalist in Cardston spoke of large scale liquidation of breeding stock.[63] The situation was not confined to southern Alberta. A year later the District Agriculturalist in more northerly Camrose commented on the chronic overgrazing of pastures and of the lamentable ignorance among farmers of forage alternatives.[64]

This alarming level of overgrazing in ranching country was paralleled by frequent and persistent calls for change among the professional agricultural community. Foremost among these spokesmen for more enlightened grazing practices were L. B. Thomson,[65] Superintendent of Manyberries and later Swift Current Dominion Research Stations, and his on-site colleague, S. E. Clarke, an agricultural scientist specializing in forage crops and pasture studies. Throughout the 1930s both men were regular speakers at the W.S.G.A. Conventions.[66] Between them, they hammered home the concept of differentiated ranching practices necessitated by variable topography, climate and grass cover. By using visual references and statistics based on ongoing research at their own facilities, Clarke and Thomson defined a new road for the floundering ranching industry. In a ground-breaking speech at the 1936 W.S.G.A. Convention, Thomson addressed the problem of overgrazing. After referring to a study being undertaken to compute the value of land for grazing, Thomson laid the contentious issue bare for the first time when he said, "In the rating capacity of grazing lands, it should be on the basis of production value rather than on acreage alone"[67] (Figure 4).

Figure 4. Percheron mares on the Bar U Ranch. The carrying capacity of this range in the foothills was much higher than that of the grass shown in Figure 1 in the drier short grass prairie to the east. Yet the rental paid for grazing leases failed to recognize these contrasts. (Glenbow Archives, Calgary, Canada, ND-8-75)

Thomson's point was not lost on the debt-burdened ranchers across southern Alberta's short grass country, and in particular on George Ross[68] of Aden. Ross, who was already recognized as a leader and innovator in the industry through his work in establishing the Red Label Feeders Association in the late 1920s, was no stranger to the financial difficulties associated with large scale ranching enterprises.[69] His family ranch holdings had expanded well beyond their original Milk River location before being curtailed by low prices and diminishing returns. And, while there is no proof that he had previously entertained the same notion as expressed by Thomson, there is every probability that he had been thinking along those lines. He was certainly quick to act. Shortly after Thomson's address, Ross initiated the formation of the Short Grass Stock Growers' Association (S.G.S.G.A.) in Medicine Hat in July, 1936. After dividing the short grass country of 30,000 square miles into 12 zones, each headed by a spokesman, the meeting passed its first resolution calling for the provincial government to rate grazing lands on their earning capacity in relation to livestock values.[70] By January, 1937, the association had organized its forces sufficiently to approach Hon. N. E. Tanner, Minister of Lands and Mines.[71] Implicit in its suggestion to Tanner was the pledge of some 54 ranchers representing over one million acres of leasehold land to submit to a voluntary experiment of a new tax on production should it be approved. Tanner proved to be sympathetic and promised to undertake a survey with a view to classifying leasehold lands in terms of their productive capacity. Four months later, the S.G.S.G.A. was able to report to its membership that:

> *A signed agreement has been made with the Provincial Government to submit the control of grazing land to a board representing the Government and stockmen . . . to administer this land on a production basis.*[72]

Up to this time, the actions of the S.G.S.G.A. to secure rentals based on production had the complete endorsement of the W.S.G.A. Indeed, many southern Alberta ranchers held membership in both associations.[73]

By the end of 1937, the notion of rentals being based on production seemed a foregone conclusion. Time seemed to be the only problem. Tanner felt that a two-year survey would provide the necessary information "so that rentals may be placed on a more permanent basis, comparative with the producing and earning capacity of the land."[74] However, it was not until July 1939 that a special committee was appointed consisting of representatives from the S.G.S.G.A. and the provincial government to investigate and recommend on the best ways of protecting the natural grasslands (hereafter cited as *Grazing Rates Report*).[75]

At this stage, it was clear that high hopes were held for pending change in the way lease rentals were assessed. Before it began its investigation, the special committee was well aware of the ranchers' promise to participate in the experimental plan, and further, was of the opinion that this option would be open to any in the industry.[76] In fact, a preliminary formula for the new assessment had already been worked out.[77] As for the W.S.G.A., it seemed to give its blessing to the forthcoming study by noting that "the need for a permanent land policy . . . is felt by the grazing industry," and that the results of the investigation were "awaited with keen interest."[78]

The study took two years and was conducted under the direction of Graham Anderson, the Provincial Grazing Appraiser and a man described by the W.S.G.A as the best man for the job.[79] The investigation was extensive and wide-ranging, and though it focused mainly on the short grass country its findings were advertised in advance as being of general significance. When released in 1941, the *Grazing Rates Report* certainly presented itself as a well-researched, insightful document with important implications for both the government and the livestock industry.[80] Included in its several recommendations were long-range security of leasehold tenure, the establishment of a Grass Conservation Commission, and an affirmation of the need to shift leasehold rentals from a flat rate to one based on production and market price.

Given the thoroughness of the report and the ranchers' initiative and co-operation in producing it, the industry reaction to it must have astounded Government officials. For the *Grazing Rates Report* received scant attention from both the W.S.G.A. and the S.G.S.G.A. upon its release and was subsequently ignored altogether. The *Canadian Cattlemen,* the official voice of the W.S.G.A., after giving the report a brief mention of the back

page of its September, 1941 issue[81] proceeded to ignore it completely, opting instead to publish in four parts the findings of the federal government's *Grassland Investigations in Alberta, Saskatchewan and Manitoba*[82] which discussed many of the issues contained in the *Grazing Rates Report* but which did not deal with leasehold rentals. It should be added that the former report seemed to buttress the short grass growers' argument for differentiated rentals, noting that up to 96 acres per animal was feasible in some areas, and that overgrazing over a four-year cycle increased weed cover by 250 percent, and reduced grass cover by 25 percent and forage yield by 45 percent.

The actions of the S.G.S.G.A. seemed totally inexplicable, and contradictory to its mandate for formation. After claiming that it had achieved that which it had set out to do, it merged with the W.S.G.A. Yet, when the provincial government called on its members to honor their agreement to try out the new production-based leasehold rentals on an experimental basis, it was met with bland indifference and non-compliance. Only two ranchers of the original 54 volunteered, and no one else from outside the S.G.S.G.A.[83]

The reasons for this sudden loss of interest in the new leasehold formula had nothing to do with the formula itself, it being public knowledge before the investigation had begun.[84] Essentially the new proposal called for the government to take an annual royalty of 10 percent[85] of the cost of production to be measured by multiplying the average annual gain of beef on grass (250 pounds) by the average market price of cattle at the Calgary Stockyards between July and December, and dividing that figure by the assessed carrying capacity of the land. As George Ross had pointed out in the late 1930s, adoption of this new formula would reduce rentals in the short grass country measurably.[86]

The W.S.G.A.'s reluctance to accept the *Grazing Rates Report* had some validity. First, it worried about the implications of the recommendations of the Grass Conservation Commission.[87] Second, it feared that the government really wanted to impose a tax on all production *in lieu* of a general land tax.[88] Third, and most importantly, it had recently been successful in achieving a cherished ambition in 1939–40 by negotiating new lease regulations with the provincial government that guaranteed twenty-year security of tenure and which reinforced the maximum flat rental rate of 4 cents per acre.[89] In the light of the *Canadian Cattlemen's* description of the regulations as being "as near as we could come to getting all we asked for,"[90] any question of a shift to a production tax was clearly unnecessary. Finally, it could be argued that W.S.G.A. members in the higher-carrying-capacity areas of the foothills were of the opinion that the new tax was to be limited to the zone delineated by the S.G.S.G.A's focus of attention.

The reasons why the S.G.S.G.A. lost interest in a proposal that it had promoted so energetically were rooted solely in pragmatic concerns, and were guided by financial motives rather than by the principles of effective grass management. When George Ross devised his formula in the late 1930s, he based it on an average market price of 2 cents per pound for range cattle at the Calgary Stockyards. He was exaggerating but not by much. Figures given in the *Grazing Rates Report* quoted an average market price for all cattle at the Calgary Stockyards at about $3.30 per hundredweight.[91] This latter price translated into a much lower rental rate under the new formula, namely 1.65 cents per acre in the short grass country. However, commencing in 1939, and fuelled further by wartime demand, cattle prices began rising dramatically. They topped $5.00 per hundredweight in 1939, and $6.00 a year later. By the time the *Grazing Rates Report* was released in late 1941, prices were over $7.00. Suddenly, George Ross' new formula for setting rental rates became an unattractive alternative. At $7.00 per hundredweight, lease rates in the short grass country would have been 3.50 cents an acre, significantly more than ranchers' flat rate in the dryland-zoned areas. The other side of the equation, that would see low rentals in adverse times, and which had driven the efforts of the S.G.S.G.A., was conveniently overlooked. It was also likely that the stockmen had decided to play the waiting game. Realizing that they had given their approval for the government to change the lease formula from acreage to production, they knew it was just a matter of time before the issue was forced.

By the end of 1943, the Hon. N. E. Tanner, the provincial Minister of Lands and Mines, was prepared to do exactly that. He had already gone ahead with his plans of dividing the province into carrying-capacity zones as recommended in the *Grazing Rates Report*.[92] Three such zones had been demarcated. A 50 to 1 ratio (one animal per 50 acres) delineated the short grass country of southern Alberta and the drier areas of the east. Along the heavily grassed foothills 24 to 1 was considered a fair allocation while most of central Alberta and a narrow trough extending south through High River and opening up in the Milk River country south of Lethbridge was designated at 32 to 1.[93] By the beginning of 1944, Tanner was ready. On 14 January 1944 he wrote to the W.S.G.A. asking for its recommendations respecting government grazing policies in the post-war period.[94] Tanner followed up his request with a critical article which appeared in the March 1944 issue of the *Canadian Cattlemen*. He referred to the government's commitment to the ranching industry illustrated by its recently enacted regulations providing for security of tenure, and to the cooperation between his ministry and the ranchers in devising the new production tax on leaseholds. He then castigated the short grass ranchers saying that "this plan has been submitted to the members of the Short Grass Stock Growers' Association but to date it is regretted that the plan has not received more favourable consideration."[95] Tanner left no illusions about his perception of the situation:

> *It is well remembered by all that during the 1930s the present flat rental rate was high in comparison to the price of beef and drought conditions that prevailed at that time. It was during this period that many of the ranchers got in arrears in their rental which made it very difficult to carry on both from the standpoint of ranchers, as lessee, and the Department, as lessor. Today the same flat rate of rental is charged as in the late nineteen thirties, yet the price of livestock has increased considerably during the same period. The ranching industry will never become stabilized as long as the rental costs are fixed and the selling price of livestock and the quantity of grass vary from year to year.*[96]

The W.S.G.A. was not impressed. Faced with cattle prices that were still rising, it attempted to counter Tanner by suggesting as its first recommendation for the post-war policy, a procedure which would allow ranchers to gradually become owners of their leases. The present flat rate on acreage was endorsed as the best alternative to the above. As for the new Production Tax, a warning was issued that it "should be thoroughly tested by experienced operators before being considered as a general policy."[97] Bolstered by the support of its membership at the W.S.G.A. Annual Convention of 1944, the Grazing Committee responded to a government request, and journeyed to Edmonton in October 1944 to present their views.

The Grazing Committee met on 12 October with a government that had clearly made up its mind with respect to the adoption of the Production Tax.[98] After flatly rejecting the Committee's recommendation for outright lease purchases, Department of Lands and Mines officials were equally unreceptive to other suggestions which included a universal experimentation period, and the isolation of the south-east area of the province for a longer trial period. When the Grazing Committee continued to hedge on accepting a tax based on production, the deputy minister responded by hinting strongly at substantial increases in the flat rate. Only then did the Grazing Committee bow to the inevitable. The Production Tax on leaseholds was accepted for a period of 10 years commencing in 1945 and subject to review at the end of a five-year period.

The W.S.G.A. was not surprised by the outcome. President Thomas Usher told the membership that the decision came as no surprise, and that "it was apparent that the Department favoured basing grazing charges on the production method."[99] He exhorted members to give the new measure their full support,[100] and indicated the fact that carrying rates had been conservatively appraised, and ultimately would be established on an individual lease basis. He also referred to the appeal process as protecting ranchers from inaccurate carrying capacity appraisals.[101] Still, it was a bitter pill to swallow particularly given the market price of $8.87 per hundredweight that was used to establish the three levies. From a maximum flat rate of 4 cents per acre between 1940–44, ranchers in the 24 to 1 carrying capacity zone were levied 9.25 cents per acre in 1945; those in the 32 to 1 zone paid 7 cents per acre while even those in the 50 to 1 zone accepted a rate of 4.5 cents per acre, a figure higher than the previous maximum. Over the next seven years, the levies continued to rise until by 1951, the three rates were 25.25 cents, 19 cents and 12 cents an acre based on a market price of $25.24 per hundredweight.

With some modifications, this process of assessing lease rentals remained in place for the next fifty years. Its flexibility protected both the rancher and the grasslands, and ended the long prevailing notion that land was a uniform product that could be measured in terms of gross acreage. It took debt, land degradation and low prices to impel producers to seek this new solution. The credit for same, however, belonged to the provincial government which, operating on high moral ground, could easily claim long range vision as its guiding principle. That these lofty ideals derived immediate fiscal benefit through rising prices was an irony that few ranchers would appreciate.

Wild West Shows and the Canadian West

Lorain Lounsberry
Glenbow Museum, Calgary

In 1996, when I began my research for Glenbow Museum's The Canadian Cowboy Exhibition (June–October 1997), I would not have thought there was enough material on this topic to merit investigation. But then I came across a photo in Glenbow's archives: a photo of Jim and Stastia Carry from Kew, Alberta. (Figure 1) The date of the photo is about 1925, and the couple is outfitted in wild-west-style gear, seated within an outdoor carnival setting. Soon after, another photo of Stastia Carry in fancy cowgirl attire appeared in the Calgary newspaper—she had just died in nearby Turner Valley at the age of 95. I was interested, and hoped to get her story from the friends and relatives she left behind. With help, the family was contacted, and an appointment set up. We were not prepared for the rich treasure trove of photos and archival material that we found on that visit. Scrapbooks filled with photos and newspaper clippings, letters, contracts, playbills, route cards, programs—all about Jim and Stastia Carry, wild-west performers from Kew, Alberta. A fascinating story began to unfold before us about Jim Carry, a talented Canadian cowboy from Kew, and Stastia Cross, an American performer who had soaked up stories about the west at the knee of William Cody—Buffalo Bill himself. The Carrys' career in the wild-west arena spanned the late teens through to the 1930s, and took them on the show circuits through the States and Canada. They crossed paths with many others in the same business, some of them from Canada. Perhaps the wild-west-show phenomenon in Canada was worth a closer look.

I began a quest for more information, and my inquiries spread across Canada, went into the United States, over to Europe, and back again to Calgary. I found many interesting people, collected some interesting stories, and borrowed some wonderful material for exhibit in Glenbow's Canadian Cowboy Exhibition. But stories about the Real Wild West phenomenon in Canada are still popping up, and many questions and ideas are yet to be answered and investigated.

By exploring a sampling of the Canadian stories and events, we begin to see that a distinctive variation of the Real Wild West show did develop in Canada.

Figure 1. Jim and Stastia Carry, wild-west-show performers, were from Kew, Alberta.
(Glenbow Archives, Calgary, Canada, NA-3123-2)

A closer look at Jim and Stastia Carry's memorabilia (now split between Glenbow Museum, and private hands) suggested that these two western performers found work in a number of formats: as individual employees with a show; as a contract act; or as a contracted show, with their own employees. They spent most of their performing careers as specialty contract acts, Jim as a rope artist, Stastia as a trick rider. They found work with traveling circuses and carnivals, and later with rodeos. For a couple of seasons, 1926–1927, they contracted with The Alberta Stampede Company, a large company with Calgary origins which travelled across Canada and into the north eastern U.S. putting on a western show and rodeo.

At this point, my research efforts turned to Circus World Museum in Bariboo, Wisconsin. They have a good record of the American circuses and carnivals, but for help with the Canadian businesses, they directed me to a semi-retired carnival man who was collecting the Canadian history. Al Stencell had good information on eastern areas, where he lived, but had not yet tackled the prairies in any depth. He reiterated what the Circus World Museum staff had said: that wild-west shows were very popular into the 1920s, and were usually the big 'back-end' show with a carnival, or a feature act with the circus. Stencell also put me in touch with an operating wild-west show in Ontario, the Bishop's 4B Ranch Wild West Shows. A family-run business in 1997, they billed themselves as the last touring Wild West Show in North America. I soon learned that they had been in business since 1914, and that Tom Bishop, the originator of the show, had been inspired as a youngster in England, about 1887, to go west by none other than Buffalo Bill Cody himself.

Buffalo Bill Cody keeps appearing in these stories, and reappeared in stories gathered later. William Cody was, after all, the originator of the genre that became known as the 'Wild West Show.' Reading the voluminous histories available about Cody, you quickly learn that Cody never used the word show in his title: it was 'The Real Wild West.' The word REAL was most important because from the outset in 1882, Cody intended to illustrate the true American West, using people who had lived the life and experienced the adventures. Cody hired real cowboys and real native peoples (mostly Sioux), and individuals who were famous in western history—people such as Sitting Bull, a medicine man whose people defeated General Custer and company, and Gabriel Dumont, right hand man to Riel during the 1885 rebellion in Canada. These members of the company were larger than life heroes, like Cody himself. But most of Cody's troupe was neither rich nor famous when they were hired—they were regular people who had skills you needed to succeed in the western cattle country.

Cody's colorful, thrilling display of the wild west was a smashing success in the crowded cities of eastern North America and Europe at the end of the nineteenth century. When Cody's Real Wild West came to town, everyone came out to see the spectacular street parade. They saw exotic

western costumes, stagecoaches, wild buffalo, long horned cattle, and Buffalo Bill himself in full regalia blasting glass balls out of the air with his rifle.

With the purchase of a ticket, the audience was entertained in the arena with the grand entry of all the performers, and then the main events: races, shooting acts, fancy roping, military exhibitions, 'cowboy fun' (rodeo events), and a flamboyant melodrama with lots of gunplay illustrating the winning of the west. The show closed with a grand, final ride-by salute from all the performers.

To our modern senses, this seems very familiar, and even slightly corny. But try to imagine yourself living in the 1890s, in a crowded city. The environment is blackened and polluted by industrialization. If you have work, it is probably repetitive manual labor, with little chance for advancement. In this world, Buffalo Bill Cody's Real Wild West display would have been mind-blowing. Dashing cowboys with big Stetson hats and riding boots, tall Sioux warriors in full feather headdress, fiery horses: these images were burned into the memories of thousands. The action was fast, and even the painted stage scenery suggested a fabulous land, uncluttered by 'civilization.' For those dreaming of a new chance, of glamor and adventure, the 'Wild West' seemed to offer escape and hope for the future.

Cody toured through Calgary near the end of his career in 1914, and even then he drew adoring crowds (Figure 2).

> *Buffalo Bill, the most romantic personality on this continent to-day. White haired, red shirted, his sombrero shading a most striking countenance, neatly booted as ever, the man who has stirred the emotions of millions rode through the ranks of thousands of his admirers.*[1]

Buffalo Bill Cody's Real Wild West had an immense, and immediate impact on those who saw it. Like kids in the 1990s, who mimic the current super hero of film or TV, the young and not so young began to imitate what they saw in Cody's Wild West arena.

In the Canadian west, an increasing number of stories have surfaced which identify the wild-west show as the motivating factor for moving west. For instance, in the late 1880s, young Al Griffin from Cedar Rapids, Michigan saw Cody's show, and ran away from home to join a wild-west show. Griffin eventually found his way to Alberta, and settled down to homesteading. Another lad named Hodgson saw Cody's show in England. Hodgson taught himself the dangerous art of trick riding and became an accomplished stunt rider in the circus. He, too, found his way to Alberta, and performed as 'Kid Hodgson' at the first Calgary Stampede in 1912. Hodgson stayed in Alberta and took up ranching. And in Rochester, New

Figure 2. Buffalo Bill Cody visited Calgary in 1914 with the Sells–Floto Circus.
(Glenbow Archives, Calgary, Canada, PA-3405-2)

York, young Guy Weadick was inspired by Buffalo Bill Cody's Wild West. Weadick taught himself trick and fancy roping, and headed west on the wild-west show circuit. By 1912, Weadick launched Calgary's first Stampede exhibition. Fired by Buffalo Bill's romantic images and stirring action, these young men pursued the dream of the wild west, headed for the geographic west, and ended up in Alberta.

But not all the wild-west action was imported. There are stories about a wild-west-style showman around Calgary in the early years around 1900. His name was Milt Dowker, and although he did a bit of ranching in the Millarville area south of Calgary, he was more interested in the wild-west-show business.

Dowker was a small man who let his hair grow long, wore a leather Stetson, and sported a white handled revolver. Nicknamed 'Wild West' Dowker, the feisty rancher enjoyed imitating the style of his role model, Buffalo Bill Cody. Dowker was good stunt rider, and would do some Roman riding himself, standing on a pair of horses, one foot on each horse, to the delight of the crowd. Dowker put together a show which featured steer roping, steer riding, and a comic steer-rustling act. But bronc riding Lee Marshall was the star of the show. Marshall was tall, good looking, and a superb rider. He was a true working cowboy, and good at his job. He was also handy with a bullwhip. With a crack of that whip, Marshall could safely snap paper out of a man's mouth. Dowker enjoyed a couple of successful seasons in southern Alberta, then travelled his show to the east. He folded his tents after only a brief run. He returned to Alberta in 1903, and eventually settled down to farming.

Cowboy competitions had been regular, unscheduled happenings in southern Alberta's ranching country since the first two bronc busters challenged each other. By about 1910, rodeo was beginning to be a profitable as well as popular spectator sport. In Medicine Hat, rancher and rodeo lover Ad Day invited the best cowboys to get together and put on a show for the Dominion Day celebrations in 1911. He took the winners from that show to Winnipeg, where they put on an impressive show of the cowboy art. Tom Three Persons of the Blood Reserve was in that select group. Buoyed with success, Day traveled to the U.S. planning to set up some dates for his western show. However, American interest in Canadian rodeo was disappointing, and Day gave up the idea.

As can be seen, there has always been a lot of talent in the Canadian West. For those with a flare for showmanship as well as talent, the lure of the wild-west arena was strong. The pay was better—at least three times the going rate for a cowboy in the 1920s. The work was less demanding, and less time-consuming. It also offered travel, adventure and more opportunities for fun—an ideal job for the footloose and fancy-free. It is little wonder that it appealed to young and talented Jim Carry of Kew, Alberta.

Jim Carry could have seen a number of traveling shows that visited the Calgary area before 1915. In 1905, the specialty act featuring bulldogger Will Picket and his manager Guy Weadick played both the Airdrie fair and Calgary Exhibition. Others, like the Miller 101 Ranch Wild West that played Calgary in 1908, were full-blown rodeo exhibitions with wild west acts and glitter. Jim Carry had perfected his trick and fancy roping after World War I, and found work in a number of the smaller traveling shows that abounded in the 1920s. By the 1920s, the American shows were smaller, and usually connected with carnivals for the circuit of the agricultural fairs: Dakota Max's Wild West played Saskatoon in 1923, and in 1927 Leon Lamar's Wild West played the Canadian prairie circuit, including Calgary. By this time, the Calgary Stampede had become an annual event, and one newspaperman reported wryly that having a Wild West show playing Calgary was like sending "coals to Newcastle."

Jim Carry traveled with Dakota Max, but was with Gollmar Brothers Circus on the American circuit when he met and married fellow performer Stastia Cross. The Carrys spent the next decade of their performing careers as specialty wild-west contract acts—Jim as a trick and fancy rope artist, and Stastia as a trick and fancy rider.

The Carrys weren't the only Canadians working the wild-west arena. In Ontario, English emigrant Tom Bishop developed a wild-west show much like that staged by his role model, Buffalo Bill Cody. Like so many others, Buffalo Bill's Real Wild West had inspired Bishop. As soon as he and his brother were able, Tom Bishop moved west to become cowboys. The Bishops lived the cowboy life for a couple of seasons in Alberta, but eventually settled in Ontario. There, Tom's ability as a horse trainer put him in the local spotlight. By 1914, he and his family had put together an immensely popular show for the local town. Bishop saw Buffalo Bill's Real Wild West one more time before Cody died in 1917. The influence of Cody's original show formula was obvious in the Wild West that Bishop developed. Colorful acts highlighted the cowboy and 'Indian,' while a stirring melodrama showed the winning of the West, American style.

Modest success did await a number of other operators based in western Canada. Buff Larkin and his troupe of cowboys from the Hanna, Alberta region enjoyed a brief summer fling with wild-west-show business in 1914. In Saskatchewan, the McDougald Brothers of Prongua, Saskatchewan toured the province with local talent for several seasons in the 1920s. No doubt more homegrown Canadian talent awaits discovery in the fine print of the local newspapers, or the handwritten reminiscences of pioneers.

However, it was imported American talent that made the most lasting impact in western Canada. Guy Weadick was born in Rochester, New York, but was turned on to the wild west of Buffalo Bill at an early age. Weadick learned the cowboy skills, and proved himself on the ranches, including Alberta's McIntyre ranch in 1904. A self-taught trick and fancy roper,

Figure 3. The design of this *Calgary Herald* newspaper advertisement for the 1912 Calgary Stampede is based on wild-west show posters.

(*Calgary Herald*, 3 September 1912)

Weadick worked both the wild-west arena and the vaudeville stage. He was a promoter and a persuasive talker. As early as 1908, Weadick saw great potential for a big western show in Calgary, the centre of Alberta's ranching community. The idea was good, but even Harry McMullen, Canadian Pacific Railway agent, said the time was not right.

But by 1911, things had changed. Settlers had been streaming into the Canadian West for several years—it was the time for Weadick's western show. McMullen contacted Guy, who gladly took up the challenge. Weadick went looking for financial backers, and found support in a group of influential ranchers. Weadick sold his dream to these ranchers—the dream of a reunion of the pioneers who had made the Canadian West: a parade of history, with the real people who had blazed the trail, a celebration, and lots of cowboy fun. According to Weadick, there was to be none of the old "villainy," "circus tinsel, nor far fetched fiction." Weadick and his backers saw their frontier pageant as an "educational, historical, and thrilling entertainment." The formula and the very words Weadick used were vintage 'Buffalo Bill.' Weadick's promotional blitz in the newspapers also reflected his wild-west show roots (Figure 3). Pretty ranch girls, rough and tough cowboys, excitement and pageantry were used to lure the crowds, and sell the tickets.

That first Calgary Stampede in 1912 had many similarities to Cody's classic wild west show format. The opening parade; the daily arena events: races, trick riding and roping, steer roping, riding and bulldogging, and bronc riding; and the grand finale ride-by and presentation of characters to the audience.

However, unlike Cody's Wild West show, the people who performed at that first Calgary Stampede were not employees or contract acts, although more than a few were from the wild-west circuit. Weadick planned to lure top-notch competitors with the biggest cash prizes ever offered at a rodeo. The best of the contestants won impressive cash prizes, and world championship titles. The professionals from the wild-west circuit were the big winners in the competitions, but a few talented locals, such as Tom Three Persons, also made spectacular wins.

Weadick's rodeo-style prize system was an important departure from Cody's Wild West format. Weadick also decided to eliminate the 'far-fetched fiction,' the large melodrama which was the highlight of Cody's performance. Cody had designed the action play to illustrate the 'winning of the west' through strength, gunplay, and victory over the original inhabitants of the land. The usual scenario was an armed military force coming to the rescue of pioneers besieged by natives. At the Calgary Stampede, firearms and sharp-shooting were given little promotion or coverage; the only quasi-military force in evidence were the North-West Mounted Police who rode in the parade; and the 'Indians' not only headed the parade, but also shared the billing in the rodeo arena.

Weadick was invited to organize the show for a third time in 1923. This time he got the whole city involved, encouraging both individuals and businesses to dress western in honor of days gone by. Weadick also introduced the chuckwagon races, an idea he had tried out in New York. The exciting, dangerous event captured the friendly rivalry of the roundup, and caught on easily in cowtown Calgary.

By the late 1920s, The Calgary Stampede had found a basic format that lasted for years. Reminiscing in 1948, Weadick called The Stampede a

Figure 4. Jim and Stastia Carry's wild-west arena is seen on the left in this photo of Conklin and Garrett's carnival at Nelson, British Columbia, in 1925.
(Glenbow Archives, Calgary, Canada, PA-3457)

"truly Canadian National epic of the days of the Old West."[2] Guy Weadick had created a new, Canadian formula for the Real Wild West.

The formula was successful, and others soon copied it. Notable among those who followed the formula was Peter Welsh, a Calgary horse dealer. Welsh and his sons were famous for their show-jumpers in the Canadian horse-show circuit in the early 1920s. He saw the success of the small wild-west shows playing in Ontario, so Welsh figured the paying public would go wild for the 'real thing.' Like Weadick, Welsh thought on the grand scale. He contacted big cities such as Vancouver, Winnipeg, Toronto, and Montreal and proposed to organize a rodeo for them. He bought up the best rodeo stock, invited the biggest names in rodeo from ranch country on both sides of the border, and put his Alberta Stampede Company into motion. His roster of rodeo stars included the infamous bucking horses Midnight, Gravedigger, and Tumbleweed, and the famous cowboys Pete Knight, Norman Edge, Slim Watrin, Paddy Ryan and Dick Cosgrave. Jim

and Stastia Carry signed on with Welsh as a contract act to add some wild-west pizzazz to the events. At each of the locations, the Carrys performed their specialty roping and riding acts, and were paid a fee of $450 per venue for the two of them. The cowboys were not on contract, but were kept on the string with the chance to win up to $1,000 per week in prize money generated from gate receipts.

Welsh's show was huge, approaching the size of the big original wild-west touring shows. The cost of transportation was enormous, and the logistics in a short summer season were complex. Welsh's first year was a fabulous success. But the success was not to be repeated. Poor weather and competing entertainment opportunities combined with huge overhead costs forced the company into bankruptcy in Toronto in 1927. Stranded in Toronto, the Welsh family stayed there. Most of the cowboys found ways to get back to the Canadian West. Jim and Stastia Carry easily picked up work for the rest of the 1927 season. The Sells–Floto Circus was playing in the area, and was glad to add the experienced performers to their wild-west-section. The Stampede formula continued to work in Calgary, in the heart of ranching country, but by the 1920s, the time of the big traveling western

show was over. Operational costs were high, and the novelty quickly wore off for the public. Besides, they could see western excitement in the new movie theatres, and they didn't have to brave the weather to do it.

However, there was still a market niche for the smaller versions of the wild-west show that traveled with the circus or carnival. In fact Jim and Stastia Carry had formed their own company in 1925. A. J. Carry's Real Wild West was a modest show. The 16-member troupe put on expert rifle shooting, knife throwing, whip handling, fancy roping, catching from one to six head of horses with one throw of the rope, fancy riding, trick riding, bronc riding, comedy riding and a clown act. Their comedic skits echoed the accepted humor of the times, and championed the Anglo–Saxon cowboy at the expense of other cultures. There were no melodramas showing the 'winning of the west' in the Carrys' show, no doubt partly because they required big staging elements such as a cabin, stage-coach or wagon. These props were expensive and difficult to transport. Figure 4 shows their wild-west-show arena set up at the back of the carnival lot in Nelson, British Columbia in 1925. The Carrys had signed on with Conklin and Garrett All Canadian Shows. They joined the carnival in Drumheller, Alberta for the summer tour through the western provinces and north-western U.S.

By the 1930s even these modest shows were in difficulty, facing not only the reduced economy of the depression but also the rising popularity of the cinema. The 'western shows' that did survive were the rodeos. Since the 1930s, they have grown into a professional sport whose biggest audience is still found in the ranching country of North America. And not least amongst these rodeos is the one which calls itself—in the promotional style of the old wild west-show—The Greatest Outdoor Show on Earth: The Calgary Stampede.

The adventure and fresh start promised by the 'Wild West' may have diminished over the years, but it has not altogether disappeared. You can still find proof of its power in the 1990s by talking to the tourists, and even some of Alberta's newer residents. Two examples come to my mind—one about an acquaintance from Switzerland who grew up on stories of the west, and moved here to fulfil his dream. He experienced the 'old west' by riding from Alberta to Mexico on horseback. Now he makes his home in Calgary, and makes a living in construction. The other story is about German-born Frank Heldke. Frank was an avid fan of Karl May, the popular German author who wrote about the 'Wild West' during Buffalo Bill Cody's era, 1880–1900. Heldke also read the western dime novels churned out in the late 1940s by Billy Jenkins. A fellow-German, Jenkins had been inspired in the 1910s by Buffalo Bill Cody to go 'West' and find the cowboy life. Fired by these vivid western stories, young Heldke taught himself rope tricks and set up a mini wild-west show in his parents' back yard. By the 1960s, Frank Heldke decided to leave the tensions of cold-war Europe, and find a freer lifestyle. He chose Calgary, because it was featured in a Billy Jenkins' western novel. Heldke expected to find the old west, but Calgary in the 1960s was not, of course, the wild west of his imagination. Frank put away thoughts of the wild west, and settled down as a graphic artist with the *Calgary Herald*. When he retired, Heldke took up trick roping again, changed his name to Holt, and in the 1990s, is in demand as a trick and fancy rope artist in Calgary.

In 1997, a new Alberta-based western show finished a successful first season. Pat Provost, rancher, stockman, tour promoter and member of the Blood Tribe created his Wild Horse Show and Buffalo Chase as a tribute to the horse, and recognition of its importance in his native culture. Provost was also responding to the comments of the visitors to Head-Smashed-In Buffalo Jump Interpretive Centre: they wanted to see some live buffalo, some live action. In the tradition of Buffalo Bill's Wild West, Provost planned a re-telling of the story of the horse, and a re-enactment of a buffalo hunt on horseback. Like Cody, Provost has given shape to the west of the imagination.

Buffalo Bill Cody's Real Wild West had powerful, long-lasting effects world-wide. He had created a mythic west, which drew people to the North-American West. Cody's mythic west was based on stories from the American West he knew. He repeated the 'winning of the west' stories in his action packed melodramas, which demonstrated and supported progress through violence. As historian Richard Slotkin points out in *Gunfighter Nation: the Myth of the Frontier in 20th Century America*, Cody's melodramas came to represent American beliefs, and reflect its morality.[3]

Cody's show also spawned many imitators. In examining a few of the Canadian imitators, it appears that the big melodramas have been consciously omitted. Could this reflect an attempt to create a variation on the myth of the west?—a Canadian version? Perhaps it is unwise to draw conclusions from such a small sample, and without further research into the development of the American rodeo. However, there are a few comments and facts that do indeed support this act of myth manipulation.

In 1911, Guy Weadick was looking for money to back his frontier pageant. He promised that there would be none of the old 'villainy,' or 'far-fetched fiction.' He dropped the melodrama from the arena show. Weadick was also careful to use the big parade to illustrate that progress in the Canadian West was peaceful. It was a colorful pageant, arranged as a time line of history in western Canada. Weadick recalled that first parade in a radio program broadcast in 1948. The words he used to describe that historical pageant illustrate his educational intent. First came the 'noble savages,' in all their splendid finery; then pioneer missionaries and Hudson's Bay Company traders; then the 'nefarious' whiskey traders, followed 'naturally' by the North-West Mounted Police in their bright scarlet tunics; next, the ranchers and cowpunchers and finally people and businesses of modern Calgary of 1912.

Weadick's parade did sketch Alberta's history, but in its simplistic arrangement, it also promoted the myth of peaceful progress in the Canadian West. The North-West Mounted Police, clad in scarlet, were placed in the parade as the mediators between the 'pre-civilized' Canadian West and the peaceful frontier of the cowboys and ranchers. These agents of the federal government, the Royal North-West Mounted Police, were still very much around in 1912, enforcing the peace throughout the western provinces. And, contrary to general beliefs, there was a lot of work for the police to do. Assault, robbery, rustling, murder, discriminatory acts, resentment of control by foreign investors, resentment of an eastern based government—and the list goes on. The real Canadian West was not a totally peaceful society. But in a booming economy, with a record number of newcomers settling in the west, it was a good business decision to promote the image of a peaceful frontier. This promise of peaceful progress would be reassuring and appealing to the new and potential immigrants who were flooding the Canadian West. It was also good advertising for businesses such as the Canadian Pacific Railway, and local suppliers who depended on the newcomers for their livelihood.

The format adapted by Weadick and the organizers of the first Calgary Stampede reinforced the positive aspects of the Canadian West, as might be expected. Perhaps it also helped shape the myth of the Canadian West as a peaceful frontier. And although the Calgary Stampede did not travel, foreign visitors and media did spread the word, even in 1912. Further research may help determine just how much influence Guy Weadick's 'truly Canadian National epic of the days of the Old West' had on the nation's image of itself.

There was more 'Wild West' in Canada than I expected. Even this cursory look uncovered a wide range of personal stories that were directly influenced by Buffalo Bill Cody's Real Wild West. During the teens and 1920s, the focus of this study, the wild-west show had lost much of its size and appeal in comparison to its glory days of the 1880s to 1900. But it still offered an exciting alternative for a few talented cowboys and cowgirls, such as Jim and Stastia Carry of Kew, Alberta. And in the hands of Guy Weadick, the wild-west show format was reshaped to support and promulgate a uniquely Canadian image: that of the peaceful frontier.

The Canadian Cowboy Exhibition

Richard W. Slatta
North Carolina State University

From late June through October 1997, 'The Canadian Cowboy' rode the polished halls of the Glenbow Museum. The 743 square-meter (8,000 square-foot) exhibit attracted an international audience, spawned an exciting conference on ranching history, and gave rise to a variety of other museum activities. Donna Livingstone, Stephen Dundas Smith, Lorain Lounsberry, Melanie Jkorlien, and Dennis Slater comprised the museum team that mounted this colorful, enjoyable, educational exhibit.

Curators developed three aspects of the cowboy in different areas of the exhibit: 'The Working Cowboy,' 'The Performing Cowboy,' and 'The Imaginary Cowboy.' Large, colorful murals painted by Murray Kimber provided powerful visual introductions and summaries of each theme. History buffs would be most drawn to the authentic artifacts of ranch life depicting 'The Working Cowboy.' Recreations of a bunkhouse and a ranch-house kitchen offered a look at cowboy living and eating quarters. The kitchen table included a large, revolving 'lazy susan' that would quickly whisk food to a hungry cowhand without interrupting anyone else's meal. A fully outfitted chuck wagon showed how hands dined while out on the range. A touch-screen monitor let visitors see and hear the voices of ranch people on today's range. Would-be hands could sit in one of two saddles to see how a cowboy spent much of his day.

Popular culture—advertising, films, pulp fiction, and television—have created the most widely known and enduring images of cowboys. The exhibit's section on 'The Imaginary Cowboy' showcased the diverse characteristics attributed to cowboys by the popular media. Large, colorful advertisements covering two walls featured cowboys hawking a bewildering range of products. A mini-theater, complete with old-time wooden, fold-up seats, occupied the middle of the exhibit area. Here visitors could settle back and watch B-western film clips that some adults may have viewed in the 1930s and 40s at a local theater. Adjacent stood a wonderfully reproduced early 1960s rumpus room, complete with kitschy western decor. Cowboy heroes of the time appeared in clips shown on a black-and-white console television set of the era.

Curators supplemented this nostalgic trip back in time with some very special artifacts from several cowboy heroes. Visitors could enjoy seeing Buffalo Bill Cody's Stetson hat and leather fringed jacket. Other items included a pair of Gene Autry's colorful boots and the rifle John Wayne used in the 1939 classic 'Stagecoach.' 'The Performing Cowboy' exhibit featured artifacts, costumes, and historic photographs from wild west shows, rodeo, dude ranches, and, of course, the storied Calgary Stampede. Fans could take a seat in a mini-grandstand and watch rodeo action from the 1996 Canadian Rodeo Finals on a large-screen monitor.

Creative touches adorned many areas of the exhibit. Life-sized, painted wooden cutouts highlighted a number of 'Canadian Cowboy Legends.' Such cutouts recognized the contributions of John Ware (ex-slave become cowboy and rancher), Tom Three Persons (native rodeo star), Stastia Carry (wild-west show trick rider), Lorne Greene (Canadian actor who played 'Pa' Cartwright on 'Bonanza'), and others. Multi-level captioning briefly identified exhibit items in large type, and, for the true history buff, presented additional interpretive and factual material in small type. Handouts, such as a bibliography of books about cowboys and a handsomely produced 36-page program, provided visitors with additional information they could carry away with them.

Ancillary projects extended the reach and substance of the exhibit. 'The Performing Cowboy' included a listening area where visitors would hear music performed by a variety of cowboy and cowgirl singers. The Glenbow gathered these and other songs into a delightful compilation called 'Word from the Range: A Canadian Cowboy Collection.' The 22 songs, totaling 72 minutes, provide a wonderful history and summary of Canada's musical cowboy heritage. Several of the songs add musical elements to our historical understanding. Wilf 'Montana Slim' Carter sings of the 'Calgary Roundup' (otherwise known as the Stampede). 'Half Mile of Hell' is Ian Tyson's tribute to the Stampede's world-famous chuck wagon races. 'High Rider,' sung by Diamond Joe White, is a musical biography of John Ware, Alberta's most famous black pioneer rancher. Other songs, traditional and modern, celebrated various aspects of rodeo and ranch life.

The Glenbow also hosted a gathering of students of cowboy life, the 'Canadian Cowboy Conference: New Perspectives on Ranching History.' Papers presented at the stimulating conference comprise this book. Special children's and family activities, such as trail rides and craft making provided educational entertainment for the general public. Among other things, children created a six-by-eighteen-foot cowboy mosaic using 30,000 candy gumballs. The museum also mounted a supplemental display of cowboy art from its permanent collection. The display featured works by Charles M. Russell, Frederic Remington, Mort Kunstler, and others. A lobby exhibit presented paintings by 'Cowboy Artists of the OH,' a famous, historic Alberta ranch.

Postscript

'He Country in Pants' No Longer— Diversifying Ranching History

Sarah Carter
University of Calgary

While the Canadian Cowboy Conference showcased some of the most recent research on ranching history, it also highlighted areas where there has been neglect. Our knowledge has become broader, richer and deeper in recent years, but there are certain groups and subjects that remain on the margins. In particular the history of women and Aboriginal people in ranching and the cattle industry is poorly understood. While class or social stratification is being addressed by several scholars, there is as yet little serious attention to other categories such as race, ethnicity and gender. The earliest scholars of ranching history in Western Canada, L. G. Thomas and Sheila Jameson, included women in their studies, but since that time there has been little serious academic interest.[1] Two recent popular books, *The Cowgirls* by Candace Savage, and *Writing the Range*, by Thelma Poirier indicate that interest is now turning to the topic of women.[2] (Calgary's 1999 Cowboy Festival was a salute to the women of the West and it featured 'cowgirl heroine' Dale Evans who sparked a stampede of autograph seekers.) Mary Lou LeCompte's *Cowgirls of the Rodeo: Pioneer Professional Athletes* is an intriguing study of the participation of women in rodeo on both sides of the 49th parallel.[3] Although they initially (from the 1890s) competed directly against men in such events as steer roping, trick roping, trick riding, and Roman racing, cowgirls were increasingly excluded from most rodeo events, and by the mid-20th century they were relegated mainly to decorative roles, although in recent years there have been concerted efforts to provide women with new competitive opportunities.

It appears that the history of women in the American West has received more serious scholarly attention than have women in the Canadian West.[4] There is a great deal of scope for comparative work, and new approaches to such old questions as 'does the border matter?' 'Well-bred' British women such as Isabelle Randall and Evelyn Cameron, who ranched with their husbands in Montana, wrote about the same experiences as their counterparts to the north: vast landscapes, isolation, riding horses, breaking colts, branding calves and working in gardens.[5] American women's

responses to this life varied just as they did among ranch women to the north; Randall was not as happy as Cameron. Yet in considering the 'Women's Wests' there are intriguing differences that also beg further exploration. One is that Western Canada does not have even a pale counterpart of an Annie Oakley, a Calamity Jane, or a Belle Starr, who defied conventional behavior during their lives, and afterward went on to further fame in dime novels and Hollywood westerns.

In the Canadian West, serious and sustained study of women and the cattle industry/ranching remains to be done. A popular assumption that continues to prevail is that women weren't really there. In his classic book *The Cowboy* (1936), Philip Ashton Rollins clearly expressed this idea, and although he was writing about the American West, this notion has perhaps to an even greater extent flourished north of the 49th parallel.[6] Rollins explained that only incidental mention would be made of women in the book as:

> *women were so relatively few in number in the Cattle Country as collectively not to have been an important factor in either its social life or the formation of its opinions. The Range described itself as a 'he country in pants.'*[7]

Although Rollins had to admit (contradicting himself) that women did live on ranches, and that some even ran ranches, he claimed that their greatest contribution was at the cookstove, and that all of these women remained invisible. Obeying "the custom which Range femininity imposed on all its members, [they] fled to the kitchen the instant a visitor had received his welcome." A cherished myth of an entirely masculine ranching culture and cattle industry has proven difficult to dislodge. Just how and why this myth came to be so entrenched, despite ample evidence that women were there, would be a fascinating study for the gender historian.

The earliest women on ranches, on both sides of the border, were Aboriginal women—Kainah, Siksika, Piegan, Lakota, Métis. Prosperous Montana rancher Granville Stuart was married to Awbonnie Tookana, a Shoshoni woman. Simon Pepin, Quebec-born cattleman and founder of Havre, Montana was married to Rose Trottier, a Métisse from Manitoba. They had five children and ran the Diamond-B Ranch of about 9,000 acres. A number of Lakota women married non-Aboriginal cattle and horse ranchers in the Wood Mountain district of present-day Saskatchewan. They brought many skills to this enterprise that were foreign to most Euro-Canadian women: riding, breaking horses, skinning, tanning and butchering. This important aspect of the history of ranching in western Canada is brought to light in a recent Canadian Museum of Civilization exhibit and companion book *Legends of Our Times: Native Cowboy Life* by Morgan Baillargeon and Leslie Tepper.[8] Clara Spotted Elk, a member of the

Figure 1. A ranching couple: A. P. Welsh and Mrs. Welsh, team up to make hay on their ranch in the early 1890s. Mrs. Welsh had been presented at court in London the year before she came to Canada. (Glenbow Archives, Calgary, Canada, NA-3163-2)

Tse-tsehese-stahase community in Lame Deer, Montana, pointed out in this book that Aboriginal women have long been involved in ranching on reservations and reserves.[9]

There was a great diversity of women on ranches. Marie Rose Smith, a Métis woman, worked alongside her husband Charley from 1877 to maintain their Jug Handle Ranch, 30 miles from Fort Macleod where they also raised 17 children. Marie Rose was a keen observer of ranch life and her (often eccentric) neighbors and she wrote about and published her experiences.[10] Evelyn Cartier (Galt) Springett, from Montreal spent ten years (1893–1903) at the New Oxley Ranche close to the Porcupine Hills where her husband was manager. In her memoirs she described herself as initially quite hopeless and dependent on her 'servant' Eliza.[11] Yet she soon found herself keeping a large garden and a chicken house, and undertaking such activities as hauling gravel from the river-bed a mile away in addition to caring for her two children. As a manager, her husband did not care to own cattle himself, but she invested in a small herd and had her own 'Circle Arrow' brand. Evelyn Springett wrote that she "might have grown to love the freedom of the West almost too well had my husband only liked it better."[12] In her memoirs, she descriped her love of spring on the prairie, the appearance of the wild geese, the brown grass turning to green and the crocuses that covered the sunny slopes (Figure 1).

Evelyn Springett's memoirs remind us that there were also women who worked as servants or maids on many of the early ranches, an aspect of social stratification within ranching society that has not received serious study. A servant 'problem' plagued this strata of society. White women who

came west as servants quickly found themselves with offers of marriage. Mary Macleod, wife of Colonel James F. Macleod, talked about this problem in an 1889 letter.

> *The Fews are having an awful time with their servants—those they brought out left in a very short time and then Mrs Scobie brought what was thought to be a splendid woman for them from Toronto, she very soon kicked up her heels, married Perry and they both left.*[13]

Agnes Skrine, also wrote about the problem of the 'vanished maid' in her "A Lady's Life on a Ranche," published in 1898.[14] She found herself doing an average of two hours housework a day, and had to get by with just a cook, as she:

> *made the usual mistake of bringing out a maid from home; but when in course of time the mistake rectified itself, and she went the way of all womankind in the West, I took to the broom and duster, and was surprised to find what a calmness descended on my spirit with release from the task of supervision.*

Evelyn Cochrane of the Little Bow or CC Ranch had a persistent 'problem' with the English governesses hired for her son Arthur. Three of them married Alberta cowboys not long after arrival in the West. A Mr. Wilders married the first governess. In 1894 John MacEwan, foreman at the CC, married the second governess, Kate Harrison, and the young couple moved to their own homestead. In 1896 MacEwan's partner, George Blake, married Louisa Lockton, the governess who had replaced Miss Harrison. According to a local history, Evelyn Cochrane said, "Enough of this losing governesses!" and the family went back to England, only coming out for the summer months.[15]

There remains much to learn about the lives of women on cattle and horse ranches. Their work likely varied dramatically depending upon abilities, background, necessity, the size and nature of the operation, the season, their class or station, and without doubt these roles changed over time. Women participated in both cattle ranching activities, and in the domestic and related service economy. They moved between the commercial and domestic domains, as did men. (Contrary to the masculine imagery of ranching and cowboy life, the West was a place where men participated in the domestic sphere, cooking, cleaning and washing for themselves, and sometimes for women.)[16] There were women who co-owned and ran ranches, such as Agnes Bedingfeld, who, with her son Frank, established a ranch at Pekisko (it was sold in 1919 to Edward, Prince of Wales, becoming the E.P. Ranch).[17] Lady Ernestine Hunt, eldest daughter

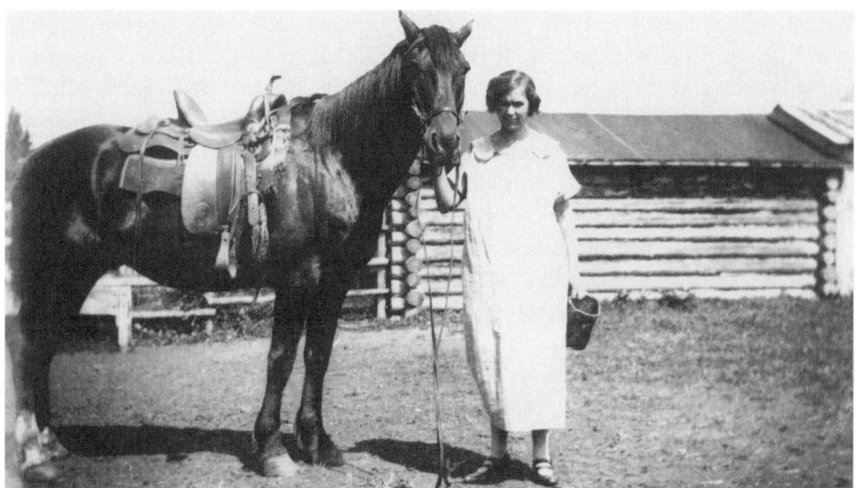

Figure 2. Monica Hopkins and her saddle horse at her Millarville, Alberta ranch, possibly about to feed the hens, ca 1914. (Glenbow Archives, Calgary, Canada, NA-4347-1)

of the Marquis of Allesbury, leased 40,000 acres southwest of Calgary to raise horses in 1906.[18] Monica Hopkins left a vivid account of how she worked with her husband to establish their ranch/farm near Priddis from 1909.[19] (Figure 2) She kept poultry and a vegetable garden, and she assisted with the care of the sheep and other chores. Some women regularly worked with the cattle. At age 15 in 1907, Violet Pearl Sykes was a visitor at the Spencer Ranching Company on Milk River, Alberta. She loved horses and the outdoors, and the cowboys put her to work helping to hold the herd of cattle which had been gathered by the roundup.

> *Then one day Jim Turner said 'cut out that steer and put him out of the other side of the herd.' Was I ever scared but I did not dare show it. Old Sammy [her horse] was a perfect cut horse so into the herd of one thousand or more cattle I reined the old horse to the one that was to be taken out. Sammy did the work while I was riding for all I was worth. The herd hold boys were all watching to see how I made out which must have met with their approval and satisfaction because after that, they really put me to work whenever I went to the round-up.*[20]

She also helped by

> *hazing the broncs, this work is to wrap the halter shank of the bronc around the horn of my saddle and lead the bronc for awhile to get it used to be [sic] ridden outside of the corral. After a few times like this the horse is ridden with the bridle.*

Violet Sykes continued to work with horses and cattle following her marriage to Emery Lagrandeur who was a champion rodeo competitor. Many women were accomplished riders used to long hours in the saddle. In the summer of 1894, for example, it was noted in the Edmonton *Bulletin* that Lula Short, a school teacher in Edmonton, would go on a visit home to High River and that she would make the trip of 240 miles on horseback, and alone.[21]

Local histories and other sources make it clear that ranch women worked with livestock, built houses and outbuildings, kept gardens, pickled and preserved, made butter, cheese, soap, vinegar and potato yeast. They also raised children and were critical in organizing community and church activities. As Philip A. Rollins so astutely observed, they also spent long hours at the cookstove but this is not the full story. The story of Katherine Austin and her husband Frank of Thornhill Ranch near Pincher Creek could serve as just one example of the life of an ordinary woman.[22] They were both from the province of Quebec and he came west first, working as a cowboy, and in time acquiring his own land, a herd and horses. Katherine arrived in 1901 and they married in Lethbridge that year. She spent the winter of 1902 alone with Myra, her first baby, and cared for the livestock while her husband was away working for a lumber company. There were problems at first as the milk cow was only familiar with men and refused to be caught until she put on her husband's clothes. In later years, Myra wrote that her father and mother "worked long hours with primitive machinery doing what they could manage themselves. As long as there was open range they depended largely on cattle for their chief income. By milking a small herd of cows, dual purpose shorthorns, the butter and eggs paid for groceries, the taxes and other incidentals of living." Katherine made excellent butter which she sold weekly in Pincher Creek. She didn't like riding but was a competent driver of a team. Both parents worked for their church and community. Katherine was the secretary of the Anglican Women's Auxiliary and she belonged to the Women's Institute. When you consider the life of an ordinary woman in ranching country, like Katherine Austin, it is hard to believe just how the conclusion could have been reached that this was 'he country in pants.' It has been only through the highly selective use of evidence that the idea of a masculine ranching culture has been created and sustained.

Russell Bennett, of the Shoderee Ranch on Waterton river, and author of *The Compleat Rancher*, presented a somewhat different perspective from that of Rollins.[23] He stressed that this was a way of living 'as a family' and it was based upon the interdependence of husband and wife. He was not describing the large cattle outfits of the 1880s in the days of the open range, but rather the family-sized ranch. Although throughout the book he portrays men as central and dominant on the family-sized ranches, he nonetheless wrote in his conclusion that

> *the interdependence of husband and wife enforces consultation... and there will not be many decisions taken without concurrence. These decisions will range from the casual to the important—from such matters as what beef to kill to the question of whether to purchase more land.*[24]

The kind of ranch described by Bennett is closely related to those Henry Klassen described in his paper on the Rocking P and Bar S where the roles played by women included ownership, financial management and decision making, as well as labor. Women's involvement in the cattle industry continued throughout the 20th century, and it continues today, but in Canada there are no detailed studies of the nature of their work and how this has changed over time. Women continue to work as cowhands, to own cattle, manage ranches and do the daily work of ranching. But as Elizabeth Maret argues in *Women of the Range: Women's Roles in the Texas Beef Cattle Industry*, these roles have always been more narrow and circumscribed for women than for men, and if anything there are increasingly fewer opportunties for women.[25] Women are, however, represented in occupations within the cattle industry that involve computer technology, reproductive technology and communications technology.

Another topic worthy of much more detailed study is the involvment of Aboriginal people in cattle ranching, rodeo and associated topics. Once again this evidence has always been there, but it has been overlooked because of a cherished myth of non-Aboriginal people that 'Indian' and 'cowboy' were somehow mutually exclusive. You could be one or the other, but not both. The book and exhibit mentioned above, *Legends of Our Time: Native Cowboy Life,* will do a great deal to help break the stereotype of the Indian *versus* the cowboy. The focus is on the contribution of people of the northern plains and plateau to ranching and rodeo. A variety of topics are covered, including the special and sacred relationship with animals—the buffalo, the deer and the horse, and how this is expressed in equipment, clothing, and narrative. Another book that has helped to break down this stereotype is Peter Iverson's *When Indians Became Cowboys: Native Peoples and Cattle Ranching in the American West.*[26] On many reservations there was a promising start to the cattle business, but there was intensive pressure to lease grazing land to non-Native interests. Federal 'wisdom' continually intervened at the expense of Indian reservation ranching as the government worked to lease out tracts to non-Native companies. At places such as Pine Ridge the Lakota cattle business experienced a downturn during the years of the First World War as large outside cattle companies took control. Iverson includes a discussion of the modern era of Indian cattle ranching, and of Indians and rodeo.

In his presentation at the Canadian Cowboy Conference, Peter Wesley, of the Nakoda (Stoney) First Nation, provided us with vivid insight into

aspects of this history, including oral traditions of first sightings of cattle, and of the winter of 1906. He also spoke about how on the Morley reserve there were skilled practitioners of animal medicine, many people with expert knowledge of horses, and some of the best rodeo cowboys in the province. Ben Calf Robe's *Siksika: A Blackfoot Legacy* contains descriptions of the involvement of the Siksika in ranching and cowboy life.[27] Hugh Dempsey has written a biography of one of the best known Alberta cowboys, Tom Three Persons, a bronc-riding champion of the Calgary Stampede from the Kainah (Blood) reserve.[28] Dempsey's book, *The Golden Age of the Canadian Cowboy: An Illustrated History*, contains rich descriptions and photographs of Métis and Indian cowboys.[29] On southern Alberta reserve communities there was considerable involvement in the cattle industry. In his biography of James Gladstone, Dempsey described the history of the cattle industry on the Blood reserve.[30] This was thriving by 1917, when they had 4000 head, but three years later the numbers were reduced to a pitiful few, largely because of federal government policies that permitted thousands of non-Blood cattle and sheep to overgraze the reserve, without the consent of the Blood. Similarly the Piegan were successful at cattle ranching, and had acquired a sizeable herd by the years of World War I. These efforts were hampered by government policies that allowed the incursion of non-Native ranchers' cattle on the reserve, through the leasing of tracts of their land without Piegan consent, through the construction of the Crow's Nest branch line, and through problems with water shortage that were never addressed (instead water was diverted to enhance non-Native agriculture).

The ongoing research efforts undertaken by Parks Canada in connection with the establishment and operation of the Bar U National Historic Ranch have included some promising exploratory work on the contribution of Aboriginal people to ranching. An oral history project conducted in 1992–93 included interviews with Stoneys from the Eden Valley Reserve who played a significant role in the life of the Bar U for a long period (Figure 3). As Simon Evans has shown in his study *The Burns Era at the Bar U Ranch*, many ranches benefited enormously from their historic connections with local Native communities, and with specific families.[31] For generations they provided a pool of temporary skilled labor, helping with branding, fencing, and haying. There were families that tended to have special ties with particular ranches.

There are many aspects of the lives of the Indian cowboy in Western Canada that deserve further study. Some of these are brought to light through an examination of the 1939 experiences of eight expert rodeo cowboys from Alberta reserves that sailed to Australia to take part in Sydney's Royal Agricultural Society of New South Wales rodeo. The eight were Frank Many Fingers and Joe Young Pine from the Blood Reserve, Douglas Kooteney and Johnny Left Hand from Morley, Edward One Spot and George Runner from Tsuu T'ina, and Joe Crowfoot and Joe Bear Robe

Figure 3. Branding on the Bar U Ranch, ca. 1919–20. Stoney Indians played a significant role in the life of this and other foothills ranches. They provided a pool of temporary skilled labor for activities like branding.
(Glenbow Archives, Calgary, Canada, NB-16-263)

from Siksika. Their trip received a great deal of press coverage, but there is a much more complex story behind the headlines that was not told, and that reveals a great deal about the way in which government policies and the Indian Act restricted basic freedoms and economic and cultural opportunities. To obtain permission to participate in the Sydney rodeo, the delegation had to seek the approval of Indian agents, the Inspector of Indian agencies, the Secretary of Indian Affairs in Ottawa and the Minister of Mines and Resources (at that time responsible for Indian Affairs). Most of the members of this formidable bureaucracy worked at this time to discourage the participation of Aboriginal people in rodeo.[32]

The trip of the rodeo cowboys required complex negotiations that took place over many months and produced voluminous correspondence. Until the 1930s the Department of Indian Affairs had only very rarely, and very reluctantly allowed those defined as 'Indian' under the Indian Act to travel to take part in exhibitions, performances or stampedes outside of the country, despite numerous invitations. Officials also wanted to discourage them from taking part in such events at home.[33] The central rationale was that the fair environment was seen as an improper influence. In 1914 the Indian Act was amended to include punishment for Indian participation (without the consent of the Superintendent General of Indian Affairs or his agent) in "any show, exhibition, performance, stampede or pageant in aboriginal costume." In 1933 the words "in aboriginal costume" were struck from this subsection, but it remained the law until 1951 that there would be no participation in shows and exhibitions without the consent of government officials.

The trip to Australia was protested by the Indian agent at Morley, Dr. W. B. Murray, as he felt it would be a too much of a diversion, and he was also trying to discourage rodeo participation in the community.[34] During the 1930s the people of Morley had begun to stage their own stampede, and the agent wasn't happy about this. The Inspector of Indian Agencies for Alberta, C. P. Schmidt agreed, telling two delegates from Australia that participation in "rough and risky" rodeo events was not encouraged.[35] He didn't mind the "colorful pageantry idea . . . going back to and beyond the days of the signing of treaties with the Indians, which was done in a most peaceful and friendly way with such color and glad rags as could be displayed." In the editorial pages of one Alberta paper the concern was raised that the Australia trip of the rodeo stars would set a bad example for the younger generation who now wanted to "spend every available minute practicing their riding, roping and racing."[36]

Despite the obstacles, the trip was made and newspaper accounts suggest that the Indian cowboys created a sensation 'down under.' The Mayor of Sydney greeted them upon arrival (Figure 4). They were taken on kangaroo hunts, and learned the art of boomerang throwing. They brought home five trophy cups and numerous individual prizes, even though they were forced, by Australian competition rules, to ride in English hunting saddles. They were not permitted to compete equally, however. They were allotted teams for the chuckwagon races which were not equal to the outfits they had to compete with, but the great disappointment was "the refusal of the management to allow the Indians to compete with the American, Australian and Canadian cowboys in the regular events, [confining] them to putting on displays among themselves." And the Indians were not there just as cowboys, like the other cowboys. Twice a day for twelve days they paraded in traditional costume headed by their escort, RCMP constable S. J. Leach, and inhabited a tipi village. Each night they put on displays of 'tribal dancing.'[37] All of this proved to be even more popular than their displays of rodeo expertise. They were visited by a million people, and were offered other bookings in Australia and New Zealand, which they were unable to accept. Eddie One Spot said "From the questions constantly asked, visitors at the exhibition appeared astonished that we were not savages. They were surprised that we all spoke English and were educated, and took an interest in the same things that they did."[38] Overall however, it seems that the eight overlooked or dismissed any negative aspects of the trip. They seemed to enjoy the opportunities to meet with other indigenous people. They went ashore at Suva (Fiji), New Zealand, and Honolulu. At Suva they were

Figure 4. A group of rodeo cowboys from Alberta reserves leaving to take part in events in Australia, 1939. (Left to right): Frank Many Fingers and Joe Young Pine, from the Blood reserve; Douglas Kootenay, from Morley; Edward One Spot, from Tsuu T'ina; John Lefthand, from Morley; Joe Crowfoot and Joe Bear Robe, from Siksika; Jim Starlight from Tsuu T'ina; and Corporal S. J. Leach, R.C.M.P.
(Glenbow Archives, Calgary, Canada, NA-480-10)

particularly interested in the type of archery and fish-spearing practised by the Fiji natives, and they brought back more than a dozen bows and arrows.[39]

The experience of the eight cowboys in Australia illustrates that Indian cowboys had to contend with and negotiate constraints and limitations that did not apply to others. Levels of permission were required to allow them to travel, and once there they were not permitted to compete equally. They could not simply appear as cowboys; half of their time and more was spent as 'Indians.' They also earned the disapproval of influential southern Alberta non-Aboriginal people, who felt that the eight were not good role models for a younger generation, but whose 'kindly advice' often resulted in diminished opportunities for residents of Indian reserves. As warned in one editorial column, "Now that eight of the top ranking Indian rodeo stars have won themselves a trip half way around the world, it will be still

more difficult to convince the embryo braves that their time should be spent in learning to write, read, build a shed or guide a plough." Studies of Indian reserve ranching both in Canada and the U.S. also indicate that there were obstacles and interventions distinct from those faced by other ranchers that served to undermine success in the cattle industry. As I argued in my book about agriculture on Indian reserves, non-Aboriginal people in Western Canada found it within their interests to insist that Indians could not be farmers, despite clear evidence to the contrary, and it appears that the same conclusion may hold true for ranching.[40] Such a conclusion is preliminary, however, and this serves to highlight the many topics that deserve further study.

Postscript

Ranching History: Have We Covered the Ground Yet?

Bill Yeo
Parks Canada

When the 1997 Canadian Cowboy Conference at Glenbow came to a close, it is entirely possible that more than one of the participants wondered if there were any cow pies yet unturned in the search for 'new perspectives.' Certainly the conference had delivered on its promise: it had provided a forum for the presentation and discussion of new research since the publication of David Breen's monumental work of more than a decade before. Not only did it explore an expanded range of topics, but it was also international in scope, and it attracted a modest but attentive crowd of students, historic site and museum staff, real ranchers and the general public.

Still, there were others there who recognized how much the conference pointed to the future, as much as it had examined the past from new angles. Terry Jordan-Bychkov and Warren Elofson challenged some long-entrenched views concerning the significance of the international boundary. There is scope here for further work, particularly in the area of 'law and order' on the range. We've known for a long time that there was discontent among smallholders, squatters and Native people when the corporate ranches moved into the foothills, but tradition told us that despite occasional rumblings from these bit players, all was quiet north of the line.

Access to grass and water has always been at the root of conflict in ranching country. In this arena, we find the small stockman vs. the large rancher vs. the homesteader, but more often the enemy has been the climate. Max Foran placed this cast of characters against a background of economic crisis, of low prices, in a struggle where there is a referee of sorts, the government. Where a great deal of range is under leasehold, rent, taxes and regulations affect the margin of success or failure. We need to know more about these seemingly humdrum issues, to understand the Canadian system of stewardship for water and grass. Sherm Ewing gave us the ranchers' perspective, and he made it plain that these are very live issues indeed.

We mustn't forget the bankers. Certainly the business or management side of ranching has received more attention lately, and the results of careful study were presented at the conference. Joy Oetelaar spoke of George Lane, the seasoned master of many strategies, whose enterprises ended up in the hands of the Dominion Bank. On the other hand, so Henry Klassen told us, the Bar S and Rocking P ranches survived with help from the banks. This is another area that calls out for more work by business historians, following Klassen's example of detailed analysis of particular enterprises.

Two intriguing personalities figured in the story of the Bar S and the Rocking P. They were the daughters of founder Roderick Mcleay, two women raised to be more than helpmates and mothers, but managers in their own right and capable riders to boot. Were they unique? Probably not. Lorain Lounsberry showed us how skilled women ropers and riders made their mark in the early years of big-time rodeo, just as they had in the wild-west shows, only to be gradually marginalized. Surely there is a rich vein to be mined here.

But where are the sources? This is a vital question, given that much of the presently available material has been recycled more than once. Richard Slatta challenged us to rescue even the humblest sources that might throw light on the role of the 'supporting actors'—real cowboys, small ranchers, women and Natives. In Alberta, where even the stories of the main players have often been spun out of this stuff, new effort is needed to strengthen the foundations of new research. Where are the business records of the North West Cattle Company? What happened to the papers of George Lane and Company, a registered corporation as late as 1992? There are also valuable collections in private hands that have never been in the hands of an historian, and that have an uncertain future. Perhaps this is the frontier that most urgently needs to be pushed back, to uncover the answers to the new questions raised in 1997. When that is done, the next conference on ranching history will indeed cover new ground.

Notes on Contributors

Sarah Carter teaches history at the University of Calgary. She is the author of several books including, *Lost Harvests: Prairie Indian Reserve Farmers and Government Policy* (Montreal: McGill-Queen's Press, 1990) and *Capturing Women: The Manipulation of Cultural Imagery in Canada's Prairie West* (Montreal: McGill-Queen's Press, 1997).

Brian Dippie is a professor of history at the University of Victoria. He has written or edited 14 major books on myths, perceptions and images concerning the settlement history of western North America. His book, *Charles M. Russell, Word Painter: Letters 1887–1926* (Fort Worth: Amon Carter Museum with Harry N. Abrams, New York, 1993), won the National Cowboy Hall of Fame, Western Heritage Award, Outstanding Art Book, 1993.

Warren Elofson is a professor of history at the University of Calgary. His primary research interest has been 18th century British parliamentarians, but he was brought up on a ranch in southern Alberta and has written a number of provocative articles on the frontier environment and the ranching industry. This research has culminated in a book to be published soon.

Simon Evans recently retired from his position as a professor of geography at Memorial University of Newfoundland. Over the past 20 years he has researched and written a considerable amount on the Canadian ranching frontier. His books include *Prince Charming Goes West: The Story of the E. P. Ranch* (University of Calgary Press, 1993) and *Essays on the Historical Geography of the Canadian West* (Geography Department: University of Calgary, 1987).

Max Foran is curator at the Western Heritage Centre at Cochrane, Alberta. For more than 20 years he was a school principal in Calgary. He is author of six monographs including, *Calgary: An Illustrated History* (Toronto: John Lorimer, 1978); *Calgary: Canada's Frontier Metropolis* (Burlington, Ontario: Windsor Publications Inc., 1982); and *Citymakers: Calgarians after the Frontier* (Calgary: Historical Society of Alberta, 1987).

Terry Jordan-Bychkov holds the Walter Prescott Webb Chair in Geography at the University of Texas at Austin. He has written 10 books on aspects of historical and cultural geography. His *North American Cattle-Ranching Frontiers* (Albuquerque: University of New Mexico Press, 1993) was hailed as 'a truly magisterial work of great importance.'

Henry Klassen recently retired after a long teaching career at the University of Calgary. Over the years he has written dozens of articles on individuals and businesses in western Canada. In particular, his work on T. C. Power and I. G. Baker, and the Conrad family, all of which were based in Montana, has done much to illuminate trans-border business interaction in the late 19th century. He also wrote *A Business History of Alberta* (Calgary: University of Calgary Press, 1999).

Lorain Lounsberry currently works as a curator of human cultural history at the Glenbow Museum in Calgary, and as a freelance consultant in Alberta. She studied art history at Queen's University in Kingston, Ontario, and received her M.A. at the University of Toronto.

Alan McCullough recently retired after more than 20 years as a historian with Parks Canada. Among his innumerable assignments, it is relevant to note that he did much of the research for Fort Walsh National Historic Site, and more recently made a major contribution to the establishment of the Bar U Ranch National Historic Site.

Joy Oetelaar is a graduate student in the history department at the University of Calgary. She fell under the spell of George Lane while carrying out a newspaper search for Parks Canada on the Bar U Ranch.

Richard Slatta is a professor of history at North Carolina State University. He is the author of five books on cowboys and ranching, in particular *Cowboys of the Americas* (New Haven: Yale University Press, 1990); *The Cowboy Encyclopedia* (Santa Barbara: ABC-CLIO, 1994); and *Comparing Cowboys and Frontiers* (Norman: University of Oklahoma Press, 1997). He has also written more than 130 articles.

Bill Yeo retired from the position of Chief of Historical and Archaeological Research after 20 years' service with Parks Canada, in 1998. He was involved in the selection and acquisition of a site to commemorate the history of ranching in Canada, the Bar U Ranch National Historic Site.

Selected Bibliography

Compiled by Simon M. Evans

Introduction

The flow of publications on ranching and cowboys continues unabated. Scholarly works, local histories, personal reminiscences, books of photographs, and fictional accounts of life on the range, combine to create a considerable volume of work. This selected bibliography only includes book titles, as opposed to journal articles, and focuses on references specifically on ranching rather than including more general works on western settlement. Of course, each of the papers in the book contains a raft of detailed references to primary and secondary sources, and specialists will be drawn to these notes. However, the general reader may find the following introductory paragraphs helpful. I have attempted to provide a highly selective and opinionated 'survival bibliography,' which will certainly provide access to a variety of views and themes within the general topic of ranching. The books mentioned are all to be found in the bibliography, and publication details are therefore omitted here.

Any attempt to come to grips with the scholarly literature on ranching must start with three foundational books: Terry Jordan's *North American Ranching Frontiers,* Richard Slatta's *Cowboys of the Americas,* and Paul Starrs' *Let the Cowboy Ride.* This triumvirate play the role that books by Walter Prescott Webb, Ernest Staples Osgood, and Edward Everett Dale played for an earlier generation of scholars. Jordan traces the complex origins of ranching and sets the historical context; Slatta places the cowboy in a hemispheric and comparative framework; and Starrs, while delving deeply into the regional history of the great plains also brings the story up to the present and explains some of the current issues facing ranchers. All three books contain exhaustive bibliographies which reflect their rather different foci.

For the Canadian range, David Breen's *The Canadian Prairie West and the Ranching Frontier* remains the definitive point of departure. However, Hugh Dempsey's *The Golden Age of the Canadian Cowboy,* and chapters in Volumes 1 and 2 of *Alberta in the Twentieth Century,* edited by Ted Byfield, contain many new points of interest as well as a selection of fine images. Edward Brado's *Cattle Kingdom,* L. G. Thomas' *The Ranchers' Legacy,* and Patrick Dunae's *Gentlemen Emigrants,* also provide important background. Vivid accounts of the early years of the Canadian cattle

business by contemporaries include Leroy Kelly's *The Rangemen*, R. M. MacInnes *In the Shadow of the Rockies*, and John Craig's *Ranching with Lords and Commons.*

There is a rich vein of writing about 'cowboying' by men and women who were involved. What some of these accounts lack in literary merit they more than make up in colorful vigor. I particularly like Teddy Blue Abbott's *We Pointed Them North*, and the classic by Philip Ashton Rollins, *The Cowboy: His Character, Equipment and his Part in the Development of the West.* Fred Gipson, *Cowhand: The Story of a Working Cowboy* presents a bleak but realistic glimpse of life in the Texas cow country between the world wars. Some of these books are not very accessible so the reprinting of Fay E. Ward's wonderfully illustrated *The Cowboy at Work* is particularly welcome. William W. Savage Jr. offers a perceptive commentary on the genre in *Cowboy Life: Reconstructing an American Myth.* The Canadian range has its share of eye-witness accounts. Monica Hopkins' charming *Letters from a Lady Rancher*, Fred Ings' *Before the Fences: Tales from the Midway Ranch*, Russell Bennett's *The Compleat Rancher*, and Stan Graber's *The Last Roundup*, are just a handful of the most enjoyable. Perhaps the most recent book of this kind is David McCumber's *The Cowboy Way*, published this year. The author gave up his prestigious job to return to his roots in Montana. Not only does he detail the seasonal round on a large modern ranch, but he shows how the attitudes and expectations of the old range are still flourishing today. This is a 'must read.'

Sometimes, it seems to me that the novelist and poet can evoke 'reality' and turn on the imagination in a way that we historians and geographers fail to do. Ranching and our region has been well served in this regard. Perhaps most famous is Wallace Stegner's *Wolf Willow*, but he would have approved of Sharon Butala's *The Perfection of the Morning* and of her latest novel, *The Garden of Eden.* Guy Vanderhaeghe catches the ambiance of the Canadian–American West during the 1870s in *The Englishman's Boy*, while Jonathan Raban depicts interaction between incumbent ranchers and incoming settlers along Montana's High Line 40 years later in *Bad Land.* Larry McMurtry gets the composition of his outfit for the long drive from Texas north exactly right in *Lonesome Dove*, and creates some unforgettable characters. Cormac McCarthy's Border Trilogy has been justly lauded, but my favorite remains the opening novel, *All the Pretty Horses.* Closer to home is Ivan Doig's magnificent trilogy on the settlement of the Montana range country, *English Creek*, *Dancing at the Rascal Fair*, and *Ride with Me, Mariah Montana.* Their only real competition comes from his biographical and evocative *This House of Sky.* Finally, in a novel with an ecological theme that embraces the whole of the plains, Richard S. Wheeler pursues a much talked about vision in *The Buffalo Commons.*

The last decade has seen the publication of a number of thoughtful books on grasslands, written for lay people but examining the major

management dilemmas which face us. Don Gayton's *The Wheatgrass Mechanism* was justly popular and his *Landscapes of the Interior* is a good follow up. Richard Manning's *Grassland* is ambitious and impassioned; the subtitle tells why, "the history, biology, politics, and promise of the American prairie"! I enjoyed Marcy Houle's *The Prairie Keepers: Secrets of the Grasslands* so much that I made a pilgrimage to her Zumwalt prairie in north-eastern Oregon and found it as good as she describes. Sherm Ewing has recorded the wisdom of ranchers and range ecologists in *The Range*, and explains many modern developments in the cattle business in *The Ranch*. His informants are drawn from both sides of the Alberta/Montana boundary, but he always focuses on the land and our dependence on it. J. G. Nelson reviewed the ecological history of the Cypress Hills in *The Last Refuge*, while Barry Potyondi displays the same sensitivity to ecology in his book *In Palliser's Triangle*. In addition there are a growing number of collections of papers on environmental history. I have *A Sense of the American West* edited by James Sherow, and have particularly enjoyed the pieces in it by Dan Flores.

Of course, there are big gaps in the Canadian literature. Nowhere is this more obvious than in the realm of economic history. While Gene Gressley, Marion Clawson, Jimmy Skaggs and John T. Schlebecker, have discussed prices, business cycles, and changing tastes and markets in the United States, data on the economy of the Canadian range remains locked in government documents and reports from Royal Commissions. Moreover, we need more studies of individual ranches through long periods, like Mothershead's work on the Swan Land and Cattle Company and William Pearce's on the Matador. Dale Alsager's *The Incredible Gang Ranch*, Nina Wooliams *Cattle Ranch: The Story of the Douglas Lake Cattle Company*, and my own work on the E.P. Ranch, *Prince Charming Goes West*, are only a beginning.

Abbott, Edward Charles 'Teddy Blue' and Helena Huntington Smith. *We Pointed Them North: Recollections of a Cowpuncher*. Norman: University of Oklahoma Press, 1939.

Alsager, Dale. *The Incredible Gang Ranch*. Surrey, BC: Hancock House, 1990.

Armitage, Susan and Elizabeth Jameson (eds.). *The Women's West*. Norman: University of Oklahoma Press, 1987.

Atherton, Lewis. *The Cattle Kings*. Lincoln: University of Nebraska Press, 1961.

Baillargeon, Morgan and Leslie Tripper. *Legends of Our Times: Native Cowboy Life*. Vancouver: University of British Columbia, 1998.

Bennett, John W. *Northern Plainsmen: Adaptive Strategy and Agrarian Life*. Arlington Heights, IL: AHM, 1976.

Bennett, John W. and Seena B. Kohl, *Settling the Canadian–American West, 1890–1915: Pioneering Adaption and Community Building*. Lincoln: University of Nebraska Press, 1995.

Bennett, Russell. *The Compleat Rancher*. New York: Rhinehart and Co., 1946.

Berry, Gerald L. *The Whoop-Up Trail*. Edmonton: Applied Art Productions, 1953.

Blasingame, Ike. *Dakota Cowboy: My Life in the Old Days*. Lincoln: University of Nebraska Press, 1958.

Brado, Edward. *Cattle Kingdom: Early Ranching in Alberta*. Vancouver: Douglas and McIntyre, 1984.

Breen, David H. *The Canadian Prairie West and the Ranching Frontier, 1874–1924*. University of Toronto Press, 1983.

Bronson, Edgar Beecher. *Reminiscences of a Ranchman*. Lincoln: University of Nebraska Press, 1962.

Butala, Sharon. *The Perfection of the Morning: An Apprenticeship in Nature*. Toronto: Harper Collins, 1994.

Butala, Sharon. *The Garden of Eden*. Toronto: Harper Collins, 1998.

Byfield, Ted (ed.). *Alberta in the Twentieth Century*, Vols. 1-3. Edmonton: United Western Communications, 1991–1994.

Christianson, Chris J. *My Life on the Range*. Lethbridge: Southern Printing, 1968.

Christianson, Chris J. *Early Rangemen*. Lethbridge: Southern Printing, 1973.

Clawson, Marion. *The Western Range Livestock Industry*. New York: McGraw Hill, 1950.

Cotton, E. J. (Bud) with Ethel Mitchell. *Buffalo Bud: Adventures of a Cowboy*. Vancouver: Hancock House, 1981.

Craig, John R. *Ranching with Lords and Commons*. Toronto: William Briggs, 1903.

Cavanaugh, Catherine and Jeremy Mouat (eds.). *Making Western Canada: Essays on European Colonization and Settlement*. Toronto: Garamond Press, 1996.

Daggett, Dan. *Beyond the Rangeland Conflict: Towards a West that Works*. Layton, UT: Gibbs Smith, 1995.

Dale, Edward Everett. *Cow Country*. Norman: University of Oklahoma Press, 1942.

Dale, Edward Everett. *The Range Cattle Industry: Ranching on the Great Plains, 1865–1925*. Norman: University of Oklahoma Press, 1960.

Dary, David. *Cowboy Culture: A Saga of Five Centuries*. New York: Knopf, 1981.

Dempsey, Hugh A. *The Golden Age of the Canadian Cowboy: An Illustrated History.* Saskatoon: Fifth House, 1995.

Dobie, J. Frank. *The Longhorns.* New York: Grosset and Dunlap, 1941.

Dobie, J. Frank. *Cow People.* Boston: Little Brown, 1964.

Doig, Ivan. *This House of Sky: Landscapes of the Western Mind.* New York: Harcourt Brace, 1978.

Doig, Ivan. *English Creek.* New York: Penguin, 1984.

Doig, Ivan. *Dancing at the Rascal Fair.* New York: Penguin, 1987.

Doig, Ivan. *Ride With Me, Mariah Montana.* New York: Penguin, 1990.

Dunae, Patrick A. *Gentlemen Emigrants: From the British Public Schools to the Canadian Frontier.* Vancouver: Douglas and McIntyre, 1981.

Dunae, Patrick A. (ed.). *Rancher's Legacy: Alberta Essays by Lewis G. Thomas.* Edmonton: University of Alberta Press, 1986.

Evans, Simon M. *Prince Charming Goes West: The Story of the E.P. Ranch.* University of Calgary Press, 1993.

Ewing, Sherm. *The Range.* Missoula: Mountain Press, 1990.

Ewing, Sherm. *The Ranch: A Modern History of the North American Cattle Industry.* Missoula: Mountain Press, 1995.

Fletcher, Robert H. *Free Grass to Fences.* New York: University Publishers, 1960.

Friesen, Gerald. *The Canadian Prairies: A History.* Lincoln: University of Nebraska Press, 1984.

Frink, Maurice W., W. Turrentine Jackson and Agnes Wright Spring. *When Grass Was King: Contibutions to the Western Range Cattle Industry Study.* Boulder: University of Colorado Press, 1956.

Gardiner, Claude. *Letters from an English Rancher.* Calgary: Glenbow Alberta Institute, 1988.

Gayton, Don. *The Wheatgrass Mechanism.* Saskatoon: Fifth House, 1990.

Gayton, Don. *Landscapes of the Interior.* Gabriola Island, BC: New Society Publishers, 1996.

Gipson, Fred. *Cowhand: The Story of a Working Cowboy.* College Station: Texas A and M University Press, 1953.

Graber, Stan. *The Last Roundup: Memories of a Canadian Cowboy.* Saskatoon: Fifth House, 1995.

Gray, James H. *The Winter Years: The Depression on the Prairies.* Toronto: Macmillan, 1966.

Gressley, Gene M. *Bankers and Cattlemen.* New York: Alfred A. Knopf, 1966.

Hage, Wayne. 3rd ed. *Storm Over Rangelands: Private Rights in Federal Lands.* Bellevue, WA: Free Enterprise Press, 1994.

Harris, R. Cole and Elizabeth Phillips. *Letters from Windermere, 1912–1914.* Vancouver: University of British Columbia Press, 1984.

High River Pioneers' and Old Timers' Association. *Leaves from the Medicine Tree.* Lethbridge: Lethbridge Herald Press, 1960.

Higinbotham, John David. *When the West Was Young*. Toronto: Ryerson, 1933.

Hildebrandt, Walter and Brian Hubner. *The Cypress Hills: the Land and its People*. Saskatoon: Purich Publishing, 1994.

Hopkins, Monica. *Letters from a Lady Rancher.* Halifax: Formac Publishing, 1983.

Houle, Marcy. *The Prairie Keepers: Secrets of the Grassland*. Reading, MA: Addison-Wesley, 1995.

Ings, Fred W. *Before the Fences: Tales from the Midway Ranch*. Calgary: McAra Press, 1980.

Iverson, Peter. *When Indians Became Cowboys: Native Peoples and Cattle Ranching in the American West.* Norman: University of Oklahoma Press, 1992.

Jacobs, Frank. *Cattle and Us, Frankly Speaking*. Calgary: Detselig Enterprises, 1993.

Jameson, Sheilagh S. *Ranches, Cowboys and Characters: The Birth of Alberta's Western Culture*. Calgary: Glenbow-Alberta Institute, 1987.

Johnston, Alex. *Cowboy Politics: The Western Stock Growers' Association and its Predecessors.* Calgary: Western Stock Growers' Association, 1972.

Jordan, Teresa. *Cowgirls: Women of the American West.* Lincoln: University of Nebraska Press, 1992.

Jordan, Terry G. *Trails to Texas: The Southern Roots of Western Cattle Ranching*. Lincoln: University of Nebraska Press, 1981.

Jordan, Terry G. *North American Cattle Ranching Frontiers: Origins, Diffusion, and Differentiation*. Albuquerque: University of New Mexico, 1993.

Kelly, Leroy V. *The Rangemen*. High River: Willow Creek Publishing, 1988.

Limerick, Patricia N. *The Legacy of Conquest: The Unbroken Past of the American West.* New York: W. W. Norton, 1987.

Long, Philip S. *The Great Canadian Range*. Toronto: Ryerson Press, 1963.

Long, Philip S. *Seventy Years a Cowboy.* Billings, MT: Cypress Books, 1976.

Loveridge, D. M. and Barry Potyondi. *From Wood Mountain to the Whitemud: A Historical Survey of the Grasslands National Park Area.* Ottawa: Environment Canada, 1983.

Malin, James C. *The Grasslands of North America: Prolegomena to its History.* Gloucester, MA: Peter Smith, 1967.

Manning, Richard. *Grasslands: The History, Biology, Politics and Promise of the American Prairie*. New York: Viking Penguin, 1995.

Mothershead, Harmon S. *The Swan Land and Cattle Company Limited*. Norman: University of Oklahoma Press, 1971.

McCarthy, Cormac. *All the Pretty Horses.* New York: Alfred A. Knopf, 1993.

McCowan, Don C. *Grassland Settlers: The Swift Current Region During the Era of the Ranching Frontier.* Saskatoon: Canadian Plains Resource Center, 1975.

McCumber, David. *The Cowboy Way.* New York: Bard, 1999.

MacEwan, Grant. *John Ware's Cattle Country.* Saskatoon: Western Producer, 1974.

MacEwan, Grant. *Blazing the Old Cattle Trail.* Saskatoon: Western Producer, 1975.

MacEwan, Grant. *Pat Burns: Cattle King.* Saskatoon: Western Producer, 1979.

MacInnes, C. M. *In the Shadow of the Rockies.* London: Rivington's Press, 1930.

McKinnon, J. Angus. *The Bow River Range.* Calgary: McAra Press, 1974.

McKinnon, Lachlin. *Lachlin McKinnon, Pioneer, 1865–1948.* Calgary: McAra Press, 1956.

McMurtry, Larry. *Lonesome Dove.* New York: Simon and Schuster, 1985.

McQuarrie, John. *Cowboyin': A Legend Lives On.* Toronto: Macmillan, 1994.

Nelson, J. Gordon. *The Last Refuge.* Montreal: Harvest House, 1973.

Nanton and District Historical Society. *Mosquito Creek Roundup.* Nanton: Nanton and District Historical Society, 1975.

Oliphant, J. Orin. *On the Cattle Ranges of the Oregon Country.* Seattle: University of Washington Press, 1968.

Osgood, Ernest Staples. *The Day of the Cattleman.* Chicago: University of Chicago Press, 1929.

Patterson, R. M. *The Buffalo Head.* New York: William Sloane Associates, 1961.

Pearce, William M. *The Matador Land and Cattle Company.* Norman: University of Oklahoma Press, 1964.

Phillips, Paul C. *Granville Stuart, Pioneering in Montana: The Making of a State, 1864–1887.* Lincoln: University of Nebraska Press, 1977.

Potyondi, Barry. *In Palliser's Triangle: Living in the Grasslands, 1850–1930.* Sakatoon: Purich Publishing, 1995.

Raban, Jonathan. *Bad Land.* London: Macmillan, 1996.

Rainbolt, Jo. *The Last Cowboy: Twilight Era of the Horseback Cowhand, 1900–1940.* Helena: America and World Graphic Publications, 1992.

Rees, Ronald. *New and Naked Land: Making the Prairies Home.* Saskatoon: Western Producer Books, 1988.

Rifkin, Jeremy. *Beyond Beef: The Rise and fall of the Cattle Culture.* New York: Dutton, 1992.

Rollins, Philip Ashton. *The Cowboy: His Character, Equipment and his Part in the Development of the West.* New York: Scribner, 1922.

Rosenvall, L. A. and Simon M. Evans (eds.). *Essays on the Historical Geography of the Canadian West.* University of Calgary: Geography Department, 1987.

Russell, Andy. *The Canadian Cowboy: Stories of Cows, Cowboys and Cayuses.* Toronto: McClelland and Stewart, 1993.

Sandoz, Mari. *The Cattlemen from the Rio Grande Across the Far Marias.* New York: Hastings House, 1975.

Savage, Candace. *Cowgirls: Real Cowboy Girls.* Vancouver: Greystone Books, 1996.

Savage, William W. *Cowboy Life: Deconstructing an American Myth.* Denver: University Press of Colorado, 1993.

Schlebecker, John T. *Cattle Raising on the Plains, 1900–1961.* Lincoln: University of Nebraska Press, 1963.

Schmidt, John. *Western Stock Growers' Association: An Experiment that Worked.* Calgary: Western Stock Growers' Association, 1994.

Sharp, Paul F. *Whoop-Up Country: The Canadian American West, 1865–1885.* Minneapolis: University of Minnesota Press, 1955.

Sherow, James E. *A Sense of the American West.* Albuquerque: University of New Mexico Press, 1998.

Skaggs, Jimmy M. *Prime Cut: Livestock Raising and Meat Packing in the United States, 1607–1983.* College Station: Texas A and M University Press, 1986.

Skaggs, Jimmy M. *The Cattle-Trailing Industry: Between Supply and Demand, 1886–1890.* Lawrence: University Press of Kansas, 1973.

Slatta, Richard W. *Cowboys of the Americas.* New Haven, CT: Yale University Press, 1990.

Slatta, Richard W. *The Cowboy Encyclopedia.* Santa Barbara: ABC-CLIO, 1994.

Slatta, Richard W. *Comparing Cowboys and Frontiers.* Norman: University of Oklahoma Press, 1997.

Shepard, G. *The West of Yesterday.* Toronto: McClelland and Stewart, 1965.

Shepard, G. *Brave Heritage.* Saskatoon: Modern Press, 1967.

Sheppard, Bert. *Spitzee Days.* Calgary: McAra Press, 1971.

Sheppard, Bert. *Just About Nothing.* Calgary: McAra Press, 1977.

Starrs, Paul F. *Let the Cowboy Ride: Cattle Ranching in the American West.* Baltimore: Johns Hopkins University Press, 1998.

Stegner, Wallace. *Wolf Willow.* New York: Viking Press, 1955.

Stegner, Wallace. *The American West as Living Space.* Ann Arbor: University of Michigan Press, 1987.

Strange, Thomas Bland. *Gunner Jingo's Jubilee.* Edmonton: University of Alberta Press, 1988.

Symons, R. D. *Where the Wagon Led: One Man's Memories of the Cowboy's Life in the Old West.* Toronto: Doubleday, 1973.

Taylor, Lonn and Ingrid Marr. *The American Cowboy.* Washington, DC: Library of Congress, 1983.

Thomas, Lewis G. *The Prairie West to 1905: A Canadian Source Book.* Toronto: Oxford University Press, 1975.

Vanderhaeghe, Guy. *The Englishman's Boy.* Toronto: McClelland and Stewart, 1996.

Wald, Johanna et al. *How Not to be Cowed: Livestock Grazing on Public Lands, an Owner's Manual.* San Francisco: Natural Resources Defence Council, 1991.

Walker, Don. *Clio's Cowboys: Studies in the Historiography of the Cattle Trade.* Lincoln: University of Nebraska Press, 1981.

Ward, Faye E. *The Cowboy at Work: All About his Job and How He Does It.* Norman: University of Oklahoma Press, 1987.

Webb, Walter Prescott. *The Great Plains.* New York: Gosset and Dunlap, 1931.

Weir, Thomas R. *Ranching in the Southern Interior Plateau of British Columbia.* Ottawa: Geographical Branch, Mines and Technical Surveys, 1964.

Wheeler, Richard S. *Buffalo Commons.* New York: Tom Doherty, 1998.

Wooliams, Nina G. *Cattle Ranch: The Story of the Douglas Lake Cattle Company.* Vancouver: Douglas and McIntyre, 1982.

Wyman, Walker D. *Nothing But Prairie and Sky: Life on the Dakota Range in the Early Days.* Norman: University of Oklahoma Press, 1988.

Notes

Introduction

1. Richard W. Slatta was kind enough to write a review of the exhibition (see this volume).
2. David H. Breen, "The Canadian West and the Ranching Frontier, 1875–1922" (Ph.D. diss., University of Alberta, 1972), published as *The Canadian Prairie West and the Ranching Frontier, 1874–1924* (Toronto: University of Toronto Press, 1983).
3. L.G. Thomas, "The Ranching Period in Southern Alberta" (unpublished M.A. thesis, University of Alberta, 1935); and Patrick A. Dunae, ed., *Ranchers' Legacy: Alberta Essays by Lewis G. Thomas* (Edmonton: University of Alberta Press, 1986).
4. For discussion see Simon M. Evans, "Review Essay: Some Research on the Canadian Ranching Frontier," *Prairie Forum,* 19, no. 1 (Spring 1994): 101–10.
5. David H. Breen, Alex Johnston Memorial Lecture, Lethbridge, September 1993.
6. Robert Lecker, ed., *Borderlands: Essays in Canadian-American Relations* (Toronto: ECW Press, 1991), x.
7. See, for example, C.W. Vrooman, G.D. Chattaway, and Andrew Stewart, *Cattle Ranching in Western Canada* (Ottawa: Department of Agriculture, 1946), 9.
8. Terry G. Jordan, *North American Cattle-Ranching Frontiers: Origins, Diffusion, and Differentiation* (Albuquerque: University of New Mexico Press, 1993); Richard W. Slatta, *Cowboys of the Americas* (New Haven, CT: Yale University Press, 1990); and Paul F. Starrs, *Let the Cowboy Ride: Cattle Ranching in the American West* (Baltimore: John Hopkins University Press, 1998).
9. Dan Flores, "Spirit of Place and the Value of Nature in the American West," in James E. Sherow, ed., *A Sense of the American West: An Anthology of Environmental History* (Albuquerque: University of New Mexico Press, 1998).
10. This relationship was posited by German scholar Heinrich von Thunen in the middle of the 19th century, and has been applied to various New World situations subsequently. See Jordan, *Cattle Ranching Frontiers,* 11–13, for a summary and references.
11. Ernest Staples Osgood, *The Day of the Cattleman* (Chicago: University of Chicago Press, 1929; Chicago: Phoenix Books, 1966), 194.
12. See James H. Gray, *Men Against the Desert* (Saskatoon: Western Producer Books, 1967); and Government of Saskatchewan, *Managing Saskatchewan Rangeland,* rev. ed. (Saskatoon: Saskatchewan Agriculture and Food, 1997). A similar process occurred in the Sandhills region of Nebraska, see Starrs, *Let the Cowboy Ride,* 134–36.
13. Starrs, *Let the Cowboy Ride*, 67.

14. Census figures show that there is a large number of small ranches and a few large ones, and that the large ranches account for a disproportionate percentage of the cattle marketed. The problem for researchers in coping with 'lifestyle ranches' in their analysis parallels that of separating 'hobby farms' from commercial enterprises.
15. Of course, more than a century of grazing has changed 'natural' grasslands out of all recognition. See Sherm Ewing, *The Range* (Missoula, MT: Mountain Press, 1990).
16. Simon M. Evans, "The Origin of Ranching in Western Canada: American Diffusion or Victorian Transplant?" in L.A. Rosenvall and S.M. Evans, eds., *Essays on the Historical Geography of the Canadian West* (University of Calgary: Department of Geography, 1987), 70–94.
17. See Max Foran's paper, "The Impact of the Depression on Grazing Lease Policy in Alberta," in this volume; and John Proskie, "Trends in Security of Tenure of Grazing Lands in Western Canada," *Canadian Cattlemen,* 2, no. 1 (June 1939): 200ff.
18. Starrs, *Let the Cowboy Ride*, 67.
19. A good summary of the debate in the United States is found in Starrs, *Let the Cowboy Ride,* chap. 4: "Ranching Frontiers and the Federal Government." Dan Daggett, *Beyond the Rangeland Conflict: Towards a West that Works* (Flagstaff: Grand Canyon Trust, 1995), is a thoughtful attempt to pursue a middle ground.
20. Slatta's presentation was based on a chapter in his most recent book and was illustrated with some splendid slides. See Richard W. Slatta, "Social History in the Saddle: Trailing Cowboys of the Americas," in *Comparing Cowboys and Frontiers* (Norman: University of Oklahoma Press, 1997).
21. Slatta, *Comparing Cowboys and Frontiers,* 181.
22. Brian W. Dippie, "Charles M. Russell, Cowboy Culture, and the Canadian Connection," this volume, p. 11.
23. Wallace Stegner, *Wolf Willow* (New York: Viking Press, 1955).
24. The last biographical sketch of Lane that I am aware of was published in 1940. See C.I. Ritchie, "George Lane: One of the Big Four," *Canadian Cattlemen* (September 1940). Because Lane was owner of the Bar U Ranch from 1902 to 1925, he has become the focus of some ongoing research by Parks Canada in connection with the establishment of the Bar U Ranch National Historic Site. Resultant papers are on file at Parks headquarters in Calgary and at the ranch site. George Lane will be included in the next edition of *The Dictionary of Canadian Biography.*
25. A partial exception might be Candace Savage, *Cowgirls* (Vancouver: Greystone Books, 1996).
26. This will be explored further in the postscripts at the end of the volume.
27. Two recently published regional studies set the stage for detailed work on ranching on the plains: Walter Hildebrandt and Brian Huber, *The Cypress Hills: The Land and Its People* (Saskatoon: Purich Publishing, 1994); and Barry Potyondi, *In Palliser's Triangle: Living in the Grasslands, 1850–1930* (Saskatoon: Purich Publishing, 1995).
28. See, for example, Don Gayton, *The Wheat Grass Mechanism: Science and Imagination in the Western Canadian Landscape* (Saskatoon: Fifth House, 1990); and *Landscapes of the Interior: Re-Explorations of Nature and the Human Spirit* (Gabriola Island, BC: New Society Publishers, 1996);

Richard Manning, *Grasslands: The History, Biology, Politics and Promise of the American Prairie* (New York: Viking Penguin, 1995); Sharon Butala, *The Perfection of the Morning: An Apprenticeship in Nature* (Toronto: Harper Collins, 1994); and in fiction Richard S. Wheeler, *The Buffalo Commons* (New York: Tom Doherty, 1998).

29. At the Annual Meeting of the Association of Canadian Geographers, held at the University of Saskatoon in 1996, two 'special sessions,' each spanning several days and involving 10–15 presentations, were relevant. The first was organized by the Canadian Geomorphological Research Group and addressed "Global Changes in the Palliser Triangle." The second, organized by A.B. Beaudoin of the Provincial Museum of Alberta, was titled "The Changing Human Landscape during the Holocene on the Canadian Prairies." This series included papers on the impact of fire and on prairie climates during the 18th and 19th centuries. Much of this work is summarized in a recent article: David J. Sauchyn and Alwynne B. Beaudoin, "Recent Environmental Change in the Southwestern Canadian Plains," *Canadian Geographer,* 42, no. 4 (Winter 1998), 337–53.
30. For a very readable introduction see Ewing, *The Range.*
31. See, for example, Sarah Carter's postscript in this volume; and Catherine Cavanaugh and Jeremy Mouat, eds., *Making Western Canada: Essays on European Colonization and Settlement* (Toronto: Garamond Press, 1996).

Does the Border Matter? Cattle Ranching and the 49th Parallel

1. Derwent Whittlesey, "The Impress of Effective Central Authority upon the Landscape," *Annals of the Association of American Geographers,* 25 (1935): 85–97; David B. Knight, "Identity and Territory: Geographical Perspectives on Nationalism and Regionalism," *Annals of the Association of American Geographers,* 72 (1982): 514–31.
2. Deryck Holdsworth, "Architectual Expression of the Canadian National State," *Canadian Geographer,* 30 (1986): 167–180.
3. Terry G. Jordan-Bychkov and Mona Domosh, *The Human Mosaic,* 8th ed. (New York: Longman, 1999), 340.
4. John C. Hudson, "Cross-Border Contrasts in the Rocky Mountains, United States and Canada," *Abstracts, Association of American Geographers, 93rd Annual Meeting* (Washington, DC: Association of American Geographers, 1997), 120.
5. Hendrik J. Reitsma, "Crop and Livestock Production in the Vicinity of the United States-Canada Border," *Professional Geographer,* 23 (1971): 220–21; and his sequel, "Agricultural Changes in the American-Canadian Border Zone, 1954–1978," *Political Geography Quarterly,* 7 (1988): 23–38.
6. Simon M. Evans, "The Origins of Ranching in Western Canada: American Diffusion or Victorian Transplant?," *Great Plains Quarterly,* 3, no. 2 (1983), 79–91.
7. Andrew H. Clark, unpublished class lecture notes, University of Wisconsin, Madison, 1962.
8. Craig M. Carver, *American Regional Dialects: A Word Geography* (Ann Arbor: University of Michigan Press, 1986); Raven L. McDavid, Jr., *Varieties of American English* (Stanford: Stanford University Press, 1980).

9. Daniel J. Elazar, *The American Mosaic: The Impact of Space, Time, and Culture on American Politics* (Boulder: Westview Press, 1994).
10. See, for example, Edward B. Espenshade, Jr. et al., eds., *Goode's World Atlas,* 19th ed. (Chicago: Rand McNally, 1995), 34, 77.
11. Terry G. Jordan, *North American Cattle Ranching Frontiers: Origins, Diffusion, and Differentiation* (Albuquerque: University of New Mexico Press, 1993).
12. Simon M. Evans, "American Cattlemen on the Canadian Range, 1874–1914," *Prairie Forum,* 4 (1979): 121–35.
13. Jordan, *North American Cattle Ranching,* 159–69, 241–66.
14. Ibid., 267–307.
15. Thomas R. Weir, *Ranching in the Southern Interior Plateau of British Columbia,* revised ed. (Ottawa: Geographical Branch, Mines and Technical Surveys, 1964), 90–91.
16. Jon T. Kilpinen, "The Mountain Horse Barn," *Pioneer America Society Transactions,* 17 (1994): 25–32; Jon T. Kilpinen, "Traditional Fence Types of Western North America," *Pioneer America Society Transactions,* 15 (1992): 15–22.
17. Evans, "Origins of Ranching."
18. Terry G. Jordan, Jon T. Kilpinen, and Charles F. Gritzner, *The Mountain West: Interpreting the Folk Landscape* (Baltimore: Johns Hopkins University Press, 1997), 11, 61–62, 73.
19. As an antidote, the reader should consult Evans, "Origins of Ranching."

Charles M. Russell, Cowboy Culture, and the Canadian Connection

1. Russell's background, long ignored because Russell himself had little to say about it, is treated in Lyle S. Woodcock, "The St. Louis Heritage of Charles Marion Russell," *Gateway Heritage,* 2 (Spring 1982): 2–15, and John Taliaferro, *Charles M. Russell: The Life and Legend of America's Cowboy Artist* (Boston: Little, Brown, 1996), which utilizes the information in two invaluable manuscript sources: the Russell Estate papers in the Helen E. and Homer E. Britzman Collection, Taylor Museum for Southwestern Studies of the Colorado Springs Fine Arts Center (hereafter, Britzman Collection); and the James Brownlee Rankin Papers, Montana Historical Society, Helena (hereafter, Rankin Papers). These sources contradict the impression of a rupture between Russell and his family, and instead establish the importance of the St. Louis connections in Russell's early career as a professional artist.
2. "Russell, the Cowboy Artist, and His Work," *Butte Inter Mountain,* 1 January 1903; C.M. Russell to [Lin B. Hess (?)], n.d. [ca. 1902], Favell Museum of Western Art and Artifacts, Klamath Falls, Oregon; C.M. Russell, "A Few Words About Myself," *More Rawhides* (Great Falls: Montana Newspaper Association, 1925), 3; Buckskin Brady, *Stories and Sermons* (Toronto: William Briggs, 1905), 103; "Ledger of Old Utica Store Values Bull Team Outfit at $4,200; Russell Is Mentioned," unidentified clipping (*Great Falls Tribune*?), 28 May 28 [1930?], C.M. Russell clipping file, Great Falls Public Library (the Weatherwax store ledgers for 27 May 1885 through 1886, C.M. Russell Museum, Great Falls, show Russell still busy charging cigarettes and fixings); and "When Charley Russell Earned $84 for 2 Months'

Labor as Montana Cow Hand," unidentified clipping (1930s), Britzman Collection. The standard source on Russell's cowboy career was the autobiographical account first published in the *Butte Inter Mountain* at the beginning of 1903, and often reprinted. Russell offered other accounts that refined some details: see, for example, Nancy C. Russell to Guy Weadick, 10 May 1916, Britzman Collection, and, especially, C. M. Russell to Guy Weadick [ca. July-August 1922], in Brian W. Dippie, ed., *Charles M. Russell, Word Painter: Letters 1887–1926* (Fort Worth: Amon Carter Museum, with Harry N. Abrams, New York, 1993), 323–24. Taliaferro, *Charles M. Russell*, chaps. 4-5, provides the best account of Russell's cowboy career. The Rankin Papers include many old cowboy reminiscences of Russell; also see the J. Frank Dobie Collection, Harry Ransom Humanities Research Center, The University of Texas at Austin (C.M. Russell Miscellaneous Material). The Montana and St. Louis newspapers will continue to shed light on Russell's doings in the 1880s and early 1890s. There is still need for detailed work of the sort provided by Hugh A. Dempsey in "Tracking C.M. Russell in Canada, 1888–1889," *Montana, the Magazine of Western History,* 39 (Summer 1989): 2–15.

3. C.M. Russell to William W. Davis, 14 May [1889], and to Charles M. Joys, 10 May [1892], *Word Painter*, 16–17, 24; and untitled item, *Weekly River Press* (Fort Benton), 19 August 1891 (I am grateful to Joel Overholser for this citation). Twenty-four sketches accompanied Russell's letter to Davis, offering in rudimentary form many of his favorite cowboy themes—roping, riding, loafing, and cow camp routine. Twenty-three are reproduced in *Word Painter*, 18–23.
4. Taliaferro, *Charles M. Russell*, 91, 101; and C.M. Russell to Nancy C. Russell, 6 February 1919, *Word Painter*, 271.
5. Jane Meyer, "The Russell Gallery at Great Falls," *American Artist,* 30 (November 1966): 26; and F.G. Renner, "Rangeland Rembrandt: The Incomparable Charles Marion Russell," *Montana, the Magazine of Western History,* 7 (Autumn 1957): 28.
6. For Russell's art, see Brian W. Dippie, *Looking at Russell* (Fort Worth: Amon Carter Museum, 1987), and Peter H. Hassrick, *Charles M. Russell* (New York: Harry N. Abrams, in association with the National Museum of American Art, Smithsonian Institution, Washington, DC, 1989).
7. Charles M. Russell, "The Story of the Cowpuncher," *Trails Plowed Under* (Garden City: Doubleday, Page & Company, 1927), 3; and Con Price, *Memories of Old Montana* (Holywood: Highland Press, 1945), 139–40.
8. C.M. Russell to Philip R. Goodwin, 23 October 1907, *Word Painter*, 91; Russell to William E. Hawks, 7 May 1909, private collection; and Russell to Walt Coburn, 27 November 1924, *Word Painter*, 359. Russell did a satirical sketch in 1896 titled *Cow Puncher—New Style, A.D. 1896* (Amon Carter Museum, Fort Worth) that proves that his aversion to newfangled cowboys antedated Ford automobiles.
9. C.M. Russell to Wallace D. Coburn, 27 January 1915, and to Berners B. Kelly, 22 February 1920, *Word Painter*, 213–14, 289.
10. C.M. Russell to William R. McDonough [ca. January 1914], *Word Painter*, 186; Allis B. Stuart to James B. Rankin, 4 April 1937, Rankin Papers; C.M. Russell to Robert Stuart, 10 March 1913, *Word Painter*, 175; and Russell, "Bronc Twisters," *Trails Plowed Under*, 165–66.
11. C.M. Russell to Robert Stuart, 16 January 1907, *Word Painter*, 78–79.
12. C.M. Russell, "Story of the Cowpuncher," *Trails Plowed Under*, 2–3;

Russell, undated note to Joe De Yong, reproduced in *Persimmon Hill,* 11, no. 3-4 (1982): 77; and Russell to Charles A. Beil, 31 May 1926, *Word Painter*, 393.

13. C.M. Russell to Will James, 12 May 1920, in *Good Medicine: The Illustrated Letters of Charles M. Russell* (Garden City: Doubleday, Doran & Company, 1929), 68.
14. For *Cowboy Camp During the Roundup* as "an entire Russell collection in one painting," see Brian W. Dippie, "'... I Feel That I Am Improving Right Along': Continuity and Change in Charles M. Russell's Art," *Montana: The Magazine of Western History,* 38 (Summer 1988): 43–55.
15. Philip R. Goodwin to his mother, 9 August 1909, Philip Goodwin Collection, Harold McCracken Research Library, Buffalo Bill Historical Center, Cody, Wyoming; High River Pioneers' and Old Timers' Association, *Leaves from the Medicine Tree* (Lethbridge: Lethbridge Herald, 1960), 66; C.M. Russell note to Joe De Yong, ca. 1916, Joe De Yong Papers, C.M. Russell Museum, Great Falls; and George Lane to Nancy C. Russell, 1 October 1912, Britzman Collection. Nancy reported to Lane on 17 December that the painting, then titled *A Bronc to Breakfast* in homage to its inspiration, was "about completed." For two versions of the axe handle story see "Prince of Wales Loses a Picturesque Neighbor," *San Francisco Chronicle*, 28 September 1925, and *Leaves from the Medicine Tree*, 106.
16. For Russell's major Mounted Police subjects, see P.J.M. Pallesen, "Russell's Work and the North West Mounted Police," *Scarlet & Gold*, 73rd ed. (1991–92), 25–27; for Cameron and the Russells, Wm. Bleasdell Cameron, "The Old West Lives Through Russell's Brush," *Canadian Cattlemen,* 13 (January 1950): 11, 26, and "Russell's Oils Eye-Opener to the East," ibid. (February 1950): 26–27; and for the Magrath commission, the Charles A. Magrath Collection, Glenbow Museum, Calgary, and Alexander Johnston, comp., *The Battle of Belly River: Stories of the Last Great Indian Battle* (Lethbridge: Lethbridge Branch, Alberta Historical Society, 1966), 19–20. I am indebted to Hugh A. Dempsey, Calgary, for information on Russell and Alberta.
17. Nancy C. Russell to Henry M. Pellatt, [October] 1912, 13 November 1912, and Pellatt to Nancy C. Russell, 11 August 1919, Britzman Collection; and Alick. C. Newton to James B. Rankin, 12 January 1938, Rankin Papers. Nancy Russell's annotated copy of the 1912 Stampede catalog, Britzman Collection, notes that the four paintings Newton owned were first sold to A. M. Grenfell, London. Alick Newton's brother Denzil apparently acquired them on a visit to London (Edward B. Noyers interview, 1971, Phonotape 71.209, Provincial Archives of Alberta, Edmonton). The Newton family connection to the Prince of Wales and its fallout is explored in Jennifer Wells, "Whodunit?," *Report on Business Magazine,* 15 (March 1999): 30–32, 34, 36, 38, 40, 42, 44, 46, 48, 50, 52. For Weadick, see Donna Livingstone, *The Cowboy Spirit: Guy Weadick and the Calgary Stampede* (Vancouver: Greystone Books, 1996), and Hugh A. Dempsey, "Charlie Russell and Guy Weadick," *Russell's West,* 5, no. 1 (1997): 14–19; and for the balance of subject matter in Russell's mature work, see Brian W. Dippie, "Charles M. Russell: The Artist in His Prime," *Charles M. Russell: The Artist in His Heyday, 1903–1926* (Santa Fe: Gerald Peters Gallery, in association with Mongerson-Wunderlich, 1995), 13–22.

18. A.E. Cross to C.M. Russell, 30 December 1924; Cross to Nancy C. Russell, 29 August 1913; and Nancy Russell to Cross, 7 September 1913, Calgary Brewing and Malting Company Papers, Glenbow Museum, Calgary.
19. Douglas Hardwick to James B. Rankin, 20 February 1937, Rankin Papers; George Campbell to the author [13 June 1980], and phone conversation with the author, 8 April 1982; and letters between William B. Campbell, Mary Campbell, and Nancy C. Russell, 1914–20, Britzman Collection. On 9 November 1920 Nancy Russell wrote William Campbell that only five of all the pictures exhibited in Calgary and Saskatoon—26 all told—remained unsold. Nancy provided the name for the Indian burial scene in 1929; the Campbells had called it *The Vanishing American*, but Nancy suggested *Her Heart Is on the Ground, while Her Warrior's Heart Sleeps.* For the history of Lane and *The Queen's War Hounds*, see J.L. Ross, *The Queen's War Hounds* (Edmonton: Provincial Museum & Archives of Alberta [Museum and Archives Notes No. 7], 1971). There is some confusion as to how and when *The Queen's War Hounds* was actually given to the Government of Alberta—Dempsey, "Charlie Russell and Guy Weadick," 19, offers a variant account—but since 1968 it has been part of the Provincial Museum's permanent collection.
20. For the Prince of Wales' visit and the Russell paintings given him, see "Russell Art Exhibit Breaks Camp," *Great Falls Tribune*, 21 September 1919; "Russell Opens Exhibition in Minneapolis Today; Prince of Wales Takes Two Paintings to England," *Great Falls Tribune*, 7 December 1919; and Arthur (Duke of Connaught) to George Lane, 6 December 1919 (copy), Britzman Collection. There is some uncertainty about whether Russell did meet the prince—in Saskatoon—and when, exactly, the prince received Russell's oil. Saskatoon's mayor F.R. Macmillan wrote to the Russells on 10 September 1919 (Britzman Collection) that "His Royal Highness Prince of Wales, will inspect your pictures at the Convocation Hall, University, about two P.M. tomorrow, the 11th instant, and I shall be glad if you would be present at the University not later than 1:45 p.m. so that if H.R.H. desires Mr. Russell can be presented." Since there is no subsequent mention of an introduction, apparently H.R.H. did not so desire. Peter J.M. Pallesen, "'When Law Dulls the Edge of Chance': 1915 Painting Is the Focus of the Relationship between C.M. Russell and H.R.H. Prince Edward of Wales," *Cowboy Gazette,* 2 (May-June 1999): 1–2, states positively that "it was during his stay at the Bar-U Ranch … that he [the Prince] was presented the 1915 oil-on-canvas gifted to him on behalf of the Town of High River . . . . The presentation took place at the Bar-U Ranch and the oil-on-canvas was thereafter handed to Professor William L. Carlyle who had been appointed as manager of the EP Ranch." But the *Great Falls Tribune* reported on 7 December 1919 that the painting was presented to the prince at a farewell luncheon in Winnipeg on 11 October, when his acquisition of the E.P. Ranch next to Lane's was announced. A story in the *Manitoba Free Press* on 13 October 1919 ("Prince Becomes Real Westerner Buys a Ranch") made no mention of the Russell painting, but did note Lane's presence at the luncheon and his role in arranging the purchase of the ranch for the prince.

The prince, in a series of letters brimming with self-pity to his sweetheart back in England, made no mention of Russell in recounting his "trying day

at Saskatoon" (though he confessed to enjoying the Stampede for about one hour of the two and a half he was in attendance), while the farewell festivities in Winnipeg a month later left him "too bored for words." He also dismissed his reception in High River on 15 September as "the usual mayor & his address to reply to, 20 veterans to inspect, school children to hear sing & crowds to wave to," and made no mention of a painting being presented him in the name of the town's citizens. He did enjoy his subsequent stay at the Bar U Ranch "with a dear old man called Lane." Indeed, riding in a cattle roundup there on "a nice locally bred horse" was what persuaded him that ranching was "a real good life ... though a vewy hard one & one's got to be real tough to take it on as a living though it pays if one can make good!!" He followed up on this assessment, meeting Lane in Fort Macleod on 2 October on his return journey from the West Coast and arranging for the purchase of what would become the E.P. Ranch. "It's going to be a very good investment," the Prince wrote, "& old Lane will be able to keep an eye on it as it's next door to his!! ... it's a good move & will create a good impression in the West, which is my part of Canada" (Rupert Godfrey, ed., *Letters from a Prince: Edward, Prince of Wales, to Mrs. Freda Dudley Ward, March 1918–January 1921* [London: Little, Brown and Company (UK), 1998], 187, 206, 189–90, 202).

21. "Handsome Oil Painting Presented to Ray Knight," *Lethbridge Herald*, 29 July 1918; data provided with Richard Knight to Loretta Eubanks, 28 April 1980, Amon Carter Museum Archives, Fort Worth; and see *Word Painter*, 356, and, for the painting, Brian W. Dippie, ed., *"Paper Talk": Charlie Russell's American West* (New York: Alfred A. Knopf, in association with the Amon Carter Museum of Western Art, 1979), 198–99. Knight, after seventeen years ranching in Alberta, had decided to move to Utah and wanted a memento. Apparently the painting was his idea, and Russell, who was no portrait artist, was unenthusiastic about the commission. Joe De Yong, visiting at the Russells' home in Great Falls in 1917, noted that Russell was away in Canada: "A big cow man up there wanted Russell to make a picture of him on a favorite horse. He didn't care much about going & I guess if he'd know[n] what the fellow wanted he wouldn't have gone at all—." Joe De Yong to his parents, Sunday evening [1917], Joe De Yong Papers, National Cowboy Hall of Fame, Oklahoma City. Having moved to Utah, Knight missed Alberta and soon returned. Subsequently, the Knight-Watson Ranching Co. Ltd., headquartered in Lethbridge, used the Russell painting on its letterhead.
22. Alick C. Newton to James B. Rankin, 9 December 1937, Rankin Papers; Wyndham R. Dunstan to C.M. Russell, 31 May 1920, Britzman Collection; and, for context, Simon Evans, *Prince Charming Goes West: The Story of the E.P. Ranch* (Calgary: University of Calgary Press, 1993).
23. C.M. Russell to Granville Stuart, undated [ca. 1916], *Word Painter*, 216; Mary S. Campbell to Nancy Russell [November 1926], Elizabeth Lane to Nancy Russell, 4 November 1926, and A.E. Cross to Nancy Russell, 30 October 1926, Britzman Collection.
24. Chas. A. Beil, "C.M. Russell as I Knew Him," *Federal Illustrator,* 9 (Winter 1926–27): 22.

Not an Old Cowhand– Fred Stimson and the Bar U Ranch

1. The research upon which this paper is based was done as part of a project to develop the Bar U Ranch National Historic Site. The conclusions drawn are the author's alone.
2. Edward Brado, *Cattle Kingdom: Ranching in Alberta* (Vancouver: Douglas and McIntyre, 1984), 121.
3. Simon Evans, "George Lane: Notes on a Life," unpublished paper prepared for Parks Canada; Simon Evans, "Story Line: Bar U Ranch, National Historic Site," unpublished paper prepared for Parks Canada.
4. Grant MacEwan, *Pat Burns: Cattle King* (Saskatoon: Western Producer Books, 1979).
5. Archives nationales de Québec (ANQ), Hull, Registres d'etat civil. Protonotaire de Sherbrooke, Film 125.1, Compton Anglican Church, 1843; ANQ, CN501-0028, Greffe de D.M. Thomas, No. 404, Inventory of the Estate of Arba Stimson and Mary Smith, 29 February 1864; ANQ, CN501-0023, Greffe de C.A. Richardson, No. 8149, Will of Arba Stimson.
6. National Archives of Canada (NA), 1871 Census of Canada, Quebec, Compton County, Compton Township, Div.2, Reel C-1090. Schedule 4, p. 13, line 1; Schedule 5, p. 13, line 1.
7. J.I. Little, "Watching the Frontier Disappear: English-Speaking Reaction to French-Canadian Colonization in the Eastern Townships, 1844–90," *Journal of Canadian Studies/Revue d'études canadiennes*, 15, no. 4 (Winter 1980–81), 93–111.
8. NA, RG15, Vol. 1209, File 142709, Part 1, Cochrane to Macdonald, 17 December 1880; ibid., Cochrane to Minister of the Interior, 10 February 1881.
9. NA, RG95, Vol. 2616, The North West Cattle Company (Limited); ibid., Riley to Secretary of State, 3 September 1884.
10. "Cattle Ranching in the North-West," *Montreal Herald and Daily Commercial Gazette*, 17 June 1881.
11. Brado, *Cattle Kingdom*, 107–8; High River Pioneers' and Old Timers' Association, *Leaves From the Medicine Tree* (Lethbridge: Lethbridge Herald, 1960), 252.
12. Montana Historical Society, T.C. Power Papers, MC55, Vol. 166, File 6, Stimson to Power, 26 April 1882; ibid., Vol. 167, File 4, 28 July 1882.
13. *Leaves From the Medicine Tree*, 253–54; Brado, *Cattle Kingdom*, 110–15.
14. NA, RG15, Vol. 1209, File 142709, Part 1, M.H. Cochrane to D.L. McPherson, 7 June 1883.
15. Canada, *Sessional Papers*, 1885, No. 8, 143. *Leaves From the Medicine Tree*, 275, suggests that they sold 1000 head at $75.00 each.
16. Canada, *Sessional Papers*, 1886, No. 20b; NA, RG15, Vol. 1220, File 192192, Stock returns for the year 1891.
17. Brado, *Cattle Kingdom*, 194, 196; L.V. Kelly, *The Rangemen: The Story of the Ranchers and Indians of Alberta* (Toronto: Coles, 1980), 185.
18. NA, RG15, Vol. 1204, File 141376, Part 1, Petition, c. March 1886; NA, RG15, Vol. 1241, File 352945, Petition from stockmen of High River, 2 April 1894.

19. David H. Breen, *The Canadian Prairie West and the Ranching Frontier 1874–1924* (Toronto: University of Toronto Press, 1983), 60; "Herald Celebrates Birthday," *Calgary Herald Magazine,* 31 August 1963.
20. "Mr. Costigan's Letter and the Conservative Position," *The Gazette and Alberta Livestock Record* (Macleod), 10 April 1896; "Mr. Costigan's Letter and the Conservative Position," NA, RG15, Vol. 1210, File 145330-3, R.A. Wallace to F. Oliver, 30 November 1897.
21. NA, RG15, Vol. 698, File 345364, Part 1, Stimson to Burgess, 25 October 1893; ibid., Ryley to the Secretary, Department of the Interior, 19 October 1894.
22. Ibid., Ryley to Burgess, 21 November 1894.
23. Archives de la Cour Superieure, Montréal, 23 May 1901, No. 46, NWCC en liquidation, & H.M. Allan, liquidateur, et F.S. Stimson, requerent; ANQ, Régistre des jugements de la cour superieure, Vol. II, 1903, p. 43, No. 494, 26 February 1903; Fabre-Surveyer, ed., *Rapports de Pratique de Québec* (Toronto: Carswell Company Ltd., 1903), 31–34, 181–82, 239–40.
24. "Death of Mr. Fred Stimson," Montreal *Gazette,* 16 January 1912, 5.
25. NA, RG15, Vol. 1204, File 141376, Part 1, Pearce to Minister of the Interior, 11 November 1886; NA, RG15, Vol. 1220, File 192192, Stock Returns from Ranches in the Northwest Territories, 20 January 1890.
26. F.W. Ings, *Before the Fences: Tales from the Midway Ranch,* ed. Jim Davis, Calgary: McAra Printing Limited, 1980), 21–22; *Leaves from the Medicine Tree,* 263–69.
27. *Leaves from the Medicine Tree,* 274.
28. Harold W. Riley, "The Romance of the Ranching Industry and the Pioneer Ranchers and Cowboys," *Canadian Cattlemen,* 3, no. 1 (June 1940): 399.
29. Sheilagh S. Jameson, *Ranches, Cowboys and Characters: Birth of Alberta's Western Heritage* (Calgary: Glenbow-Alberta Institute, 1987), 61–62.
30. Calgary: Glenbow Archives, M337, J.L. Douglas, Journal, 27.
31. Norman Rankin, "Boss of the Bar U," *Canada Monthly,* 9, no. 5 (March 1911): 332.
32. NA, MG28, III, 20, Canadian Pacific Railway, Van Horne Letterbooks, Vol. 52, 324, Van Horne to Stimson, 13 November1896.
33. A. Herbert Eckford, "Wolf Hunting in the Days of the 'Open Range' in Alberta," *Canadian Cattlemen,* 9, no. 1 (June 1946): 48.
34. Harold W. Riley, "Herbert William (Herb) Millar: Pioneer Ranchman," *Canadian Cattlemen,* 4, no. 4 (March 1942): 142.
35. Brado, *Cattle Kingdom,* 119.
36. Glenbow, M337, J.L. Douglas, Journal, 35.
37. Phil Weinard, "Gives Vivid Picture of Early Days and Hardships," *Canadian Cattlemen,* 3, no. 3 (December 1940): 462.
38. Alberta Archives, Stimson Homestead File, Reels 2010 and 2011, File 173491, Statement made and sworn by Frederick Smith Stimson, 9 October 1894. She was enumerated at the ranch in both the 1891 and 1901 censuses.
39. NA, RG3, D-3, Vol. 53, File 1889-365, Reel T-2179; ibid., Vol. 66, File 1894-544, Reel T-2185.
40. Ings, *Before the Fences,* 86; Glenbow, M4652, Luxton Papers, Notes on Fred Stimson.

41. NA, MG29, D72, Vol. 1, Bowen to Macpherson, 11 January 1897. A comparison of this letter with a similar one from Mary Stimson to Lemoine, 11 January 1897, shows Mary Stimson's much more formal style.
42. *Bar U National Historic Park. Oral History Project,* Interview 024, 8; ibid., Interview 025, 2; Judea Dixon to Barbara Holliday, 30 July 1995.
43. Arni Brownstone, "Tradition Embroidered in Glass," *Rotunda: The Magazine of the Royal Ontario Museum,* 29, no. 1 (Summer 1996): 21.
44. Glenbow, M4652, Luxton Papers, Notes on Fred Stimson.
45. Arni Brownstone, "Tradition Embroidered in Glass," *Rotunda: The Magazine of the Royal Ontario Museum,* 29, no. 1 (Summer 1996): 21.

George Lane: From Cowboy to Cattle King

1. David H. Breen, *The Canadian Prairie West and the Ranching Frontier 1874–1924* (Toronto: University of Toronto Press, 1983), 12–14, 21–22, 26–32, 85–88, 94–98, 172–76; see also Lewis G. Thomas, *Ranchers' Legacy: Alberta Essays,* ed. Patrick A. Dunae (Edmonton: University of Alberta Press, 1986), 5–10, 141–49, 153–65; Sheilagh S. Jameson, "The Social Elite of the Ranch Community and Calgary," in *Frontier Calgary: Town, City, and Region 1875–1914,* eds. Anthony W. Rasporich and Henry C. Klassen (Calgary: McClelland and Stewart West, 1975), 57–70. For an alternate view, see Simon M. Evans, "The Origin of Ranching in Western Canada: American Diffusion or Victorian Transplant?" in *Great Plains Quarterly,* 3, no. 2 (Spring 1983): 79–91; W.M. Elofson, "Adapting to the Frontier Environment: The Ranching Industry in Western Canada, 1881–1914," in *Canadian Papers in Rural History,* vol. 8, ed. Donald H. Akenson (Gananoque, ON: Langdale Press, 1996), 307–27.
2. In a recent article, historical geographer Simon Evans maintains that the Americans on the Canadian range provided a great deal more than merely the ability to physically handle cattle and argues that their contribution was critical to both the establishment and survival of the major Canadian ranches. Evans, "Some Observations on the Labor Force of the Canadian Ranching Frontier During Its Golden Age, 1882–1901," *Great Plains Quarterly,* 15, no. 1 (Winter 1995): 3–17.
3. Elizabeth Sexsmith Lane, "A Brief Sketch of Memories of My Family," original typed manuscript provided by Bev Lane, 25, gives George Lane's place of birth as Boonville, Indiana. Although all previously published information lists Iowa as Lane's state of birth, including Elizabeth Lane's manuscript on file, June 1945, Glenbow Archives M652, 20, other inconsistencies lead the author to make the correction in the text. Present maps, for example, show a Boonville in Indiana but not in Iowa. See also William L. Sexsmith, "Pioneer: The Story of a Ranch and Its People," Glenbow Archives, M6088, 173. The author of this manuscript is the son of Lem Sexsmith, brother to Elizabeth.
4. Archibald O. MacRae, *History of the Province of Alberta,* vol. 1 (Calgary: Western Canada History Co., 1912), 488; High River Pioneers' and Old Timers' Association, *Leaves from the Medicine Tree* (Lethbridge: Lethbridge

Herald, 1960), 66.

5. James Knox Polk Miller, *The Road to Virginia City: The Diary of James Knox Polk Miller*, ed. Andrew F. Rolle (Norman: University of Oklahoma Press, 1960), 81–82.
6. Miller, *The Road to Virginia City*, 44, 74–88, 91; Granville Stuart, *Pioneering in Montana: The Making of a State, 1864–1887*, ed. Paul C. Phillips, originally published under title *Forty Years on the Frontier as seen in the Journals and Reminiscences of Granville Stuart, Gold Miner, Trader, Merchant, Rancher and Politician*, vol. 2 (Arthur Clark Company, 1925; Lincoln: University of Nebraska Press, 1977), 21–22, 31; Michael P. Malone, Richard B. Roeder, and William L. Lang, *Montana: A History of Two Centuries*, rev. ed. (Seattle: University of Washington Press, 1991), 89–90.
7. Malone et al., *Montana*, 157; Lewis Atherton, *The Cattle Kings* (Bloomington: Indiana University Press, 1967), 1–8, 22–24, 59–68.
8. Atherton, *Cattle Kings*, 161, 168–92, 201–05, 219–26; Malone et al., *Montana*, 151.
9. Atherton, *Cattle Kings*, 121.
10. For a discussion of reasons to prohibit firearms, see Atherton, *Cattle Kings*, 40–48. The author notes that the heavy, cumbersome six-shooter interfered with the efficiency of the cowboy. In addition, since shooting an unarmed man was regarded as murder, it was wiser to go unarmed unless positive and specific danger decreed otherwise. When weapons were carried it was primarily for defense against snakes and animals.
11. Malone et al., *Montana*, 155–56.
12. Malone et al., *Montana*, 146–51; Atherton, *Cattle Kings*, 161, 183, 219–23, 268, 272 . Kohrs also served as an elected official and as president of the Union Bank and Trust Company in Helena. The Grant–Kohrs Ranch is now a U.S. National Historic Site.
13. Terry G. Jordan, *North American Cattle-Ranching Frontiers: Origins, Diffusion, and Differentiation* (Albuquerque: University of New Mexico Press, 1993), 199–207, 294, 298.
14. Jordan, *Cattle-Ranching Frontiers*, 267.
15. Jordan, *Cattle-Ranching Frontiers*, 300–07.
16. Historian Henry C. Klassen has written extensively on the importance of Alberta-Montana economic relationships during their formative periods of development. See, for example, Klassen, "Shaping the Growth of the Montana Economy: T.C. Power & Bro. and the Canadian Trade, 1869–93," *Great Plains Quarterly*, 11, no. 3 (Summer 1991): 166–80; and "Entrepreneurship in the Canadian West: The Enterprises of A.E. Cross, 1886–1920," *Western Historical Quarterly*, 22, no. 3 (August 1991): 315, 333. See also James M. Francis, "Montana Business and Canadian Regionalism in the 1870s and 1880s," *Western Historical Quarterly*, 12, no. 3 (July 1981): 301–02.
17. Jordan, *Cattle-Ranching Frontiers*, 300; Malone et al., *Montana*, 148, 150; Gerald L. Berry, *The Whoop-Up Trail: Early Days in Alberta ... Montana* (Lethbridge: Lethbridge Historical Society, 1995), 46; Simon M. Evans, "Stocking the Canadian Range," *Alberta History*, 26, no. 3 (Summer 1978): 1–8.
18. Sexsmith, "Pioneer," 172; Frederick Ings, *Before the Fences: Tales from the Midway Ranch*, ed. Jim Davis (1936; Calgary: McAra Printing Limited, 1980), 15.

19. A.E. Cross, "The Roundup of 1887," *Alberta Historical Review*, 13, no. 2 (Spring 1965): 24.
20. Letter #46, 1 September 1885 to Hill's mother, Edward F.J. Hills Letters 1883–1885, Fish Creek, Glenbow Archives M7988.
21. Ings, *Before the Fences*, 14, "...a face that was clean and clever with quiet grey-blue eyes"; Norman Rankin, "The Boss of the Bar U," *Canada Monthly*, 9, no. 5 (March 1911): 330–31, 333. Rankin's description was more vivid. "His is a picturesque figure; an attractive personality; a double-barrelled, back-action, high-pressure, electrical dynamo at full speed; a living example of perpetual motion, mental, physical and corporal; a six-foot giant with tow-colored hair and the smile of a sister of charity." Although his colorful prose appears characteristic of an enthusiastic but uninformed urbanite, Rankin had worked as a cattle tender for the Allan ship lines and knew Lane personally. Moreover, as Publicity Commissioner of the Natural Resources Department of the CPR, he visited the Bar U in September 1911 with the editor of *The Canadian Magazine* when the Kinnemacolor Picture Co. of England made colored motion pictures of a roundup of Lane's Percherons. *High River Times*, 21 September 1911.
22. Sexsmith, "Pioneer," 172-73.
23. Ings, *Before the Fences*, 36; E.S. Lane, "A Brief Sketch," 11.
24. *Leaves from the Medicine Tree*, 121, 239; MacRae, *History of the Province of Alberta*, 489; L.V. Kelly, *The Range Men: The Story of the Ranchers and Indians of Alberta* (Toronto: William Briggs, 1913; Coles Reprint, 1980), 225, 231–32.
25. E.S. Lane, "A Brief Sketch," 11–12. Elizabeth Lane adds that, for a period of time, the doctor was fearful Lane would die unless treatment was strictly followed, and he rode daily from 30 miles away to monitor his patient. Although Lane's general recovery was good, one leg was still swollen and painful and by October, he was sent to Montreal for surgery to save the limb. The residual effect of the ordeal apparently did not prevent Lane from a very active life until his later years, when he required the use of a cane.
26. E.S. Lane, "A Brief Sketch," 12; *Leaves from the Medicine Tree*, 66–67.
27. *Macleod Gazette*, 28 February 1889, cited in Gregory E.G. Thomas, "Five Early Alberta Ranches: 1880-1905," Agenda Paper 1974-43A, Western Region, Archaeological Research Services, Parks Canada, 28.
28. E.S. Lane, "A Brief Sketch," 12.
29. E.S. Lane, "A Brief Sketch," 12-13.
30. E.S. Lane, "A Brief Sketch," 13-14; Sexsmith, "Pioneer," 205–06.
31. Sexsmith, "Pioneer," 21; *Leaves from the Medicine Tree*, 67; Lawson & Fordyce Architects, Calgary, 5 May 1910, "Plan of Bungalow for Geo. Lane, Willow Creek," Glenbow Archives, unprocessed blueprint.
32. Amanda Dow, "The Bar U Pigsty," paper on file, Archaeological Services, Parks Canada, 1993. Dow found plans for the pigsty in J.H. Sanders, *Practical Hints About Barn Building* (Chicago: Sanders, 1892), 193. The design was also unique, having been found on only two other secondary operations in North America: one at a farm outside of Chicago, in Flanagan, Illinois, and the other on Lane's Bar U Ranch, built prior to 1927.
33. Sexsmith, "Pioneer," 21–23.
34. Sexsmith, "Pioneer," 22–25.
35. Thomas, "Five Early Alberta Ranches," 29; Kelly, *The Range Men*, 281, 290, 298.

36. Simon Evans, "George Lane: Purebred Horse Breeder," Parks Canada, 1994, 14–15; Kelly, *The Range Men*, 311; E.S. Lane, "A Brief Sketch," 17-18; MacRae, *History of the Province of Alberta*, 489; Rankin, "The Boss of the Bar U," 331–32.
37. Klassen, "Entrepreneurship in the Canadian West," 317–18.
38. Klassen, "Entrepreneurship in the Canadian West," 316–20, 327.
39. Rankin, "The Boss of the Bar U," 330.
40. *Leaves from the Medicine Tree*, 34–35.
41. Frank Howard Schofield, *The Story of Manitoba*, vol. 2 (Winnipeg: C.J. Clarke Publishing Co, 1913), 40–43, 688–92; Kelly, *The Range Men*, 298.
42. *The Story of Manitoba*, 691; *Calgary Herald*, 5 February 1902.
43. J.G. Rutherford, Veterinary Director-General and Live Stock Commissioner's Report, 1909, cited in Kelly, *The Range Men*, 393.
44. Kelly, *The Range Men*, 429–30; Lane on "Scarcity of Live Stock," *High River Times*, 16 May 1912.
45. Kelly, *The Range Men*, 355, 367; Breen, *The Canadian Prairie West*, 133–35.
46. G. Lane to J.W. Greenway, 1 June 1904, Public Archives of Canada 1880–1926, M3799, Box 2, F 34, Glenbow Archives.
47. F. Oliver to C. Sifton, 4 June 1904, Public Archives of Canada 1880–1926, M3799, Box 2, F 34, Glenbow Archives.
48. Breen, *The Canadian Prairie West*, 122–24, 140, 186.
49. For a further discussion of Lane's early and extensive irrigation system on the Bar U, see Joy Oetelaar, "George Lane's Vision of Development on the Alberta Range," paper on file, Bar U Historic Site Project, Parks Canada, 1994, 25–30.
50. For a discussion of the transition from 'pure ranching' to mixed farming, see W.M. Elofson, "Not Just a Cowboy: The Practice of Ranching in Southern Alberta, 1881–1914," in *Canadian Papers in Rural History*, vol. 10, ed. Donald H. Akenson (Gananoque, ON: Langdale Press, 1996), 205–16. Although many other large-scale cattle operations cut wild hay during the early period, the progression to growing grains for feed supplement became more common after 1900 and was only fully in place by 1914. Moreover, the addition of poultry, swine and milk cows became a characteristic of many large scale operations, rather than small operators, in the second decade of the 1900s.
51. L.V. Kelly noted in 1912 that Lane and independent cattleman E.H. Maunsell saw Alberta's ranching future as "a gigantic mixed farm, stock fed throughout the winter," *The Range Men*, 52.
52. Although contemporaries uniformly refer to Lane's brusque and commanding manner, nonetheless it appears that he viewed his employees as more than simply hired labor. Rather, he understood the value and importance of their contribution to the business. For example, in 1912, Lane organized a 'reunion' on the Bar U for all the men who had run one of his outfits, Lane to W. Greig, 18 June 1912, Nanton Historical Society papers, M4689, Glenbow Archives; *High River Times*, 25 July 1912.
53. Breen, *The Canadian Prairie West*, 94–97; Klassen, "Entrepreneurship in the Canadian West," 321. While living at the Flying E, the eldest Lane children attended boarding school in Calgary. The family moved to Calgary in 1897 to more easily accommodate the education of their growing family of six, E.S. Lane, "A Brief Sketch," 15.

54. *Leaves from the Medicine Tree*, 494; Herbert Sheppard, *Just About Nothing* (Calgary: McAra Printing, 1977), 73; Bassano History Book Club, *Best in the West by a Damsite, 1900–1940* (Calgary: D.W. Friesen & Sons Ltd., 1974), 318.
55. Bert Sheppard worked for Lane in the 1920s and was one of the men who turned his experience on the Bar U training ground into a successful cattle business of his own. Nearly 80 years later, Sheppard paid tribute to his former employer, "the only cowboy who ever owned the Bar U," by commissioning a 3.5-meter bronze statue of Lane to be sculpted, *Calgary Herald*, 28 June 1997.
56. *High River Times*, 25 July 1912; *Leaves from the Medicine Tree*, 91, 135, 231.
57. Bassano History Book Club, *Best in the West*, 345–46.
58. Bassano History Book Club, *Best in the West*, 311–12.
59. Bassano History Book Club, *Best in the West*, 303, 356–57; Ken E. Liddell, *This is Alberta* (Toronto: Ryerson Press, 1952), 72–73. Stone remained closely connected to the Lane family, however. Roberts became associated with one of Lane's sons, Roy, who had established his own cattle business on some of his father's land near Bassano. Based primarily on friendship, the relationship was loosely constructed in a manner beneficial to both with Roberts generally wintering his herd with Lane.
60. *High River Times*, 17 October 1912, 5 December 1912, 30 December 1915.
61. *High River Times*, 30 November 1916; Breen, *The Canadian Prairie West,* 216–17.
62. Millar became the first manager of the Namaka farm, *High River Times*, 26 June 1912.
63. G. Lane, National Live Stock Association Address, Ottawa, February 1912, M652, Glenbow Archives. Lane represented the Western Stock Growers' Association and the Alberta Horse Breeders' Association.
64. Alan F.J. Artibise, "Exploring the North American West: A Comparative Urban Perspective," in *Cities and Urbanization: Canadian Historical Perspectives*, ed. Gilbert A. Stelter (Toronto: Copp Clark Pitman Ltd., 1990), 20.
65. *High River Times*, 30 May and 6 June 1912.
66. Guy Weadick, "Origin of the Calgary Stampede," *Alberta Historical Review*, 14, no. 4 (Autumn 1966): 20–21; Chris J. Christianson, *Early Rangemen* (Lethbridge: Southern Printing Co., 1973), 63–64; Tom Ward, *Cowtown: An Album of Early Calgary* (Calgary: McClelland & Stewart West Ltd., 1975), 478; James Gray, *A Brand of Its Own: The 100 Year History of the Calgary Exhibition and Stampede* (Saskatoon:Western Producer Prairie Books, 1985), 36–37.
67. *High River Times*, 27 July 1911 and 23 November 1911.
68. *High River Times*, 18 September 1919; 6 April 1920. Lane was instrumental in another, less well-known ranch purchase by a member of the nobility, the 5th Earl of Minto. Lord Minto had served as an aide de camp to the Governor General of Canada in 1918–19, and his father, the 4th Earl of Minto, had been Governor General from 1898 to 1904. In November 1921, Lane bought the Two Dot Ranch, near Nanton, Alberta, on behalf of the 5th Earl of Minto. The following month, Lord Minto bought one of Lane's Percheron mares and the stallion, Perfection, which had won three

Canadian championships that year, to establish his ranch as a purebred stock operation. Lane also provided Lord Minto with the service of one of his own ranch managers, Thomas Geddles. Lane had similarly accommodated the Prince of Wales, allowing Thomas Carlyle, his manager of the Bar U, to become the manager of the E.P. Ranch. *High River Times*, 13 November 1921, 11 December 1921, 22 January 1922, and 7 October 1922.

69. *High River Times*, 9 September, 21 September, and 23 September 1922. Sir Roderick and Lady Jones, traveling with the Imperial press party, spent a short holiday at the Bar U as Lane's guests. Lady Mountstephen, Mr. and Mrs. Robert Reaford, and Mrs. Meighen traveled from Montreal on the private CPR car 'Hochelaga' to the Bar U, and C.A. Bogert, general manager of the Dominion Bank, and a party of directors and other bank officials, spent the day as Lane's guests; Prince Fuishimi of Japan was a guest in 1918. Later, the Duke and Duchess of Devonshire visited the Bar U when the former served as Governor General of Canada. E.S. Lane, "A Brief Sketch," 19.
70. See various articles on this issue: *High River Times*, 3 January and 3 February 1910, 29 August 1912, and 3 May 1917.
71. A.E. Cross Papers, M1543, F 594, Calgary Glenbow-Alberta Institute Archives. Various individuals served as president of the company, including Lane in 1919. With the information at hand, I am unable to say how long Lane held this position.
72. Max Foran, *Calgary: An Illustrated History* (Toronto: James Lorimer & Company and the National Museum of Man, 1978), 120–23.
73. *High River Times*, 6 April 1911.
74. L.G. Thomas, *The Liberal Party in Alberta: A History of Politics in the Province of Alberta, 1905–1921* (Toronto: University of Toronto Press, 1959), 138.
75. *High River Times*, 3 April 1913; Oetelaar, "George Lane's Vision of Development," 30–31. It should be noted that no previously published work on Lane has made reference to his move into politics.
76. *Calgary Herald*, 8 April and 15 April 1913. One article claimed that, in order to elect Lane, local Liberals were getting ranch workers intoxicated; another, which appeared as an 'official bulletin' from Ottawa, stated local settlers were protesting that Lane was 'hogging' land fit for settlement.
77. *Calgary Herald*, 18 April 1913.
78. Thomas, *The Liberal Party in Alberta*, 144; *A Report on Alberta Elections 1905–1982* (Edmonton: Office of the Chief Electoral Officer, 1983), 25, 176; *High River Times*, 29 May 1913.
79. *High River Times*, 8 November 1917.
80. *Calgary Herald*, 17 November 1917.
81. Breen, *The Canadian Prairie West*, 30.

Tenderfoot to Rider: Learning 'Cowboying' on the Canadian Ranching Frontier During the 1880s

1. This account of Bob Newbolt's arrival and early life in Alberta is based on the work of Angus McKinnon, who interviewed the Newbolts at the Bowchase Ranch in the early 1950s. The notes he made were put away at the Glenbow until the couple had both died, and then they were written up and published in the *Canadian Cattlemen*: Angus McKinnon, "Bob Newbolt, Pioneer of 1884," *Canadian Cattlemen*, 23 (February 1960): 10ff. References used in this article are to the manuscript version at the Glenbow.
2. Thomas Bland Strange, *Gunner Jingo's Jubilee* (London: Remington, 1893); Edward Brado, *Cattle Kingdom: Early Ranching in Alberta* (Vancouver: Douglas and McIntyre, 1984), 126–36; and Patrick A. Dunae, *Gentlemen Emigrants: From the British Public Schools to the Canadian Frontier* (Vancouver: Douglas and McIntyre, 1981), 99–101.
3. Glenbow M2487, "Bob Newbolt," 5 (hereafter Newbolt).
4. Newbolt, 8.
5. Newbolt, 8.
6. My review essay, published in 1994, is already dated. See Simon M. Evans, "Review Essay: Some Research on the Canadian Ranching Frontier," *Prairie Forum*, 19 (Spring 1994): 101–10. Important new books include: Hugh A. Dempsey, *The Golden Age of the Canadian Cowboy* (Saskatoon: Fifth House, 1995); Sherm Ewing, *The Ranch* (Missoula: Mountain Press, 1995); Terry G. Jordan, *North American Cattle-Ranching Frontiers* (Albuquerque: University of New Mexico Press, 1993); Richard Slatta, *The Cowboy Encyclopedia* (Santa Barbara: ABC-CLIO, 1994); Barry Potyondi, *In the Palliser Triangle* (Calgary: Purich, 1995); and Richard W. Slatta, *Comparing Cowboys and Frontiers* (Norman: University of Oklahoma Press, 1997). See "Selected Bibliography" for more comments.
7. Jordan, *Ranching Frontiers*, 313.
8. David H. Breen, *The Canadian Prairie West and the Ranching Frontier, 1874–1924* (University of Toronto Press, 1983); Breen built on the work of Lewis G. Thomas: see Patrick Dunae, ed., *Ranchers Legacy: Alberta Essays by Lewis G. Thomas* (Edmonton: University of Alberta Press, 1986).
9. Simon M. Evans, "Some Observations on the Labour Force of the Canadian Ranching Frontier during its Golden Age, 1882–1901," *Great Plains Quarterly*, 15, no. 1 (Winter 1995): 3–18.
10. For example, the stories of more than 20 young Britons were examined. As there were 243 range workers from the United Kingdom recorded in 1891, this amounts to a 8.2% sample.
11. This phrase was used as the title of a delightful book which contains a chapter on ranching: Ronald Rees, *New and Naked Land: Making the Prairies Home* (Saskatoon: Western Producer Books, 1988).
12. Breen, *The Canadian Prairie West*, 8–14; and for a perspective from the American side of the border, Robert H. Fletcher, *Free Grass to Fences* (New York: University Publishers, 1960).

13. Gerald C. Berry, *The Whoop-Up Trail* (Edmonton: Applied Arts, 1953); and Peter Darby, "From Riverboat to Rail Line: Circulation Patterns in the Canadian West during the Last Quarter of the Nineteenth Century," in L.A. Rosenvall and S.M. Evans, eds., *Essays on the Historical Geography of the Canadian West* (Calgary: University of Calgary Geography Department, 1987).
14. *Statement Showing the Number of Cattle Entering Alberta, 1880–1885*, Public Archives of Canada, Department of Interior, RG 15, f.11007; and Canada, *Sessional Papers,* 1904, XXXVIII, Vol. B, Census of Canada, 1901,II,262. For an overall assessment see Simon M. Evans, "Stocking the Canadian Range," *Alberta History*, 26, no. 3 (Summer 1978): 1–8.
15. Simon M. Evans, "The Origins of Ranching in Western Canada: American Diffusion or Victorian Transplant?" *Great Plains Quarterly*, 3, no. 2 (Spring 1983): 83.
16. Background information on Hills' family was obtained from correspondence and an interview with his niece, Mrs. Geraldine Lamaison. Mrs. Lamaison was responsible for returning Ted Hills' letters home to Alberta when she inherited them. She sent them first to her sister-in-law, Mrs. Jean Matthews, who donated them to the Glenbow in 1989. See also High River Pioneers' and Old Timers' Association, *Leaves from the Medicine Tree* (Lethbridge: Lethbridge Herald, 1960), 75.
17. Glenbow Archives, M7988, Edward F.J. Hills letters, 1883–1885. (Hereafter this collection will be referred to as Hills and the particular letter will be identified by number and date.)
18. Hills, letter 42, 10 May 1885.
19. The remuda was the name given to the herd of replacement horses from which cowboys drew their mounts twice a day. The less familiar word 'cavvy,' derived from the Spanish *caballada*, was often used in this sense on the northern ranges. See Slatta, *The Cowboy Encyclopedia* (Santa Barbara: ABC–CLIO, 1994), 310; and Ramon F. Adams, *Western Words: A Dictionary of the Range, Cow Camp and Trail* (Norman: University of Oklahoma Press, 1944).
20. Some of his earlier letters refer to riding and jumping in the "big meadow" at home with his brother Bob. See Hills, letter 12, 30 August 1883; while in Toronto, the tedious work of learning shorthand was made easier by regular riding excursions. Hills, letter 13, 14 September 1883.
21. Hills, letter 44, 8 June 1885.
22. "Most cowhands are for ever practicing the art of roping like they planned to win the world championship next week ... roping is an occupational disease with them." Fred Gibson, *Cowhand: The Story of a Working Cowboy* (College Station: Texas A & M University Press, 1953), 48.
23. Hills, letter 43, 25 May 1885.
24. Interview with Ted Hills' niece, Mrs. Geraldine Lamaison, Pulborough, Sussex, May 1995.
25. As Dempsey points out, "Many (young Englishmen) were educated and remained in the districts for the rest of their lives, leaving behind a record of their experiences." Dempsey, *Golden Age*, 39. In this paper the emphasis is on those who made good in the Canadian West. There were some members of the contingent of privileged emigrants who have been lampooned, quite rightly, as 'chinless wimps' arrogant in their denigration of things colonial.

The activities of these 'remittance men' have given rise to much myth and many apocryphal stories which detract from the real achievements of those who contributed much to the young province. See, for example, the following stereotypical comments in a recent publication: "cowboys were amazed at how little physical work was done by many of them, especially the British contingent," and "the spectacle of grown men in packs pointlessly pursuing hounds and coyotes through the coulees must have amused western hands." Ted Byfield, ed., *The Great West Before 1900* (Edmonton: United Western Communications, 1991), 202–03. Nobody hated these black sheep more than their British contemporaries. See Claude Gardiner, *Letters from an English Rancher* (Calgary: Glenbow, 1988), 40–41; and Mary E. Inderwick, "A Lady and her Ranch," *Alberta History*, 15 (Autumn 1967): 2.

26. Later, Professor Church edited and published the letters he received from his sons. Alfred J. Church, *Making a Start in Canada: Letters from Two Young Emigrants* (London: Seeley, 1889). Herbert also wrote a book of reminiscences some twenty years after his pioneering sojourn along Sheep Creek. H.E. Church, *An Emigrant in the Canadian North West* (London: Methuen, 1929).
27. Gardiner, *Letters from an English Rancher.*
28. Glenbow Archives, M480, "Hatfield Diary."
29. The 1891 census indicates that out of ten men employed on the range, four had been born in Britain, four in Canada, and the remaining two in the United States. See Evans, "Some Observations on the Labour Force of the Canadian Ranching Frontier during its Golden Age, 1882–1901," *Great Plains Quarterly*, 15, no. 1 (Winter 1995), 3–18.
30. Lachlin McKinnon, *Lachlin McKinnon, Pioneer, 1865–1948* (Calgary: McAra, 1956); and J. Angus McKinnon, *The Bow River Range* (Calgary: McAra, 1974).
31. See Dempsey, *Canadian Cowboy*, 123–24; and J.R. Weston, "Charlie Miller of the Bar U," *Canadian Cattlemen*, 10, no. 2 (September 1947). Note that Weston spelt his subject's name wrong.
32. The next few paragraphs owe much to the patient research of Barbara Holliday of Parks Canada. See Barbara Holliday, "Herb Millar of the Bar U," *Alberta History*, 44, no. 4 (Autumn 1996): 15–21.
33. Harold W. Riley, "Herbert William (Herb) Millar: Pioneer Ranchman," *Canadian Cattlemen*, 4, no. 4 (March 1942): 164–65.
34. David Dary, *Cowboy Culture: A Saga of Five Centuries* (New York: Knopf, 1981), 276. William Savage comments: "Cowboying required no particular skills beyond the initial ability to sit a horse and pay attention. The State of Texas has made much of the superiority of its native sons in performing the mundane job of cowpunching, but a multitude of frail and pampered easterners, Britons and Frenchmen and others learned to ride and rope in short order and with equal proficiency. The work was simply more tiring than heroic, more boring than romantic." William W. Savage, *Cowboy Life: Deconstructing an American Myth* (Denver: University Press of Colorado, 1993), 5.
35. Philip Ashton Rollins, *The Cowboy: His Character, His Equipment and His Part in the Development of the West* (New York: Scribner, 1922), 23; Edward Charles Abbott, *We Pointed Them North: Recollections of a Cowpuncher* (Norman: University of Oklahoma Press, 1939), 194; and Frank Collinson, *Life in the Saddle* (Norman: University of Oklahoma Press, 1963).

36. Frederick William Ings, *Before the Fences: Tales from the Midway Ranch* (Calgary: McAra Printing, 1980), 25.
37. J. Frank Dobie, *Cow People* (Boston: Little Brown, 1964), 32. Dobie wrote of Ab Blocker, "he savvies the cow—cow psychology, cow anatomy, cow dietetic—cow nature in general and cow nature in particular."
38. Brado, *Cattle Kingdom*, 37; and *Leaves from the Medicine Tree*, 21–23.
39. Another ex-Hudson Bay man was the manager of the Quorn Ranch, the lean Irishman, John T. Barter, who Ted Hills thought so much of.
40. Glenbow Archives, M337, J.L. Douglas, "Journal of Four Months Holiday to Canada and the USA, August to December, 1886."
41. Alex Johnston, *Cowboy Politics: The Western Stock Growers' Association and its Predecessors* (Calgary: Western Stocker Growers, 1972), appendix.
42. Our knowledge of this remarkable man and the company he served has been much enhanced by the work of business historian Henry Klassen. See Henry C. Klassen, "The Conrads in the Alberta Cattle Business, 1875–1911," *Agricultural History*, 64, no. 3 (1990).
43. *Leaves from the Medicine Tree*, 173–75.
44. Dempsey, *Canadian Cowboy*, 60.
45. *Leaves from the Medicine Tree*, 44–47.
46. Phil Weinard, "Gives Vivid Picture of Early Days and Hardships," *Canadian Cattlemen*, 3, no. 3 (December 1940): 463.
47. A.B. McCullough, "Eastern Capital, Government Purchases and the Development of Canadian Ranching," *Prairie Forum*, 22, no. 2 (Fall 1997): 213–36.
48. See Elofson's paper for a forceful presentation of this point of view. Warren M. Elofson, "Adapting to the Frontier Environment: The Ranching Industry in Western Canada, 1881–1914," *Canadian Papers in Rural History*, vol. 8, ed. Donald H. Akenson (Gananoque, ON: Langdale Press, 1996), 307–27.
49. "A Pioneer Stockman," *Farm and Ranch Review* (20 September 1922).
50. For a good account of this problematic relationship see, Brado, *Cattle Kingdom*, 81–104.
51. Simon M. Evans, "Some Observations on the Labour Force of the Canadian Ranching Frontier During its Golden Age, 1882–1901," *Great Plains Quarterly*, 15, no. 1 (Winter 1995), 3–18.
52. His father was Joseph William Lane from Kentucky, and his mother, Julia Pidgeon Lane, was of Quaker stock from Pennsylvania. Glenbow Archives M651, Elizabeth Sexsmith Lane, "A Brief Sketch of Memories of my Family," June 1945; and C.I. Ritchie, "George Lane: One of the Big Four," *Canadian Cattlemen*, 3, no. 2 (September 1940): 415.
53. *High River Times*, 30 March 1916.
54. See *Leaves from the Medicine Tree*, 66, for the connection; and Ernest Staples Osgood, *The Day of the Cattleman* (University of Chicago Press, 1929), 224–26, for the technology.
55. Norman Rankin, "The Boss of the Bar U," *Canadian Monthly* (March 1911).
56. Hills, letter 46, 1 September 1885.
57. Cochrane and Area Historical Society, *Big Hill Country* (Calgary: Friesen, 1977), 318. Johnson was a friend and hunting companion of Owen Wister, who may well have used his knowledge of Johnson's life to help him create the central character of *The Virginian*, arguably the most famous western ever written.

58. Glenbow Archives, M2388, "Stair Ranch Letterbook," 350.
59. Dona B. Ernst, "The Sundance Kid in Alberta," *Alberta History*, 42, no. 4 (Autumn 1994): 10–15.
60. "W.D. Kerfoot, by Archie Kerfoot, " in *Big Hill Country*, 390.
61. See "Frank White's Diary, November 1882," reprinted in *Canadian Cattlemen* from December 1945 to March 1950.
62. "W.D. Kerfoot, by Archie Kerfoot, " in *Big Hill Country*, 390.
63. See Simon M. Evans, "Stocking the Canadian Range," *Alberta History*, 26, no. 3 (Summer 1978), 1–8.
64. John R. Craig, *Ranching with Lords and Commons* (Toronto: William Briggs, 1903), 105.
65. See McCullough, "Eastern Capital," for discussion of Cochrane, Stimson and McEachran.
66. Simon M. Evans, "American Cattlemen on the Canadian Range, 1874–1914," *Prairie Forum*, 4, no. 1 (1979): 121–35.
67. Based on my observations of the history of the Canadian range, I tend to agree with Dan Flores when he suggests that the pressures of the market place were as important as adaptations to environment. See Dan Flores, "Review of *North American Cattle Ranching Frontiers*," in *Journal of Historical Geography*, 20 (October 1994): 481.

The Untamed Canadian Ranching Frontier, 1874-1914

1. This point of view is best expressed by David Breen in his seminal work on the Canadian ranching frontier. David H. Breen, *The Canadian Prairie West and the Ranching Frontier, 1874–1924* (Toronto: University of Toronto Press, 1983). For quotations and detail, see p. 82.
2. Stanley D. Hanson, "Policing the International Boundary Area in Saskatchewan, 1890–1910," *Saskatchewan History*, 19, no. 2 (Spring 1966), 61–73.
3. T. Thorner, "The Not-So-Peaceable Kingdom—Crime and Criminal Justice in Frontier Calgary," in *Frontier Calgary: Town, City, and Region 1875–1914*, eds. Anthony W. Rasporich and Henry C. Klassen (Calgary: McClelland and Stewart West, 1975), 100–13.
4. Louis Knafla, "Violence on the Western Canadian Frontier: A Historical Perspective," in *Violence in Canada: Sociopolitical Perspectives*, ed. J.I. Ross (Oxford: Oxford University Press, 1995), 10–39.
5. Hugh A. Dempsey, *The Golden Age of the Canadian Cowboy: An Illustrated History* (Saskatoon: Fifth House, 1995), 104.
6. Glenbow Museum, "Year of the Cowboy" display, 26 September 1997.
7. M. Laviolette, "The Tame West," *Calgary Magazine* (July 1988), 8–9, 21, 47.
8. W. Beahen and S. Horrall, *Red Coats on the Prairies: The North-West Mounted Police, 1886–1900* (Regina: Centax/Printwest, 1998). The authors set out to demonstrate how, albeit with difficulty, the Mounties transformed the West and helped to turn it into a secure and stable society.
9. See, for instance, Breen, *The Canadian Prairie West*, 86.
10. Along with the evidence enlisted here the reader might consult Thorner's article cited in note 3 above.

11. Canada, *Sessional Papers,* 36, 12 (1902), n. 28, 1–2.
12. Ibid.
13. I am indebted to a former undergraduate student, Stanley Bailey, for bringing this to my attention.
14. R.C. Macleod, *The NWMP and Law Enforcement, 1873–1905* (Toronto: University of Toronto Press, 1976), 22ff.
15. See S.M. Evans, "American Cattlemen on the Canadian Range," *Prairie Forum*, 4, no. 1 (1979), 121–35.
16. Breen stresses the importance of Old World values in strengthening respect for the law; *The Canadian Prairie West*, 86. I do not disagree but I would argue that these values began to erode almost immediately on the frontier. Thorner makes this point succinctly in his article, "The Not-So-Peaceable Kingdom," 113.
17. James H. Gray, *Red Lights on the Prairies* (Toronto: Macmillan, 1973); and P. Voisey, *Vulcan: The Making of a Prairie Community* (Toronto: University of Toronto Press, 1988), 26, 162, 163.
18. "Atrocities of Outlaw Band in Assiniboia," *Calgary Herald*, 8 August 1904; Donna B. Ernst, "The Sundance Kid in Alberta," *Alberta History*, 42, no. 4 (Autumn 1994): 14; and Frank W. Anderson, *Sheriffs and Outlaws of Western Canada* (Calgary: Frontier Publishers, 1973), 53–56.
19. On 22 June 1900 the *Macleod Gazette* reported that "Jones and Nelson … have stolen over 300 head of horses and thousands of cattle from the northern ranges, all of which were driven into Canada and disposed of" ("Stock Notes").
20. Anderson, *Sheriffs and Outlaws of the Canadian West*, 53.
21. "Lynched in Montana," *Macleod Gazette*, 11 April 1885. For other such lynchings south of the border see, "Lynched in Helena," *Macleod Gazette*, 21 February 1885; and L.V. Kelly, *The Range Men*, 75th anniversary ed. (High River: Willow Creek Publishing, 1988), 75–76.
22. L. V. Kelly, *The Range Men*, 176; Canada, *Sessional Papers,* 37:11 (1904), n. 28, 58: Annual Report for E Division, 30 November 1903.
23. L. V. Kelly, *The Range Men*, 73.
24. Canada, *Sessional Papers,* 31:11 (1897), n. 15, 160: Annual Report for E Division, 1 December 1896.
25. M. Terrill, "Medicine Hat Pioneer, William Mitchell, 1878–1946," *Canadian Cattlemen*, 9, no. 3 (December 1946): 150.
26. *The Western Law Reporter*, 12 (1910): 562. See also L.A. Knafla, "Violence on the Western Canadian Frontier: A Historical Perspective," in *Violence in Canada: Sociopolitical Perspectives*, 22.
27. Terrill, "Medicine Hat Pioneer, William Mitchell," 150.
28. Breen, *The Canadian Prairie West*, 52.
29. "On Conviction," *Macleod Gazette*, 7 July 1893.
30. H. Maguire, "Cowboy Tales of 1896," *Canadian Cattlemen*, 15, no. 8 (August 1952): 39.
31. Canada, *Sessional Papers,* 41:11 (1906, 07), n. 28, 62: Annual Report for K Division, 1 October 1906.
32. Ibid.
33. Canada, *Sessional Papers,* 31:11 (1897) n. 15, P. 9: Annual Report of the Commissioner, 10 December 1896.
34. R. Burton Deane, *Mounted Police Life in Canada: A Record of Thirty-one Years' Service* (London: Cassell, 1916), 166.

35. Ibid.
36. Deane, *Mounted Police Life in Canada*, 93, 154ff; Public Archives of Canada, RG18 A1, N.W.M.P. papers, bx. 2, file 60, v. 242, f. 25, pt. 1; file 61, v. 243, f. 25, pt. 2; file 62, v. 261, f. 823; "American Cattle," *Medicine Hat Weekly News*, 3 December 1896; "Stray American Cattle," *Lethbridge News*, 7 September 1887.
37. H.C. Klassen, "The Conrads in the Alberta Cattle Business, 1875–1911," *Agricultural History*, 64 (Summer 1990): 31–59.
38. Canada, *Sessional Papers,* 33:12 (1899), n. 15, 3: Annual Report of the Commissioner, 20 December 1898.
39. Ibid.
40. Canada, *Sessional Papers,* 31:11 (1897) n. 15, P. 9: Annual Report of the Commissioner, 10 December 1896.
41. Canada, *Sessional Papers,* 32:12 (1898), n. 15, 2: Annual Report of the Commissioner, 17 December 1897.
42. Canada, *Sessional Papers,* 38:11 (1904), n. 28, 59: Annual Report for E Division, 30 November 1903.
43. Canada, *Sessional Papers,* 32:12 (1898), n. 15, 4: Annual Report of the Commissioner, 17 December 1897.
44. Canada, *Sessional Papers,* 38:11 (1904), n. 28, 6–7: Annual Report of the Commissioner, 25 January 1904.
45. Canada, *Sessional Papers,* 29:11 (1896), n. 15, 3: Annual Report of the Commissioner, 18 December 1895.
46. Canada, *Sessional Papers,* 38:11 (1904), n. 28, 59: Annual Report for E Division, 30 November 1903.
47. Anderson, *Sheriffs and Outlaws*, 54.
48. Knafla, "Violence on the Western Canadian Frontier," 22.
49. Grant MacEwan, *John Ware's Cow Country* (Edmonton: Institute of Applied Arts Ltd., 1960), 75.
50. Glenbow Archives, Stair Ranch Letter Book, M2388, 86: 29 September 1890. In September 1890 D.H. Andrews acknowledged receipt of a cheque for $440.00 for the sale of 17 steers from a rancher in Montana named Thomas Clary. He offered thanks and help for Clary on the Canadian side of the border.
51. "Range Horses," *Macleod Gazette*, 23 March 1886; "Horse Thief Captured," *Macleod Gazette*, 25 May 1886; "A Syndicate of Horse Thieves," *Macleod Gazette*, 4 April 1902.
52. G. Shepherd, "Tom Whitney of Maple Creek," *Canadian Cattlemen*, 4, no. 4 (March 1942): 156.
53. F.W. Godsall, "Old Times," *Alberta Historical Review*, 12, no. 4 (Autumn 1964): 19.
54. "All over the Range," *Macleod Gazette*, 9 November 1886.
55. Kelly, *The Range Men*, 78, 89, 108, 194.
56. Glenbow Archives, M234, Cochrane Ranche Letter Book, Diary, p. 16: 19 May 1885; ibid., 22 May 1885.
57. H.F. Lawrence, "Early Days in the Chinook Belt," *Alberta Historical Review*, 13, no. 1 (Winter 1965): 13.
58. W.R. "Bob" Newbolt, "Memoirs of the Bowchase Ranch," *Alberta History*, 32, no. 4 (Autumn 1984): 1–10.
59. H. Maguire, "Shaunavon Tales," *Canadian Cattlemen*, 13, no. 2 (February 1950): 47.

60. John G. Donkin, *Trooper and Redskin in the Far Northwest: Recollections of Life in the North-West Mounted Police, Canada, 1884–1888* (Toronto: Coles, 1973), 222.
61. "Cowboy Runs Amuck," *Macleod Gazette*, 15 July 1904.
62. "Cowboy Defies Mounted Police and is Shot," *Calgary Herald*, 13 July 1904.
63. T. Thorner, "The Not So Peaceable Kingdom," University of Calgary M.A. thesis, 1973, 65. The Prince Albert stage was also held up that summer; Donkin, *Trooper and Redskin*, 229–30.
64. H.F. Lawrence, "Early Days in the Chinook Belt," 17.
65. "A Fatal Quarrel," *Macleod Gazette*, 15 July 1885.
66. Canada, *Sessional Papers,* 25:10 (1892), n. 15: Annual Report for C Division, 30 November 1891; and Anderson, *Sheriffs and Outlaws*, 65–66.
67. Canada, *Sessional Papers,* 29:11 (1896), n. 15, 41: Annual Report for Macleod District, 30 November 1895.
68. Canada, *Sessional Papers,* 33:11 (1897), n. 15, 136: Annual Report for E Division, 1 December 1896.
69. "Dave Akers," *Macleod Gazette*, 2 March 1894.
70. Kelly, *The Range Men*, 162; see also "Murder," *Macleod Gazette*, 12 February 1891.
71. Canada, Sessional papers, 29:11 (1896), n. 15, p 93: Annual Report for K Division, 1 December 1895; and Kelly, *The Range Men*, 149.
72. "Train Robbery," *Macleod Gazette*, 26 October 1886; "A Lively Chase," *Macleod Gazette*, 11 October 1901; "Trainmen Tell Story of Hold Up on CPR," *Calgary Herald*, 13 September 1904; "How Road Agents Robbed an Express," *Calgary Herald*, 4 August 1904.
73. Kelly, *The Range Men*, 3.
74. Kelly, *The Range Men*, 134. This episode is also recounted in Dempsey, *The Golden Age of the Canadian Cowboy*, 115–16.
75. Ernst, "The Sundance Kid in Alberta," 14.
76. Newbolt, "Memories of Bowchase Ranch," 4.
77. G. Shepherd, "Tom Whitney of Maple Creek," *Canadian Cattlemen*, 4, no. 4 (March 1942): 156.
78. "A Big Drunk," *Macleod Gazette*, 16 February 1886. For other reports of this nature see "Rioting and Drunkeness," *Macleod Gazette*, 19 September 1884; "Macleod," *Calgary Tribune*, 11 November 1885; "Police News," *Calgary Herald*, 21 October 1902 and following footnote.
79. "The Six Shooter Again is Called in to Settle a Dispute," *Macleod Gazette*, 21 July 1885.
80. "Veteran Mountie Tells of Adventures in West," *Albertan*, 23 April 1942.
81. "Arrest of Indian Cattle-Killers," *Macleod Gazette*, 3 February 1883.
82. Canada, *Sessional Papers,* 25:10 (1892), n. 15, 70–71: Annual Report for K Division, 1 December 1891; see also, T.L. Chapman, "Crime and Justice in Medicine Hat, 1883–1905," *Alberta History*, 39, no. 2 (Spring 1991): 17–24.
83. John Jennings, "The Plains Indians and the Law," in *Men in Scarlet*, ed. Hugh A. Dempsey (Calgary: McClelland and Stewart West, 1975), 50–65; and "Policemen and Poachers," in *Frontier Calgary*, 87–99.
84. "Indians Shot," *Macleod Gazette*, 30 August 1887.
85. There are many incidents reported in the papers: see, for instance, "Bullets Flew Near Cardston," *Macleod Gazette*, 23 October 1903.

86. See, for instance, "Shot Him," *Macleod Gazette*, 11 January 1888; "Shot and Knifed," *Macleod Gazette*, 10 March 1893.
87. "Kooteni Indians," *Macleod Gazette*, 4 April 1888.
88. "Charcoal," *Macleod Gazette*, 30 October 1896; "Charcoal Adds Another Victim to his List," *Macleod Gazette*, 13 November 1896; "Charcoal on the Gallows," *Macleod Gazette*, 19 March 1897; and Anderson, *Sheriffs and Outlaws*, 49–51.
89. "Local Notes," *Macleod Gazette*, 22 November 1895; "Trouble in the North," *Macleod Gazette*, 4 June 1897.
90. "Foul Murder of Land-seeker," *Calgary Herald*, 4 September 1903.
91. Macleod, *The NWMP*, 136.
92. Kelly, *The Range Men*, 111–12; "In Town and Out," *Macleod Gazette*, 4 September 1882; "The Whiskey Traffic," *Macleod Gazette*, 7 December 1886; "Seized Forty Gallons," *Macleod Gazette*, 20 August 1891.
93. Canada, *Sessional Papers,* 22:13 (1889), n. 17, 16: Annual Report of the Commissioner, 10 Dec. 1888.
94. Kelly, *The Range Men*, 111.
95. Canada, *Sessional Papers,* 31:11 (1897), n. 15, 2: Annual Report of the Commissioner, 10 December 1896.
96. Canada, *Sessional Papers,* 22:13 (1889), n. 17, 16: Annual Report of the Commissioner, 10 December 1888.
97. Macleod, *The NWMP*, 134–36; Beahen and Horrall, *Red Coats on the Prairies*, 259–60; "Sent Down," *Macleod Gazette*, 12 April 1887; "Three Mounted Police Receive Stiff Sentences," *Calgary Herald*, 4 January 1904.
98. "The West of Edward Maunsell," pt. 1, ed. H.A. Dempsey, *Alberta History*, 34, no. 4 (Autumn 1986): 2–4.
99. As stated above, Thomas Thorner also provides evidence of prostitution and other crimes in his article "The Not so Peaceable Kingdom." See also Gray, *Red Lights on the Prairies.*
100. For prostitution and brawling on the farming frontier see, Voisey, *Vulcan*, 162–63.
101. Dr. Louis A. Knafla at the University of Calgary, 12 January 1999.

A Century of Ranching at the Rocking P and Bar S

1. Interviews by the author with Ernest Blades, 1 May 1991, 19 August 1997, 27 August 1997; interview by the author with Mac and Rennie Blades, 19 August 1997; interview by the author with George Chattaway, 1 May 1991.
2. Provincial Archives of Alberta, accession no. 74.32, Homestead Records, file 535112, statement made by George Emerson, 6 June 1893; *Alberta Farmer*, 9 September 1920.
3. Homestead Records, file 535112, statement made by George Emerson, 6 June 1893; *Alberta Farmer*, 9 September 1920.
4. *Farm and Ranch Review*, 5 August 1919.
5. Provincial Archives of Alberta, accession no. 74.32, Homestead Records, file 535112, statement made by George Washington Emerson, 6 June 1893; *Alberta Farmer*, 9 September 1920. See also David H. Breen, *The Canadian Prairie West and the Ranching Frontier, 1874–1924* (Toronto: University of Toronto Press, 1983), 63; Simon M. Evans, *Prince Charming Goes*

West: The Story of the E.P. Ranch (Calgary: University of Calgary Press, 1993), 33–61; W.M. Elofson, "Adapting to the Frontier Environment: The Ranching Industry in Western Canada, 1881–1914," in *Canadian Papers in Rural History*, vol. 8, ed. Donald H. Akenson (Gananoque, ON: Langdale Press, 1992), 321–22.

6. Homestead Records, file 535112, statement made by George Emerson, 15 June 1900.
7. *High River Times*, 5 November 1953; High River Pioneers' and Old Timers' Association, *Leaves from the Medicine Tree* (Lethbridge: Lethbridge Herald, 1960), 20–23.
8. *High River Times*, 5 November 1953.
9. Homestead Records, file 643040, statement made by Roderick Riddle Macleay, 22 January 1906; *Alberta Farmer*, 10 September 1931.
10. Homestead Records, file 643009, Pekisko, 12 April 1906, Rod Macleay to P.G. Keyes.
11. Ernest Blades interviews, 1 May 1991, 19 August 1997, 27 August 1997.
12. Homestead Records, file 643009, statement made by Rod Macleay, 22 January 1906; file 636996, statement made by Alexander Macleay, 21 April 1907.
13. Ernest Blades interviews, 1 May 1991, 19 August 1997, 27 August 1997.
14. Interview by the author with George Chattaway, 1 May 1991.
15. Ernest Blades interviews, 1 May 1991, 19 August 1997, 27 August 1997.
16. *Alberta Farmer*, 10 September 1931.
17. *Mosquito Creek Roundup* (Nanton: Nanton and District Historical Society, 1975), 60; *Nanton News*, 20 March 1952.
18. *Alberta Farmer*, 10 September 1931.
19. Ibid.
20. Ernest Blades interviews, 1 May 1991, 19 August 1997, 27 August 1997.
21. Calgary Land Titles Office, land records, 1916–1919.
22. *Alberta Farmer*, 10 September 1931.
23. *Mosquito Creek Roundup*, 59.
24. Ernest Blades interviews, 1 May 1991, 19 August 1997, 27 August 1997; *Mosquito Creek Roundup*, 59.
25. *Alberta Farmer*, 10 September 1931.
26. T.B. Higginson, "Moira O'Neill in Alberta," *Alberta History*, 5 (Spring 1957): 22.
27. Homestead Records, file 364504, statement made by Walter C. Skrine, 29 May1893.
28. L.V. Kelly, *The Range Men*, 75th Anniversary ed. (High River: Willow Creek Publishing, 1988), 100.
29. Homestead Records, file 364504, statement made by Walter C. Skrine, 29 May 1893.
30. Breen, *The Canadian Prairie West and the Ranching Frontier*, 64.
31. Homestead Records, file 364504, Calgary, 29 August 1894, Amos Rowe to the Secretary, Dominion Lands Commission, Winnipeg.
32. Higginson, "Moira O'Neill in Alberta," 22.
33. Homestead Records, file 364504, statement made by Walter C. Skrine, 20 July 1898.
34. Homestead Records, file 364504, statement made by Walter C. Skrine, 20 July 1898; Calgary, 23 January 1900, Walter C. Skrine to J.R. Sutherland;

High River, 13 June 1902, Walter C. Skrine to the Secretary, Department of the Interior; Calgary, 26 August 1902, Walter C. Skrine to the Secretary, Department of the Interior.

35. Quoted in Higginson, "Moira O'Neill in Alberta," 24.
36. Homestead Records, file 364504, statement made by Walter C. Skrine, 20 July 1898.
37. *Farm and Ranch Review*, 5 August, 5 September 1919; Glenbow-Alberta Institute Archives, A.E. Cross Family Papers, M1543, box 13, file 93, Calgary, 11 May 1896, W.C. Skrine to A.E. Cross; box 19, file 141, Calgary, 7 September 1900, D.W. Gillies to A.E. Cross; box 56, file 445, High River, 18 April 1901, Walter C. Skrine to A.E. Cross; High River, 21 May 1901, Walter C. Skrine to A.E. Cross; High River, 8 August 1901, Walter C. Skrine to A.E. Cross.
38. Cross Family Papers, M1543, box 56, file 445, High River, 14 June 1901, Walter C. Skrine to A.E. Cross.
39. Homestead Records, file 364504, Calgary, 2 September 1902, Walter C. Skrine to the Secretary, Department of the Interior. As a letter from George Lane, spokesperson for the ranchers in this area, to the Commissioner of Dominion Lands indicates, there was a widespread perception that an era had ended. "As one of the cattlemen of southern Alberta, I would like to call your attention to the very uncertain position we are in at the present time with the herds. For the past two seasons (1902 & 1903) settlers were crowding into the country, and what used to be our summer range is practically gone now and our cattle are confined to the hills and range country along the east slope of the Rockies. You can easily understand a man, who has some hundreds or thousands of cattle, who can neither lease nor purchase land for grazing, being in a very uneasy state of mind as to what the final outcome of his business will be if settlement still continues to crowd in upon him. In the past cattle owned in the foothills, drifted out onto the plains for the summer and the grass in the hills was then saved for the winter months, but the large settlement along the Calgary and Edmonton Railway has cut off the summer range and cattle are now practically confined to the hills all the year round." National Archives of Canada, RG15, Canada, Department of the Interior, file 145330 (part 3), 1 June 1904, George Lane to J.W. Greenway, Commissioner of Dominion Lands.
40. Homestead Records, file 1525616, statement made by Peter Muirhead, 6 February 1908; *Mosquito Creek Roundup*, 57.
41. *Mosquito Creek Roundup*, 57.
42. Ibid.
43. Ibid.
44. Homestead Records, file 1525616, statement made by Peter Muirhead, 6 February 1908.
45. Ibid.
46. *Mosquito Creek Roundup*, 57-58.
47. *Mosquito Creek Roundup*, 58.
48. Cross Family Papers, M1543, box 58, file 460, Nanton, 1 May 1905, P. Muirhead to A.E. Cross; *Mosquito Creek Roundup*, 58.
49. *Mosquito Creek Roundup*, 58, 60.
50. Calgary Land Titles Office, land records, 1916–1921.
51. *Alberta Farmer*, 10 September 1931.

52. Ernest Blades interviews, 1 May 1991, 19 August 1997, 27 August 1997.
53. Ibid.
54. Ibid.
55. *Mosquito Creek Roundup*, 60.
56. Alberta Registries, Edmonton, Macleay Ranches Ltd. file.
57. Ibid.
58. Ibid.
59. Ibid.
60. Ibid.
61. Ernest Blades interviews, 1 May 1991, 19 August 1997, 27 August 1997.
62. Ibid.
63. Ibid.
64. Ibid.
65. Interviews by the author with Clay and Pat Chattaway, 18, 19 August 1997.
66. E.A. Howes, "An Artist in the Foothills," *Trail Riders of the Canadian Rockies, Bulletin No. 53* (February 1939): 14–15. Maxine Macleay's sketches included *Heading for the High Range*, *Seeking Strays*, *Blizzard on the Range*, *Ride 'em Cowboy*, and *Day Dreaming*. With her dexterity in handling pen and ink, she made sketches that in every way resembled the real thing.
67. *Alberta Farmer*, 10 September 1931.
68. *Mosquito Creek Roundup*, 60. See also Max Foran, "The Politics of Animal Health: The British Embargo on Canadian Cattle, 1892–1932," *Prairie Forum*, 23 (Spring 1998): 1–17.
69. *Alberta Farmer*, 10 September 1931.
70. Ernest Blades interviews, 1 May 1991, 19 August 1997, 27 August 1997.
71. Ibid.
72. Ibid.
73. Ibid.
74. Ibid.
75. Alberta Registries, Macleay Ranches Ltd file.
76. *Mosquito Creek Roundup*, 60.
77. Alberta Registries, Macleay Ranches Ltd. file.
78. Ibid.
79. *Nanton News*, 20 March 1952.
80. *Nanton News*, 5 November 1953.
81. Glenbow-Alberta Institute Archives, newspaper clipping files.
82. *Nanton News*, 5 November 1953.
83. Interview by the author with George Chattaway, 1 May 1991.
84. Alberta Registries, Rocking P Ranch Ltd. file; Bar S Ranch Ltd. file.
85. Alberta Registries, Rocking P Ranch Ltd. file.
86. Alberta Registries, Bar S Ranch Ltd. file.
87. Ernest Blades interviews, 1 May 1991, 19 August 1997, 27 August 1997.
88. Ibid.
89. Ibid.
90. Ibid.
91. Ibid.
92. Ibid.
93. Ibid.
94. Ibid.
95. Ibid.

96. Ibid.
97. Ibid.
98. Ibid.
99. Ibid.
100. Ibid.
101. Ibid.
102. George Chattaway interview, 1 May 1991.
103. *Alberta Beef*, April 1994.
104. George Chattaway interview, 1 May 1991.
105. Ibid.
106. Ibid.
107. Alberta Registries, Bar S Ranch Ltd. file.
108. George Chattaway interview, 1 May 1991.
109. Ibid.
110. *Alberta Beef*, April 1994.
111. George Chattaway interview, 1 May 1991; Interviews by the author with Clay and Pat Chattaway, 18, 19 August 1997.
112. Clay and Pat Chattaway interviews, 18, 19 August 1997.
113. Alberta Registries, Bar S Ranch Ltd. file.
114. Clay and Pat Chattaway interviews, 18, 19 August 1997.
115. Ibid.
116. Ibid.
117. Interview by the author with Mac and Renie Blades, 19 August 1997.
118. Ibid.
119. Ibid.
120. Ibid.
121. Ibid.
122. Ibid.
123. Ibid.
124. For a fascinating account of ranching in Alberta from the viewpoint of the cowboys in the late 19th and 20th centuries see Hugh A. Dempsey, *The Golden Age of the Canadian Cowboy: An Illustrated History* (Saskatoon: Fifth House Publishers, 1995).

The Impact of the Depression on Grazing Lease Policy in Alberta

1. For an excellent overview of the question of lease tenure in Alberta up to 1936, see John Proskie, "Trends in Security of Tenure of Grazing Lands in Western Canada," *Canadian Cattlemen* (June 1939). Proskie was an economist with the federal Department of Agriculture, Marketing Service.
2. Statistics on leasehold acreage and the number of lessees were given annually in "The Department of Interior Annual Reports" contained in Canada, *Sessional Papers*. The trend which saw the average size of leaseholds diminish and the number of lessees increase was to continue well into the early 1900s. For example, in 1889 there were 126 leases on 2.88 million acres. In 1902, 908 leases were held on 1.272 million acres.
3. David H. Breen, *The Canadian Prairie West and the Ranching Frontier, 1874-1924* (Toronto: University of Toronto Press, 1983). Breen's superb study deals extensively with leasehold issues during this period.

4. "Grazing Leases Discussed With Thurber Committee, History of Crown Leases," *The Western Stock Grower* (July 1997). The Thurber Committee was appointed by the Provincial Government in 1996 to study the crown lease question.
5. Canada, *Sessional Papers*, "Annual Report of the Department of the Interior," No. 15b, 1912, Appendix 12, Health of Animals Branch, "The Cattle Trade in Western Canada."
6. Canada, *Sessional Papers,* No. 28, 1911, "Annual Report of the North-West Mounted Police." Report of P.C.H. Primrose, Superintendent D Division, Fort Macleod. For an excellent account of this decline, see Simon Evans, "The End of the Open Range Era in Western Canada," *Prairie Forum*, 8, no. 1 (1983): 71–87.
7. Homestead entries reached a record 44,479 in 1911. In the same year it was reported that cropped land around Fort Macleod had increased by 20% in a single year. Grain shipments from Stavely and Claresholm in the heart of ranching country totalled over 1.5 million bushels in 1911.
8. A good example was Dorsey McDaniel who, with a number of well-known southern Alberta ranchers, ran several thousand head on unleased land in the Wintering Hills area near Hussar, Alberta. McDaniel's son believes the land upon which these cattle grazed was open and not under lease at all.
9. C.H. McKinnon, *Events of LK Ranch* (Calgary: Phoenix Press, 1979), 59. This is an excellent account of the history of one of Alberta's most enduring and successful livestock enterprises. Consisting mainly of detailed reminiscences, particularly those of family patriarch, Lachlan McKinnon, the narrative chronicles the evolutionary nature of ranching in Alberta.
10. Canada, *Sessional Papers,* No. 15b, 1912, "Annual Report of the Department of the Interior," Appendix 12, Health of Animals Branch, "The Cattle Trade in Western Canada."
11. For information on the Ranch Inquiry Commission, see Breen, *The Canadian Prairie West and the Ranching Frontier,* 188–94; for copy of the 1913 Grazing Regulations, see Glenbow, Cross Fonds Box 70, file folder 554.
12. In 1919 for example, the government issued relief to southern Alberta farmers in the form of groceries and feed. The year previous (1918), the federal and provincial governments together with the C.P.R. reached an arrangement by which feed was shipped to cattle at a 50% reduction. In the same year, under this arrangement, 182 hay-making outfits moved north while over 86,000 tons of hay moved south. Alberta, *Department of Agriculture, Annual Reports* (1918, 1919).
13. See "Regulations Governing Grazing Lands in the Provinces of Manitoba, Saskatchewan, Alberta, and the Peace River Tract in the Province of British Columbia." Established by Order in Council, 12 April 1922.
14. Cross Fonds, Box 118, file folder 955.
15. Certainly, the W.S.G.A. took the credit for the new amendments. Writing to the membership, W.S.G.A. President Dan Riley noted that, "Arrangements have now been made for securing 21 year closed leases to take the place of the 10 year lease now in force ... and was a result of several trips to Ottawa by your delegates and could not have been secured except through an agency such as your association, commanding as it does universal respect and confidence." Cross Fonds, Box 118, file folder 954, letter dated 5 May 1925.

16. Gross leasehold acreage had been steadily rising since the formation of the Province in 1905, partly as a result of farm abandonments after 1920 but mostly because of the increasing amount of marginal land being sought after for grazing purposes. 1.551 million acres were under lease in 1906; 1.737 million acres in 1910; 2.563 million acres in 1918; and 2.925 million acres in 1923.
17. "Regulations Governing the Leasing of Grazing Lands," O.C. 656-31, 18 June 1931.
18. Glenbow, Western Stock Growers Association Papers (hereafter cited as W.S.G.A. Papers) Box 2, file folder 11, "E.D. Hardwick, Chairman, Grazing and Taxation Committee of the W.S.G.A. to the Directors of the W.S.G.A., April 15, 1932."
19. At the time of the transfer of natural resources to the Province, the several long-term leases granted by the Dominion Government continued to operate as such. As late as 1936, 1,790 Dominion leases covered 2.029 million acres in comparison to 992 Provincial leases on 1.122 million acres. By the mid 1940s all long-term grazing leases in Alberta were under provincial control.
20. This is not to say the whole issue of taxation was not worrisome in this early period. In 1908 the Federal Inspector of Ranches blamed some of the ranchers' abandonment of their leases as being due to "the dread of a provincial tax." See Report of Albert Helmer, in Canada, *Sessional Papers,* Number 25 of 1908, "Annual Report of the Department of the Interior." In Breen, *The Canadian Prairie West and the Ranching Frontier,* 161, the author documents an incident whereby two homesteaders offered to sell their land to A.E. Cross, using as an inducement the fact that they could petition a school district which would then force him to pay school taxes.
21. The source of this statement was Albert Helmer, federal Supervisor of Grazing. See The Western Heritage Centre Library, C. Graham Anderson, Grazing Appraiser, Department of Lands and Mines, Province of Alberta in *Grazing Rates Report, Short Grass Area of Alberta*, compiled with the cooperation of the Short Grass Stock Growers' Association (1941), 71.
22. Cross Fonds, Box 114, file folder 918.
23. *We'll All Be Buried Down Here: The Prairie Dryland Disaster 1917–26*, ed. David C. Jones, Historical Society of Alberta, vol. 6 (Alberta Records Publication Board, 1986), 37–38. The farmer in question was giving evidence before the Board at Youngstown on 15 December 1921.
24. Alberta, *Department of Municipal Affairs Annual Report* (1921–29). Leases were generally located in areas designated for taxation purposes as Municipal or Improvement Districts.
25. Cross Fonds, Box 117, file folder 943, "A.E. Cross to George Hoadley, Minister of Agriculture, Province of Alberta, June 7, 1924."
26. W.S.G.A. Papers, Box 2, file folder 11. The resolution was passed at a meeting in Medicine Hat on 30 June 1928.
27. This crushing tariff exceeded the already burdensome Fordney-McCumber tariff of 1922 and amounted to a 30% levy on exported cattle to the United States. Shipments to the United States from Canada dropped from over 160,000 in 1929 to less than 10,000 in 1931. In Alberta the reductions were even more dramatic. From 27,650 in 1929, the number dropped to just 48 in 1931 and a year later no cattle left Alberta for the United States.

See *Canadian Cattlemen* (June 1938). According to the Alberta Department of Agriculture, prices immediately dropped after the imposition of the tariff by between $1.00-2.50 per cwt, followed by another decline a few months later of between $2.00-2.50 per cwt. See Alberta, *Department of Agriculture Annual Report* (1930).

28. Alberta, *Department of Agriculture Annual Report* (1930). Arrears on Dominion lease rentals alone amounted to $39,771.44 at the time of transfer of natural resource to the Provinces. See *Canadian Cattlemen* (June 1938).
29. F. Albert Rudd, "Production and Marketing of Beef Cattle from the Short Grass Plains Area of Canada" (Master's thesis, University of Alberta, 1935), 63.
30. L.B. Thomson, "Costs of Beef Production," *Canadian Cattlemen* (June 1938): 42. Thomson at the time of writing was Superintendent of the Experimental Station at Swift Current, but was referring to experiments undertaken at Manyberries during his tenure as Superintendent. The survey represented cattle numbers in excess of 50,000.
31. *Calgary Albertan*, 27 November 1933. The editorial gave a selling price of 2.5 cents per pound and a production cost of 6 cents per pound.
32. Canada, *Sessional Papers*, No. 25 of 1916 "Annual Report of the Department of the Interior," Report of the Inspector of Ranches. In his report for the year 1916, the Inspector wrote that "owing to the exceptional crop of 1915 the granting of leases for grazing purposes is getting more difficult to settle satisfactorily as much land that was heretofore looked upon as worthless from an agricultural standpoint is now being entered for that purpose." See *Sessional Papers*, number 25 of 1917, "Annual Report of the Department of the Interior."
33. The findings of this Board, entitled "Report and Recommendations of the Southern Alberta Survey Board," were published in *The Calgary Herald* on 6 February 1922. Generally, the Board was optimistic on the agricultural future of southern Alberta particularly if its extensive irrigation recommendations were implemented. That the Board was not really interested in the pivotal role of ranching in southern Alberta was evidenced by the words of one of the Board members. C.A. Magrath in a letter to A.E. Cross on 15 February 1922 responded to Cross's urging not to abolish the lease system by saying, "My view at the time was that a few million dollars would be invested in cattle with practically no addition to the population of the country." Cross Fonds, Box 114, file folder 918. Fortunately for the ranchers, the Board's recommendations were never implemented. A change of governments in Ottawa buried the issue and the stockmen were able to successfully advance their cause for longer closed leases.
34. Cross Fonds, Box 114, file folder 918, "A.E. Cross to C.A. Magrath, Member of the Southern Alberta Survey Board, March 7, 1922."
35. See Jones, *We'll All Be Buried Down Here*. Using contemporary documents, Jones graphically describes the impact of drought and floundering cash crop agriculture on the economic and social fabric of southern Alberta. One result was the increase in leasehold acreage by almost one third between 1918 and 1930.
36. S.E. Clarke, "Pasture Investigations in the Short Grass Plains of Saskatchewan and Alberta," *Scientific Agriculture,* 10, no.10 (June 1930): 731–49.

37. One has only to read the Sessional Papers during the period. Heavy emphasis was placed on crop experiments. In fact, all forage experimentation was discontinued during the First World War.
38. Clarke, "Pasture Investigations," 733.
39. Cross Fonds, Box 69, file folder 544, "A.E. Cross to W.J. Roche, Minister of the Interior, December 3, 1913." Cross was replying to a letter from Roche on 20 November 1913 asking him for his opinion on the new grazing regulations.
40. See S.E. Clarke, J.A. Campbell, and J.B. Campbell, *An Ecological and Grazing Capacity Study of the Native Grass Pastures in Southern Alberta, Saskatchewan and Manitoba*, Publication No. 738, Technical Bulletin 44, Department of Agriculture, Division of Forage Crops, Dominion, Experimental Station, Swift Current, Saskatchewan, 4; W.S.G.A. Papers, Box 1, file folder 9, Resolution passed at 31st Annual Conference, Calgary, 30 March 1927.
41. The station was located 18 miles south and 9 miles east of Manyberries, and comprised 18,000 acres typical of the 80,000 square miles of short grass country.
42. See Clarke, "Pasture Investigations." Clarke was the agrostologist at Manyberries at the time he wrote the article; also L.B. Thomson, Superintendent of Manyberries Research Station, Address to Canadian Society of Animal Production, Eighth Annual Meeting, June 1936, "Carrying Capacities and Beef Production," in *Farm and Ranch Review* (August 1936): 3.
43. Of particular interest in the area of forage and regrassing was the nutritious and palatable Crested Wheat Grass. For good contemporary discussion on the origins of the use of Crested Wheat Grass in Western Canada, see W. Moore, "Our Experience With Crested Wheat Grass," *Canadian Cattlemen* (June 1939).
44. "Monthly Price Good Butcher Steers, Toronto, 1920-1938," *Canadian Cattlemen* (September 1938). The average price of $19.59 in 1920 dropped dramatically the following year to $7.58, and fell below $7.00 in 1923 and 1924 before recovering slightly and then exceeding $10.00 in 1928–29. In sharp contrast, the average price between 1931 and 1938 was $5.50. These Toronto prices were higher than what would have been realized in regional markets like Calgary.
45. Alberta, "Report of the Livestock Supervisor," *Department of Agriculture Annual Report* (1931).
46. Alberta, "Report of the Livestock Supervisor," *Department of Agriculture Annual Report* (1932).
47. Alberta, "Report of the Livestock Supervisor," *Department of Agriculture Annual Report* (1933).
48. "Interview with Dr. J.W. Grant MacEwan, Professor of Animal Husbandry, University of Saskatchewan, 1928–46, Dean of Agriculture, University of Manitoba, 1946–51," Calgary, 20 August 1997. MacEwan himself was heavily involved in animal nutrition research at the time, and frequently published his findings in *Scientific Agriculture* in the early 1930s. He later published extensively in *Canadian Cattlemen* where he served for a time as Associate Editor. 'Canner cow' was used to describe those low-grade animals whose meat was to be used for canning purposes.

49. L.B. Thomson, "Costs of Beef Cattle Production," *Canadian Cattlemen* (June 1938): 42. Thomson at the time was Superintendent of the Dominion Experimental Farm, Swift Current, Saskatchewan. It was felt that profits were assured only when ranchers had over 50% of their equity in cattle
50. W.S.G.A. Papers, Box 2, file folder 11. See Address by L.B. Thomson, then Superintendent of Manyberries Research Station, 11 May 1935. According to Thomson, land costs on producing 100lb beef represented 12% of total costs; a similar figure for grain was 6%.
51. See W.S.G.A. Papers, Box 13, file folder 121, "Brief on Grazing Lands," Short Grass Stock Growers Association, 1937. Another economic survey in 1938–39 put land charges and rentals as 19% of production in the short grass country. See *Canadian Cattlemen* (December 1940): 485.
52. Figures abstracted from the Department of Lands and Mines Annual Reports suggest that well over 1000 leases were cancelled between 1935 and 1940. One result of these cancellations was the establishment of Provincial Grazing Reserves. By 1944 there were 3 such reserves totalling 223,500 acres running 3,933 head of cattle plus another 10 reserves run by approved grazing associations.
53. The above statistics were abstracted from Alberta, *Department of Municipal Affairs, Annual Report* (1927–42).
54. *Canadian Cattlemen* (September 1938).
55. The responses were many and varied. Federally, the Prairie Farm Rehabilitation Act, 1935, provided for a long-range scheme of land regeneration through regrassing and water conservation. The Provincial Special Areas Act, 1938, admitted the need for special treatment in markedly disadvantageous areas. Special Fodder, Freight and Marketing policies were put into place to help farmers and ranchers. For example between 1937 and 1941, over a million pounds of forage seed were distributed in Alberta.
56. Cross Fonds, Box 126, file folder 1012, Correspondence dated 6 September 1934. See also *Farm and Ranch Review* (October 1935): 4.
57. See W.S.G.A. Papers, Box 13, file folder 121, "Circular to Membership, January 25, 1937"; also J. Harvie, Deputy Minister, Department of Lands and Mines, "Alberta's Grazing Policy," *Canadian Cattlemen* (September 1938). In typical fashion, the W.S.G.A. was self-congratulatory over its role in securing these arrangements. See *Farm and Ranch Review* (June 1937): 9.
58. Not all leasehold areas in the Province had the same rates. Generally the maximum of 4 cents an acre was paid in the foothills area while rates in the more arid short grass country were lower.
59. Harvie, "Alberta's Grazing Policy."
60. A good example occurred in 1937 when the W.S.G.A. Board of Directors' Meeting referred to "the shocking figures supplied by the Department of Lands and Mines on January 30 as to the number and proportion of leaseholders in arrears of rentals and taxes." See W.S.G.A. Papers, Box #2, file folder, 11, "Minutes of Board of Directors' Meeting, March 30, 1937."
61. Alberta, *Annual Report of the Department of Lands and Mines*, "Reports of Grazing Supervisor, 1931, 1935, 1936."
62. Ibid., 1936.
63. Alberta, *Department of Agriculture Annual Report*, 1936, "Reports of the District Agriculturalists."
64. Ibid., 1937.

65. Known as 'LB,' Thomson, according to Grant MacEwan, was a no-nonsense, very capable and highly respected administrator. MacEwan remembers him as the only Western agriculturalist "who Jimmy Gardiner (federal Agriculture Minister) would ever listen to."
66. L.B. Thomson, "Costs of Production and Land Charges," 1935, "Carrying Capacities and Beef Production," 1936; S.E. Clarke, "A Study of Our Range Pastures," 1929, "The Differences Between Grass in the East and in the Foothills," 1932, "Providing Feed For Range Livestock," 1935, "Leaseholds and Production Costs," 1937.
67. W.S.G.A. Papers, Box 2, file folder 10. Thomson's words were echoed by Clarke in an address to the 1937 Convention.
68. Ross is a fascinating figure. The son of a rancher, Ross learned to fly during the First World War and afterwards became one of, if not the first cattleman to use his own plane for business activities. He served for several years on the executive of the W.S.G.A. including a term as President. He was also Chairman of the Canadian Council of Beef Producers and a member of the federal advisory Wartime Prices and Trade Board. Ross died at his Milk River ranch in 1956.
69. In the late 1920s, Ross conducted what many thought was a stupid experiment when he shipped several feeders to farms around Saskatoon to be tended by rural children. The success of the experiment confounded his critics. One carload sold at 17 cents per lb., well over the current market price.
70. See *Farm and Ranch Review* (July 1936); also *Canadian Cattlemen* (July 1939) for S.G.S.G.A.'s President George Ross's statements re founding reasons.
71. W.S.G.A. Papers, Box 2, file folder 11, "George Ross to N.E. Tanner, January 20, 1937."
72. W.S.G.A. Papers, Box 2, file folder 10, "Proceedings of W.S.G.A. 41st Convention, May 25-27, 1937."
73. Ibid.
74. W.S.G.A. Papers, Box 2, file folder 11, "N.E. Tanner to W.S.G.A., November 16, 1937."
75. C. Graham Anderson, Grazing Appraiser, Department of Lands and Mines, *Grazing Rates Report, Short Grass Area of Alberta,* compiled with the co-operation of the Short Grass Stock Growers' Association (1941), 9–12.
76. See W.S.G.A. Papers, Box 2, file folder 10, "Preamble to Resolution passed at W.S.G.A. 41st Convention, 27-28 May, 1937."
77. See "Grazing Rates Report," 10–11; George Ross, "New Approach to the Economics of Lease Rentals and Taxes," *Canadian Cattlemen* (September 1938).
78. *Canadian Cattlemen* (March 1940).
79. Graham Anderson was certainly well-qualified. He had been Assistant Supervisor of Grazing, Dominion Department of the Interior, and in 1924 had written a thesis on Range Management as part of his graduate work at the University of Saskatchewan.
80. The Report covered 237 pages and was based on over 100 interviews and 70 written briefs (one by L.B. Thomson). During its investigation, the committee had studied grazing regulations in several American states as well as in Argentina, Australia, New Zealand and South Africa. It had also worked in close co-operation with the Manyberries Research Station.

81. *Canadian Cattlemen* (September 1941). The Report's lack of mention in subsequent issues indicated that it had been conveniently forgotten.
82. See J.A. and J.B. Campbell, "Grasslands Investigations in Alberta, Saskatchewan and Manitoba," *Canadian Cattlemen* (March, June, September, December, 1942).
83. W.S.G.A. Papers, Box 2, file folder 12, "N.E. Tanner to W.S.G.A. Board of Directors, January 14, 1944." The 54 members who had originally said they would be part of the production tax experiment represented 1,045,000 acres of leased land. See "Grazing Rates Report," 9. Though not documented, it is likely that George Ross was one of the two who did volunteer.
84. See "Grazing Rates Report," 10–11; Also, Ross, "New Approach to the Economics of Lease Rentals and Taxes."
85. The government made a half-hearted effort to secure a 12.5% royalty, but certainly the popular opinion among stockholders was that the royalty would be set at a maximum of 10%. Some years later the royalty was lowered to 8%.
86. W.S.G.A. Papers, Box 13, file folder 121, "Brief on Grazing Lands," compiled by the Short Grass Stock Growers Association (1937).
87. W.S.G.A. Papers, "Board of Directors Meeting, October 22, 1941."
88. W.S.G.A. Papers, Box 2, file folder 11, "Resolution passed at 42nd Convention, 2-3 June, 1938."
89. See "Revised Alberta Lease Regulations," *Canadian Cattlemen* (March 1940); Alberta, *Department of Lands and Mines Annual Report* (1940). It is interesting that while the three-year cancellation clause remained in effect, this long contentious issue had ceased to be of concern. The soil surveys which had followed the provisions of the new Land Act in 1939 had clearly classified the true agricultural potential of land.
90. See "Revised Alberta Lease Regulations," *Canadian Cattlemen* (March 1940); W.S.G.A. Papers, Box 2, file folder 11.
91. Abstracted from "Grazing Rates Report," 178.
92. On 3 April 1939, the Legislature of Province of Alberta had passed an important new Act, "An Act to Amend and Consolidate the Provincial Lands Act," Chapter 10, *Statutes of Alberta*, 1939. This Act abolished the old Homestead System and replaced it with an Agricultural Leasing policy. The Act also directed the Minister of Lands and Mines to divide the Province for land utilization purposes.
93. Later a 40 acre to one animal zone was added to include most of the area north of Edmonton. See Glenbow, "Alberta, Grazing Capacity and Grazing Rates, 1951," Map.
94. W.S.G.A. Papers, Box 2, file folder 12, "Tanner to Chairman of W.S.G.A. Grazing Committee, January 14, 1944."
95. N.E. Tanner, "Alberta's Grazing Policy," *Canadian Cattlemen* (March 1944).
96. Ibid.
97. W.S.G.A. Papers, Box 2, file folder 13, "Report of Grazing Committee, W.S.G.A. Annual Convention, June 15-16, 1944."
98. For details, see W.S.G.A. Papers, Box 2, file folder 13, "Meeting With Government and Grazing Committee, October 12, 1944."
99. *Canadian Cattlemen* (December 1944).

100. Ibid. Usher's words were conciliatory. "This may seem a pretty drastic change for some, but I would ask all our members to give the plan a fair trial before passing judgement on it."
101. Following the first year of the new arrangement, the Department of Lands and Mines reported on its satisfactory implementation, noting that very few ranchers had resorted to the appeal process. Alberta, *Department of Lands and Mines Annual Report* (1946). The Department was correct up to a point in that objections were expressed mainly in terms of carrying capacity appraisals. The real issue at stake was not so much the objections but the fact that ranchers realized that the era of flat rates was gone forever and that the production tax was a *fait accompli*.

Wild West Shows and the Canadian West

1. *Evening Albertan*, 25 July 1914.
2. CBC Radio, "Origins of the Stampede," 25 July 1948.
3. Richard Slotkin, *Gunfighter Nation: The Myth of the Frontier in 20th Century America* (New York: Atheneum, 1992).

Postscript 'He Country in Pants' No Longer—Diversifying Ranching History

1. See Lewis G. Thomas, *Ranchers' Legacy*, ed. Patrick A. Dunae (Edmonton: University of Alberta Press, 1986); Sheilagh Jameson, "Women in the Southern Alberta Ranch Community, 1881–1914," in *The Canadian West*, ed. Henry C. Klassen (Calgary: University of Calgary Comprint Publishing Co., 1977), 63–78; and Sheilagh Jameson, *Ranches, Cowboys and Characters: Birth of Alberta's Western Heritage* (Calgary: Glenbow Museum, 1987).
2. Candace Savage, *Cowgirls: Real Cowboy Girls* (Vancouver: Greystone Books, 1996), and Thelma Poirier, *Writing the Range* (Calgary: Fifth House, 1997).
3. Mary Lou LeCompte, *Cowgirls of the Rodeo: Pioneer Professional Athletes* (Chicago: University of Illinois Press, 1993).
4. For a recent overview of historical writing about women in the Canadian West, see Anne Leger-Anderson, "Canadian Prairie Women's History: An Uncertain Enterprise," *Journal of the West*, 37, no. 1 (January 1998): 47–59. For a recent sampling of work on the American West, see Elizabeth Jameson and Susan Armitage, eds., *Writing the Range: Race, Class, and Culture in the Women's West* (Norman and London: University of Oklahoma Press, 1997). On ranching women, see Teresa Jordan, *Cowgirls: Women of the American West* (1982; reprint, Lincoln and London: University of Nebraska Press, 1992).
5. Isabelle Randall, *A Lady's Ranche Life in Montana* (London: W.H. Allen and Co., 1887), and Donna M. Lucey, *Photographing Montana 1894–1928: The Life and Work of Evelyn Cameron* (New York: Alfred A. Knopf, 1991).

6. Philip Ashton Rollins, *The Cowboy: An Unconventional History of Civilization on the Old-Time Cattle Range*, foreword to the rev. ed. Richard W. Slatta (1992, 1936; reprint, Norman: University of Oklahoma Press, 1997).
7. Ibid., 34–35.
8. Leonard Lethbridge, Harold Thomas, and Thelma Poirier, "At Wood Mountain We Are Still Lakota," in *Legends of Our Time: Native Cowboy Life*, eds. Morgan Baillargeon and Leslie Tepper (Vancouver: University of British Columbia Press, 1998).
9. Clara Spotted Elk, "Women and the Ranching Life," in *Legends of Our Time*, eds. Baillargeon and Tepper.
10. Glenbow Archives, Marie Rose Smith Papers, typescript manuscript, "Eighty Years on the Plains." Marie Rose Smith's life story was serialized in the *Canadian Cattlemen*. A version of her life is also presented in Jock Carpenter, *Fifty Dollar Bride: Marie Rose Smith—A Chronicle of Metis Life in the Nineteenth Century* (Sidney, BC: Gray's Publishing, 1977).
11. Evelyn Cartier Springett, *For My Children's Children* (Montreal: Unity Press, 1937).
12. Ibid., 103.
13. Glenbow Archives, Mary Ella Inderwick Papers, correspondence from Mary Macleod, 9 April 1889.
14. Moira O'Neill (Agnes Skrine), "A Lady's Life on a Ranche," *Blackwood's Edinburgh Magazine* (January 1898): 3.
15. Nanton and District Historical Society, *Mosquito Creek Roundup* (Calgary: Friesen Printers, 1975), 42–44. See also Simon Evans, "Labour Force and Wages: 'CC' Ranch" (Calgary: Parks Canada, 1993, unpublished).
16. Jeanne Kay, "Landscapes of Women and Men: Rethinking the Regional Historical Geography of the United States and Canada," *Journal of Historical Geography*, 17, no. 4 (1991): 435–52.
17. Simon Evans, *Prince Charming Goes West: The Story of the E.P. Ranch* (Calgary: University of Calgary Press, 1993).
18. Hugh A. Dempsey, *The Golden Age of the Canadian Cowboy: An Illustrated History* (Saskatoon: Fifth House Publishers, 1995), 38–39.
19. Monica Hopkins, *Letters from a Lady Rancher*, intro. Sheilagh Jameson (Halifax: Goodread Biographies, 1983).
20. Violet Pearl Sykes, "Memoirs of a Cowboy's Wife," Provincial Archives of Alberta.
21. *Edmonton Bulletin*, 9 July, 1984.
22. Pincher Creek Historical Society, *Prairie Grass to Mountain Pass: History of Pincher Creek and District* (Pincher Creek: Pincher Creek Historical Society, 1974), 4–7.
23. Russell H. Bennett, *The Compleat Rancher* (1946; reprint revised, Minneapolis: T.S. Denison and Co. Inc., 1965).
24. Ibid., 246.
25. Elizabeth Manet, *Women of the Range: Women's Roles in the Texas Beef Cattle Industry* (College Station: Texas A & M University Press, 1993).
26. Peter Iverson, *When Indians Became Cowboys: Native Peoples and Cattle Ranching in the American West* (Norman and London: University of Oklahoma Press, 1994).
27. Ben Calf Robe with Adolf and Beverly Hungry Wolf, *Siksika: A Blackfoot Legacy* (Invermere: Good Medicine Books, 1979).
28. Hugh A. Dempsey, *Tom Three Persons* (Saskatoon: Purich Publishers, 1997).

29. Dempsey, *The Golden Age of the Canadian Cowboy.*
30. Hugh A. Dempsey, *The Gentle Persuader: A Biography of James Gladstone, Indian Senator* (Saskatoon: Western Producer Prairie Books, 1986).
31. Simon Evans, *The Burns Era at the Bar U Ranch* (unpublished manuscript, 1997).
32. National Archives of Canada (NA), Record Group 10 (RG 10), Records relating to Indian Affairs, volume 4010, file 253,430.
33. See Keith Regular, "'Red Backs and White Burdens': A Study of White Attitudes Toward Indians in Southern Alberta" (unpublished M.A. thesis, University of Calgary, 1985).
34. NA, RG 10, vol. 4010, file 253,430, Dr. W.B. Murray to the secretary, Indian Affairs branch, 24 July 1938.
35. NA, RG 10, vol. 4010, file 253,430, C.P. Schmidt to the secretary, Indian Affairs branch, 2 September 1938.
36. NA, RG 10, vol. 4010, file 253,430, Indian Affairs scrapbook of clippings (1930s).
37. *Calgary Herald*, 6 May 1939, 8 May 1939. See also George H. Gooderham, "Joe Crowfoot," *Alberta History*, 32, no. 4 (1984): 26–28.
38. *Calgary Herald*, 8 May 1939.
39. Ibid.
40. Sarah Carter, *Lost Harvests: Government Policy and Indian Reserve Agriculture* (Montreal: McGill-Queen's Press, 1990).

Index

A

A7 ranch, 51, 68
Aboriginal people, 155. *See also* Indians; Natives; cattle ranching, 161–2, 167; rodeos, 161; women, 156–57
Akers, Dave, 92
Alberta Flour Mills, 57
Alberta Horsebreeders' Association, 55
Alberta Stampede Company, 141, 148
Alberta Stock Growers' Association, 48, 53, 55
alcohol, xiii, 93. *See also* whiskey; consumption, 98; and gun violence, 91; liquor offences and trade, 81, 95; permits, 95–97; prohibition, 95; and roundups, 96
Allan, Sir Andrew, 76–77
Allan family, 33–34, 36
Almighty Voice (Cree Indian), 95
American cowboys, 77; in Canadian bars, 94; as foremen and managers, 66; origins, 79; wild west shows, 145
American Midwest, 7, 58
Anchor P Ranch, 121
Anderson, Graham, 133
Andrews, D. H., 77
"Architectural Expressions of the Canadian National State" (Holdsworth), 1
Artibise, Alan J., 56
assault. *See* law and order
Austin, Frank, 160
Austin, Katherine, 160
Autry, Gene, 154

B

Baillargeon, Morgan, 156
Bank of Montreal, 104, 108, 112
Bar S, xiii, 74; acquired and run by Rod Macleay, 106, 108; bequeathed to Maxine Macleay, 112–13; Clay Chattaway, president, 117; consolidation into Macleay Ranches Ltd., 109; founder, Walter Skrine, 101, 106; George and Maxine Chattaway, 116–17; help from banks, 168; under Peter Muirhead, 107–8; sold to Pat Burns, 108; women's roles, 161
Bar U, 25
Bar U National Historic Ranch, 31, 162
bar-room gunfights. *See* law and order
Battle of Belly River, The, 23
Bear Robe, Joe, 162
Beaverslide haystacker, 8, 10
Bedingfeld, Agnes, 158
beef bonanza, 45, 66, 74
Beil, Charles A., 25, 27
Bennett, R. B., 57
Bennett, Russell, 160
Benton and St. Louis Cattle Company, 74
Big Fire Ranch, 121
Big Four, xii, 24, 31, 76
Bigland, Mary, 78
Bird, Manerd, 121
Bird, Shauna (Blades), 121
Bishop, Tom, 141, 145
Bishop's 4B Ranch Wild West Shows, 141
Blackstone, Mr., xi
Blades, Dorothy (Macleay), 113–15, 118, 121; as Macleay, Dorothy, 109–13
Blades, Ernest, 113–15, 118, 121
Blades, Justin, 121
Blades, Lynnie, 121
Blades, Mac, 118, 121
Blades, Renie (Jones), 119, 121
Blades, Rod, 121

Bodmer, Karl, 14
boosterism, 56
booze. *See* alcohol; whiskey
Borderlands: Essays in Canadian-American Relations (Konrad), viii
borders, vii–viii, viii, x, xii, 2–7, 10, 33, 93, 155; Alberta-Montana, 59; cross-border relationships, xiv; cross-boundary movements, 5; and dairying, 5; and human occupance, 1; and land use, 1; liquor trade and, 95; significance of, 167; six-shooters and, 91
Borein, Edward, xi
Bow River Valley, 6
Bowen, Nellie, 39
Breen, David H., vii, viii, 65, 87, 167
Britons. *See* Englishmen
Bronc to Breakfast, 22
buckaroos, 6, 18, 189
Bucking Bronco, 20–21
Buffalo Bill. *See* Cody, William (Buffalo Bill)
buffalo raising, 120
Bureau of Land Management, x
Burns, Pat, xi, 24, 31–32, 49, 56, 71, 80, 108–9
Burns Era at the Bar U Ranch, The (Evans), 162

C

Calf Robe, Ben, 162
Calgary, 81–82, 109, 142; bar disputes, 92; Texan imprint, 6
Calgary Albertan, 127
Calgary Exhibition, 145
Calgary Herald, 57, 151
Calgary Herald and Alberta Livestock Journal, 34
Calgary Stampede, xi, 17, 23–24, 27, 31–32, 56, 142, 144–45, 147, 150, 152, 154, 162; cash prizes, 147; and Cody's wild west show, 147
California system, 5, 64; impact on Canada, 6–7; material culture, 6; vocabulary, 6
Cameron, Evelyn, 155
Cameron, William Bleadsell, 23
Camp Cook's Troubles, 22, 24
Campbell, William B., 24
Campbells, 26
Canadian Cattleman, 133–35
Canadian Circle outfit, 74
Canadian Coal and Colonization Company's 76 Ranch, 70
Canadian Cowboy Conference: New Perspectives on Ranching History, vii, viii, xiv, 154–55, 161, 167
Canadian Cowboy Exhibition, vii, 139, 153–54
Canadian Northern Railway, 56
Canadian Pacific Railway, 96; holdups, 93
Canadian Percheron Society, 55
Canadian Pictorial and Illustrated War News, 82
capital, 45, 56, 109, 121; Eastern, xii, 45; Great Britain, 66; risk capital, x, 66, 76
Carlyle, S.G., 130
Carlyle, William, 57
carnivals, 141, 149
Carry, Jim, xiv, 139–40, 144, 149–50, 152; memorabilia, 141
Carry, Stastia, xiv, 139–40, 145, 149–50, 152, 154; memorabilia, 141
Carson's Men, 24
Carter, Sarah, 169
Carter, Wilf (Montana Slim), 154
Case, Joe, 106
Casey, Bob, 92
Catlin, George, 14
cattle: Alberta foothills, 65; breeding in American West, 46; breeding up, 79; British derived breeds, 7; of British origin, 46; feed lots, 80; genetic research, 117; Hereford crosses, 115–17, 119; Iberian cattle, 5–6; range stock deterioration, 53; reproductive technology, 161; scrub, 5; shorthorn cattle, 46; winter feed, 5, 7, 46, 52, 54, 79
cattle ranching. *See* ranchers and ranching
cattlemen. *See* ranchers and ranching
Cattlemen's Protective Association, 55
cavvy, 198n

cavvyard, 6
CC Ranch, 68
Charcoal (Blood tribe), 95
Chattaway, Chris, 118
Chattaway, Clay, 117–18
Chattaway, George, 113, 116–17
Chattaway, Maxine (Macleay), 116–17; as Macleay, Maxine, 110, 112–13
Chattaway, Morgan, 118
Chattaway, Pat (Jevne), 117–18
Chattaway, Scott, 118
Chattaway family: education, 118
Chicago stock market, 52
Chicago stock yards, 71
Chicago's World Columbian Exposition, 13
Christensen, Carl, 112
chuckwagon races, 147
Church brothers, 68
Circle Ranch, 89
Circus World Museum, 141
circuses, 141, 149
Clark, Andrew, 4
Clarke, S.E., 131
class, 155
Clines, Roy, 55
Cochrane, Billy, 91
Cochrane, Evelyn, 158
Cochrane, James, 78
Cochrane, Senator Matthew Henry, 33, 76–77
Cochrane, W. F., 76
Cochrane Ranche, 47, 51, 74, 76, 78, 86
Cody, William (Buffalo Bill), 12, 139, 141–43, 145, 147, 150, 154; Buffalo Bill Cody's Real Wild West, 141–42, 144, 151–52
community pastures, 128; reseeding, x
Compleat Rancher, The (Bennett), 160
Conklin and Garrett All Canadian Shows, 150
Connaught, Duke of, 23
Conrad Brothers, 50, 74, 77
conservation, 117, 119, 121. *See also* range degradation; regrassing, 129; water, 129
Conservative government, 124
Conservative party, 57; Calgary District Conservative Association, 34; ties with cattle companies, 53
Cooper, Nancy. *See* Russell, Nancy
corporate ranches, 76
Cosgrave, Dick, 148
cow sense, 66, 72, 76
Cowan, Roy, 70
Cowboy, The (Rollins), 156
Cowboy Camp During the Roundup, 19, 22
cowboy competitions. *See* rodeos
Cowboy Conference, viii, xiv. *See* Canadian Cowboy Conference: New Perspectives on Ranching History
cowboy culture, xi, 11, 14; cowboy of the imagination, vii; cowboy social history, xi; cowboy *versus* Indian, 95; Hollywood cowboys, 15; material culture, xi, 6–7, 64; performing cowboy, vii; working cowboy, vii
Cowboy Festival, Calgary, 1999, 155
Cowboys of the Americas (Slatta), ix
Cowgirls, The (Savage), 155
Cowgirls of the Rodeo: Pioneer Professional Athletes (LeCompte), 155
Craig, John, 76, 79
crops: alfalfa, 49; cash crop agriculture, 124, 127–28; crop farming, xiv; dryland farming techniques, 124; forage crops, 131; grain growing, 55; grass, 123; grass, unimproved, x; hay and fodder crops, x, 47; mechanical mowers, 47; mixed farming, x; wheat farming, 5; wild hay production, 46, 76
Cross, Alexander S., 51
Cross, Alfred Ernest, xi, 24, 26, 31, 47, 56, 70, 111, 126, 128; finances, 51
Cross, Stastia. *See* Carry, Stastia
Crowfoot, Joe, 162
cultural geography: borders and, 1

D

Dacotah, Peter, 92
Dakota Max'x Wild West, 145
Dakotas, 65; political ideologies, 5
Day, Al, 144
Dempsey, Hugh A., 81, 162

Depression. *See* Great Depression
Diamond O, 51
Dippie, Brian, xii, 169
Douglas, Charlie, 73
dovetailed notches, 10
Dowker, Milt, 144
Drumheller, Dan, 7
Dry Belt Ranchers' Association, 126, 128
Dubois, John F., 86
Dubois brothers, 90; rustling and intimidation, 81
dudes, 61, 71. *See also* greenhorns; newcomers
Dumont, Gabriel, 141
Dunlap, Jim, 76
Dutch Henry gang, 84, 90

E
E. P. Ranch, 31, 56
Eastern Canada: aspiring cowboys from, 70; risk capital, 66, 76; as source of labor, 65, 70
Edge, Norman, 148
Elofson, Warren, xiii, 167, 169
Emerson, George, 33, 71–72, 76, 101; partnership with George Lane, 102; partnership with Rod Macleay, 102, 105
end-only hewing, 10
Englishmen, 79; as butt of westerners' jokes, 61; on Canadian range, 68; in United States, 72
E.P. Ranch, 25, 32
ethnicity, 155
Evans, Dale, 155
Evans, Simon, xii, 4, 6, 162, 169
Ewing, Sherm, vii, 167

F
family ranches, 160; medium sized, xiii
Fares, W. H., 52
farming sector: roots in, 52
fencing, 7, 46–7, 64, 79
Ferris, Mary, 74
Fisher, James, 86
Fletcher, Edward'Tex', 92
Flores, Dan, ix
forage crops, 129, 131
Foran, Max, xiv, 167, 169
Ford, Robert, 47, 49, 76–77
Fordney-McCumber tariff, 111
foremen, 45. *See also* instructors; non-commissioned officers; as American influence, 43; experienced Americans as, 76
forest reserves, 109, 115–16, 120, 126
Fort MacLeod, 6, 93–94
Fort Macleod Gazette, 34
Fort Whoop-Up, 96
forty-ninth parallel. *See* borders
Franklin, Johnny, 55
Frewen, Moreton, 77
Frields, G. W., Doc, 76
frontiersmen: as leaders, 72, 74
Fuller, Jim, 73

G
Gardiner, Claude, 68
Gates, William, 7
gender, xiv, 84, 155
George Lane and Company, 168
George Lane Attacked by Wolves (painting), 22
Glass, Charlie, 115
Glenbow Museum, vii, 139, 153
Glendenning, Jack, 73
gold, 72, 77, 745; Virginia City, Montana, 45
Golden Age of the Canadian Cowboy, The (Dempsey), 82, 162
Gollmar Brother Circus, 145
Goodwin, Philip R., 22
Gordon, Ironside and Fares, 31, 50, 53; Mule Creek Ranch, 109
Gordon, J. T., 50–52
government, 65; lease rentals, 137; leasehold system, 66, 123; Liberal government, 53; Provincial government, 125; Provincial grazing regulations, 125; regulations, 123, 128; regulations, 1914, 124; Social Credit government, 131
Grass Conservation Commission, 134
Grassland Investigations in Alberta, Saskatchewan and Manitoba, 134
Gravedigger, 148

reciprocity, 57; and Robert Ford, 47; six-shooter, 91; social life, 49; success on Chicago market, 55; typhoid infection, 48; United States army, 77; Willow Creek Cattle Company, 50; winter feeding, 54; work horses, 50
Larkin, Buff, 145
lassos, 18; hemp, 6; rawhide, 6, 18
Laugh Kills Lonesome, 25
Lavarro, Jesus, 76
law and order, 45, 84, 92, 97, 99, 167. *See also* guns; six-guns; assault, 98; Cowboy cavalry, 82; family and, 97; gambling, 81; gun fights, 91–94; intimidation, 81; liquor, 81, 93; Native-white violence, 95; networks of thieves, 88; peaceful frontier, 152; police inadequacies, 84; progress through violence, 151; property crimes, 81; ranchers' feuds, 92; retaliation, 90; rustlers and rustling, 81, 84, 86–90, 95; shooting, 93–95; smuggling trade, 96–97; thieves and outlaws, 82
Leach, S.J., 164–65
leases and lease systems, x, xiv, 66, 74, 77, 123, 128–29, 212n; 1881, x; arrears in rentals and taxation, 130; closed leases, 53, 124; leasehold management, 129; legislation, 54; long term, 124, 211n; production, 133; security, 124; Western Canada, 33
LeCompte, Mary Lou, 155
Left Hand, Johnny, 162, 165
Legends of Our Times: Native Cowboy Life (Baillargeon and Tepper), 156
Leon Lamar's Wild West, 145
Let the Cowboy Ride (Starr), ix
Liberal party, 54, 57–8
livestock experiments, 128
Livingstone, Donna, 153
Longbaugh, Harry, 78. *See also* Sundance Kid
Lounsberry, Lorain, xiv, 82, 153, 168, 170
Lynch, Tom, 33, 63, 73, 76, 94
Lyon, George, vii

M

MacEwan, Grant, 130
Macleay, Dorothy, 109–10, 112–13; as Blades, Dorothy, 113–15, 118, 121
Macleay, Laura, 104, 109
Macleay, Maxine, 110, 112–13; as Chattaway, Maxine, 116–17
Macleay, Rod, 102, 106; acquired Bar S, 106; bank credit, 108; born, 103; children Dorothy and Maxine, 105; death, 113; debt, 109; family identity, 122; Hereford-Galloway-Angus cross, 106; John Ware Ranch, 104; Macleay Ranches, 109; married Laura Sturtevant, 104; partnership with George Emerson, 102, 105; purchased TL Ranch, 105; Riddle & Macleay Bros. Ranch Co., 103–4; Rocking P, 104; sole ownership of Rocking P, 105; started raising horses, 106; start-up capital, 104; and tariff barriers, 111; will, 112
Macleay Ranches Ltd., 109; Great Depression, 111; management structure, 110; postwar period, 112
Macleod, Colonel James F., 98
Macleod, Mary, 158
Macleod Gazette, 87
Magrath, Charles A., 23
major domo, 6
mange, 53
Mankiller, 20
Many Fingers, Frank, 162, 165
Manyberries Research Station, 127, 129, 131
Mapiatow Ranch, 121
Maret, Elizabeth, 161
markets: British, 55; Chicago, 55; home, 55; Winnipeg, 55
Marshall, Lee, 144
Mauldin, James, 51
Maunsell, E. H., 50
mavericks, 6, 86–88
Max, Dakota, 145
May, Karl, 150
McCullough, Alan, xii, 170
McDonald, Ben, 48
McDonald, George, 48

McDougald Brothers, 145
McDougall, David, 47
McDougall, John, 47
McIntosh, Duncan, 48
McKay, Gilbert, 92
McKinnon, Charles, 55, 73
McKinnon, Lachlin, 70
McLean, A. J., 24, 56
McLean, Hon. Archie, xi
McMullen, H. C., 56
McMullen, Harry, 146–47
"Medicine Line," xii
Medicine Tree, 74
Meinsinger, Jim, 71
Midnight, 148
"Midwest Triumphant, The" (Jordan), 64
Midwestern system, xiii, 5, 7, 10, 46–47, 59, 64–65, 79
Military Colonization Company Ranch, 61, 70
Millar, Charlie, 31, 39, 48, 55, 70, 79; as greenhorn, 71
Millar, Herb, 31, 51–52, 70
Miller 101 Ranch Wild West, 145
Minesinger, Jim, 33
Mitchell, C. R., 58
mixed farming, x, 55, 124, 194n
Mix-Up, A, 22
Montana, 7, 11, 22, 47, 65, 76; business practices, 45; cattle country of, 43; cowboy culture, 11; and established cattlemen, 45–6; goldfields, 72, 77; mountain horse barn, 10; pastoral methods, 45; as place of origin, 70, 78; smuggling, 96
Montana Stock Growers' Association, 47
Morley reserve, 162
Morton, Cal, 71
Mosquito Creek, 77
mountain horse barn, 9–10
Mounties. *See* North-West Mounted Police
Muirhead, Peter, 107–8
Murray, Lou, 73
Musselshell Roundup, 22
myths, xi; about the West, 81; of Canadian west, xiii; of masculine ranching culture, 156; of the orderly society, 82; of peaceful progress, 152

N

Namaka farm, 55
Natives, 49. *See also* Aboriginal people; Indians; Native-White violence, 95; as skilled labor, 162
Nelson-Jones gang, 84, 90
Nesbitt, Alex, 55
New Oxley Ranche, 157
Newbolt, Bob, 61–3, 67, 70–71, 79, 94
newcomers, 66–67. *See also* dudes; greenhorns; and necessary skills, 65
Newsom, A. V., 50
Newton, Alex, xi
Newton, Alick C., 23
night herding, 12
Noble, C.S., 55
non-commissioned officers, 71–73, 76. *See also* foremen; instructors
North American Cattle Ranching Frontiers (Jordan), ix, 63
North West Cattle Company, 33, 47, 51, 71, 74, 78, 168
North West Territories, 61; cattle in, 66; lease system, x
North West Territories Act of 1875, 95
North-West Mounted Police, xiii, 22–24, 47, 73, 83–84, 90–95, 97, 147, 152; alcohol consumption, 98; inadequacies, 84; Russell's studies of, xii; as symbol of law and order, 81

O

Oetelaar, Joy, xii, 170
Oliver, Frank, 53–54
One of the Rough String, 20, 24
One Spot, Edward, 162, 164–65
O'Neill, Moira, 107
oreanna, 6
Osgood, Ernest Staples, ix
Otelaar, Joy, 168
overgrazing, 131. *See* range degradation
Oxley Ranche, 74, 76
Ozeroff, Norma, 118

P

Palliser's Triangle, xiv
Parks Canada, vii
pastures: fences and fencing, 46–47; rotating, 117, 120, 129; seasonal shifting of, 46–47; studies, 131
Patterson, James (Pat), 76
Patterson, Jim, 76, 91
Pearce, William, 57
Pellat, Sir Henry Mill, 23
Pepin, Simon, 156
Percherons, 50–51, 55
"Performing Cowboy, The," 153–54
Picket, Will, 145
Pierson, Bert, 55
Pincher Creek, 68
Pinhorn, Stanley, 76
Pirates of the Plains, 24
plainsmen, 66, 78–79
Poirier, Thelma, 155
popular culture, xi, 153
population: origins of, 1–2, 67
Porteous, Scotty, 106
Powder River Cattle Company, 77
Primrose, P.C.H., 124
Prince of Wales, 24, 31–32, 56–7
Prohibition, 15
prostitution, 81, 98
Provincial Grazing Reserves, 214n
Provost, Pat, 151
Purcel, Lee, 92

Q

quarter horses, 120
Queen's War Hounds, The, 23–24

R

race, xiv, 155; racial friction, 81; racial strife, 95; white/native violence, 95
rancherie, 6
ranchers and ranching, ix, 64, 131; American influence, 43, 47; American Midwest, 58; boom, 33; and the border, 5; British influence, 10; Britons, 43; California, 5; Canada's institutional environment, 65; Canadian as distinctive, 10; corporate ranches, 76; dude ranches, 154; and Eastern Canadians, 43; economic and political influence, 45; experienced rangemen, 66; family ranches, 160; and homestead system, 124; land base, ix; Midwestern, 5; Montana experience, 47; neglect of livestock, 5; North-West Territories, 66; open-range system, 5, 86, 88; political and legislative framework, vii; public land, x; Rocky Mountain cultural/pastoral practices, 46; scrub cattle, 5; Siksika, 162; and social elite, 58; stock pens, 46–47; summer range, 53; and territorial elite, 45; Texas, 5; trail driving days, 65; types of, 5; winter feed, 5, 46, 52, 54, 79
ranching frontiers, viii, 64; evolution of, vii; mythology of, 71–72
ranching systems, ix; California system, 5–7, 64; foothills of Alberta, viii; interior valleys of British Columbia, viii; Midwestern system, 5, 7, 10, 46–47, 59, 64, 79; short-grass prairies, ix; Texas system, 5–6, 64
Ranchmen's Club in Calgary, 24, 36
Randall, Isabelle, 155
range degradation, 128, 130–31. *See also* conservation
range feminity, 156
range labor force, 55; Aboriginal women, 156; American cowboys, 65–66, 77; characteristics of, 65; dudes, 61, 71; from Eastern Canada, 65, 70; experience on western American range, 43; foremen, 43, 45, 76; frontiersman and, 72, 75; greenhorns, 63, 66, 71; immigrant cowboys, xii; instructors, 66–7, 72, 79; newcomers, 65–7; non-commissioned officers, 71–3, 76; plainsmen and, 66, 78–79; professional cowboys and, 66; wages, 111; women, 155–61, 168
range management, 128–29
Range Mother, 22
rangeland crime. *See* law and order
Rankin, Norman, 36

Ray Knight Roping a Steer, 25
Real Wild West, 148
Real Wild West show: distinctive Canadian variation, 139
reciprocity, 32, 57
Red Label Feeders Association, 132
Reitsma, Hendrik, 3
Remington, Frederic, 154
remuda, 198n
Riddle, Douglas, 103
Riddle, Stewart, 109–10
Riel, Louis, 141
Riel Rebellion, 67, 82, 95
Riley, Dan, 105
Riley, Harold, 36, 70
River Bend Ranch, 74
Riverside Ranch, 51
Roberts, Ezekiel Stone, 55
Rocking P Ranch, xiii, 121; bequeathed to Dorothy Macleay, 112; consolidation into Macleay Ranches Ltd., 109; Ernest and Dorothy Blades, 113–16; founder, George Emerson, 101–2; help from banks, 168; management by Blades children, 118–22; Rod Macleay, 102–6; women's roles, 161
Rocky Mountain Rangers, 82
rodeos, 141, 144, 148, 150, 154. *See also* wild west shows; cowgirls, 155; exhibitions, 145; riders, 17, 162
Rollins, Philip Ashton, 156, 160
rope. *See* lassos
Ross, George, 73, 132, 134–35
Ross, Walter, 70
Royal Agricultural Society of New South Wales rodeo: Indian cowboys, 162–65
Royal Bank of Canada, 112, 117
Royal Ontario Museum, 39
Runner, George, 162
running irons, 87
Russell, Charles M., xi, xii, 154, 184n; Alberta patrons, 184n; as artist, 12–14; authenticity, 14; born, 11; California buckaroos, 18; Canadian commissions, 23; Canadian connections, 22, 24; Chicago's World Columbian Exposition, 13; exhibition, Dore Galleries, 23; exhibition in Calgary, 23; family, 11, 13; funeral, 25; Hollywood cowboys, 15–17; and Imperial Institute, 25; Indian paintings, 23–24; Judith Basin roundup, 11; marriage, 13; as memorialist, 19; Montana themes, 11, 22; nature painitings, 20; North-West Mounted Police, 22–4; and Prince of Wales, 24; as puncher, 12; riding and roping, 19, 22; rodeo riders, 17–18; as wrangler, 12
Russell, Nancy, xi, 23–24, 26
rustlers and rustling, 81, 84, 88–90, 95; by Canadian ranchers, 86; Dutch Henry gang, 84; Nelson-Jones gang, 84; reign of terror, 84; small ranchers, 87; Sundance Kid, 84; Wood Mountain area, 81
Ryan, Paddy, 148

S

saddles, 17–18; single-cinched Visalia, 6
Savage, Candace, 155
Schlosser, Blake, 121
Schlosser, Ethel, 121
Schlosser, Monica (Blades), 121
Schmidt, C.P., 164
settlement, x, xiv, 53, 207n; colonization projects, 61; farm abandonments, 211n; farming families, 128; homestead system, 216n; pioneer farmers, x; pressure from, 124; regulations, x
Sexsmith, Lem, 49
shooting. *See* law and order
Short, Lulu, 160
short grass country, 124
Short Grass Stock Growers' Association (S.G.S.G.A.), 132–35
Sifton, C. J., 86
Sifton, Clifford, 54, 124
Siksika: ranching and cowboy life, 162
Siksika: A Blackfoot Legacy (Calf Robe), 162
Single Handed, 23
Sioux, 74
Sitting Bull, 141

six-guns, 90–91, 94, 192n
Skrine, Agnes, 158
Skrine, Walter, 74, 107; founded Bar S, 101, 106; sold Bar S to Peter Muirhead, 107
Skrine brothers, 68
Slate, Dennis, 153
Slatta, Richard, ix, xi, 168, 170
Slotkin, Richard, 151
Smith, Marie Rose, 157
Smith, Mary Greely, 39
Smith, Stephen Dundas, 153
smuggling trade, 96
Snipes, Ben, 7
social stratification, 155, 157
South West Stock Association, 34
Southern Alberta Survey Board, 126–27
Spalding, James, Inspector, xi
Spanish windlass, 6–7
Spencer Brothers, 88–89
Spotted Elk, Clara, 157
Springett, Evelyn Cartier (Galt), 157
Stairley, Wallace, 25–26
Stanley, Lord (Governor-General), 38
Starr, Paul E., ix
Stegner, Wallace, xii
Stencell, Al, 141
Stimson, Fred, xii, 29–41, 52, 67, 71, 74, 79; and Allans, 34; Bar U, 32; buying cattle in Montana, 33; Conservatives, 34; contribution to ranching, 39, 41; death, 34, 39; family, 32; first visit west, 33; as host, 36, 38; leases, 33; marriage, 39; and Mel Zimrose, 36; native peoples and culture, 39; North West Cattle Company (NWCC), 33–34; outsider status, 32; roundups, 34, 36; South West Stock Association, 34; stories about, 33, 38–39; as storyteller, 32, 38, 41
Stimson, Mary (Greely), 39, 78
stock associations, 46, 73, 76
Stoney cowboys, vii
Strange, Major General, 61, 70
Stuart, Granville, 77, 156
Studies of Western Life, 12
Sturtevant, Laura. *See* Macleay, Laura
Sundance Kid, 84, 94. *See also* Longbaugh, Harry
Sykes, Violet Pearl, 159–60

T

Tanner, N.E., 132–33, 135–36
tariff barriers, 111, 126
taxation, 130–31, 211n; production tax, 134–36
Taylor, Sheriff C. WAllace, 86
teachers. *See* instructors
Templeton, J. G., 50
Tepper, Leslie, 156
Texans in Canada, 6
Texas system, 5–6, 64
Thomas, L.G., vii, 155
Thomson, Edmund, 105
Thomson, L.B., 131
Thorner, Thomas, 81
Three Persons, Tom, 144, 147, 154, 162
Tight Dally and a Loose Latigo, A, 22
TL Ranch, 121
Tookana, Awbonnie, 156
toponyms, 10
transcontinental railways, 5
Trottier, Rose, 156
Tumbelweed, 148
Tyson, Ian, 154

U

United States Forest Service, x
University of Calgary, vii
Uppingham public school, 61, 67
Usher, Thomas, 136

V

Vale, Charlie, 48
Van Horne, William, 38
Victor Ranch, 49
Voisey, Paul, 84
3vs Ranch, 114–15

W

Waiting for a Chinook, 12–13
Wake, Walter, 48
Walker, Colonel James, 78
Ward, David, 107
Ware, John, 6, 31, 68, 154

Watrin, Slim, 148
Watt, Walter, 73
Wayne, John, 154
Weadick, Guy, 23, 56, 145–46, 151–52; Canadian formula for Real Wild West, 148
Weinard, Phil, 38, 71, 74–75
Weir, Thomas, 7
Welsh, Peter, 148
Welsh family, 149
Wendick, Guy, 144–45
Wesley, Peter, vii, 161
Western art tradition: authenticity, 14
Western Stock Growers' Association (W.S.G.S.), xiv, 124–26, 130–31, 133–34, 136; and erosion of grazing lands, 129
When a Left Handshake Is the Safest, 24
When Horses Talk War There's Small Chance for Peace, 20
When Indians Became Cowboys (Iverson), 161
When Law Dulls the Edge of Chance, 23–25
When the Plains Were His, 23
whiskey, 85, 92, 95. *See also* alcohol; trade, 97; traders, xii, 81
Whiskey Smugglers Caught With the Goods, 23–24
White, Diamond Joe, 154
White, Frank, 70, 78
White, J. D., 82
Whittlesey, Derwent, 1
Whoop-Up Trail, 47, 71
Wideman, Betty, 121
Wild Horse Show and Buffalo Chase, 151
wild west shows, xiv, 139–50, 154. *See also* rodeos; and moving west, 142; smaller versions of, 149
Wilde, Sergeant A. B., 95
Wilder, Bert, 55
Willow Creek roundup, 48
Winder, George, 48
Winnipeg, 5, 52
Winnipeg Stampede, 23–24
winter feed, 5, 7, 46, 52, 54, 79
women, 155; Aboriginal, 156–7; Bar S and Rocking P, 168; British, 155; cattle industry, 156; communications technology, 161; computer technology, 161; servants, 157; skills, 156
Women of the Range: Women's Roles in the Texas Beef Cattle Industry, 161
wool subsidy, 13
"Word from the Range: A Canadian Cowboy Collection," 154
"Working Cowboy, The," 153
Writing the Range (Poirier), 155
Wyoming Stock Growers' Association,46

Y

Yeo, Bill, 170
Young Pine, Joe, 162, 165

Z

zig-zagged log pasture fence, 7
Zimrose, Mel, 36